THE COMPLETE JUGGLER

DAVE FINNIGAN
AKA "PROFESSOR CONFIDENCE"

ILLUSTRATED BY BRUCE EDWARDS

WITH SPECIAL CONTRIBUTIONS
BY TODD STRONG
TECHNICAL CONSULTANT: ALLAN JACOBS

VINTAGE BOOKS
A Division of Random House • New York

A VINTAGE ORIGINAL, February 1987
FIRST EDITION

Library of Congress Cataloging in Publication Data
Finnigan, Dave.
The complete juggler.
"A Vintage original."
1. Jugglers and juggling.   I. Strong, Todd.
II. Jacobs, Allan.   III. Title.
GV1559.F49   1987   793.8   86-40158
ISBN 0-394-74678-3 (pbk.)

Manufactured in the United States of America
10 9 8 7 6 5 4 3 2 1

THE COMPLETE JUGGLER

**This book is dedicated to
The International Jugglers' Association,
an organization with a heart—
and a funny bone**

TABLE OF CONTENTS

Acknowledgments

In 1976 when I first learned to juggle, I looked around for equipment to use and for a step by step guide from bumbling beginner to adept master. Neither was available.

Almost a decade later, juggling equipment is available in many sporting good, toy, magic and theatrical supply stores; and in many book stores you can find a scarf or beanbag set with instructions. But that guide book I dreamed of never appeared, and I had to learn the hard way, gathering bits and pieces of information from here or there.

Well, here it is, the book I needed when I began to juggle. This book contains over 1,000 separate illustrations and the cumulative skill and spirit of 4,000 years of juggling history. Even though it is called "complete," no book is ever finished and I look forward to input from you for the next edition.

Thanks go to my many teachers:

To John Ross, who inspired me to learn to juggle—

To Carlo, who taught me the Cascade—

To Greg Albert who showed me the pattern for four—

To Roger Dollarhide who gave me the secret for five balls the "easy" way—

To Joe Buhler who had the patience to teach me to pass clubs—

To Reverend Chumly whose sidewalk circus inspired me to perform—

To Rudy Benton whose classroom magic inspired me to teach—

To Mark Sutherland who gave me the idea to teach juggling with scarves—

To George Nissan who told me to "grow slowly and go for quality"—

To Won Israel with whom I've shared over 300 stages—

To Barret Felker, a touring partner "non pareil"—

To Richard Powers, Ray Fryson, Chris Breed, Barbara Szwek, Linda Page and Rick Masters, who watch the shop when I go off to have fun—

To Lottie Brunn, John Webster, Robert Stuverud, Amy Adams, Rainbow Piper, Ken Chen and Todd Strong, who shared their skills for our illustrations —

To Rich Chamberlin, for his help with the glossary—

To Anne Freedgood and the team at Random House for their faith and patience—

To the Board of the International Jugglers' Association and the many IJA members who helped design the Achievement Awards system—

To my mom who wanted me to be a doctor, and my dad who might have preferred a stockbroker, thanks for letting me be myself—

But most of all to Thelma and Davy, who tolerated the thump-thump-thump while Daddy learned to play, and the long periods of silence when he ignored their needs to write this book.

As you can imagine, a book like this is a team effort. I would like to give thanks to special contributor Todd Strong who stimulated the project with his original manuscripts which became the Devil Stick and Diabolo chapters, and to Allan Jacobs, past U.S. national team and solo juggling champion, for his valuable consultation and critiques. John Dobleman, Johnathon Whitfield, Mike Vondruska and Ken Burke all made contributions to the Juggling Games chapter. Our layout assistant was Tom Wetzel. Most important is the skillful and exciting artwork and layout by Bruce Edwards giving life to mere words.

Dave Finnigan
"Professor Confidence"
Edmonds, WA

THE
COMPLETE
JUGGLER

JUGGLING AND YOU

Juggling is a series of challenges. The first challenge is simply to throw one object from hand to hand following a specific pattern. Once you can throw one, you can exchange two; and after you can exchange two, you can juggle three. If you have three objects under control you can begin to play with the infinite variations found in this book and in your imagination.

Jugglebug is dedicated to introducing as many people as possible to the joy of juggling. Almost anyone can juggle. It is not an art form reserved for circus people, but is a physically and mentally relaxing form of recreation which can help you to discover and to nurture your innate coordination. Once you have learned how, juggling, like swimming, is impossible to forget. So it is a skill that you can keep for life. Unlike most sports, juggling is completely portable and you can do it almost anywhere either alone, with a partner, or in a group.

Another characteristic of juggling is its rhythmic, almost musical nature. It can have the same calming effect on your spirit as playing or listening to good music. For many, juggling is a form of meditation, of integrating mind, body, and spirit.

Juggling is an infinite art form. The patterns you can weave in the air with 2, 3, 4, 5, or more balls, rings or clubs or with 2, 3, 4, 5, or more people are beyond reckoning. Each time you learn a trick you see or think up a new one; and you are continually extending the upper limit (or "leading edge") of your capability. After a month or a year or a decade of juggling one thing stands out—how far ahead you are compared to where you were when you started or where you ever thought you could be. What looked impossible just a while ago is now a part of your routine and now something far more difficult appears impossible. The horizon retreats endlessly before you. Jugglers are very supportive of one another. Each person is at a level determined by his or her ability and by the amount of time and energy given over to juggling. Unlike other

3

activities, in juggling you can plan for and experience your own growth. Once you have conquered the basic "cascade" pattern you will also be able to overcome any nervousness about juggling in front of others. Dropping the balls is not a sign of clumsiness, it is a sign of progress, showing that there is growth going on.

At Jugglebug we suggest you carry your equipment with you at all times, in your executive brief case or your junior executive backpack. Your bumper sticker or any of the achievement pins will identify you as a juggler. When you meet a fellow juggler don't hesitate, get out your equipment and share information. Let's fill the hallways of office buildings, parks and freeway rest stops with jugglers.

Some sports seem to foster impatience, a sense of frustration and the sort of destructive competition which makes half the participants in any event into losers. You will find that juggling can help you to develop patience, self-confidence, and an ability to work smoothly with others. There are no losers, and you only compete with yourself.

Most of all juggling is joyous. It is a release of energy in the form of creativity which gives instant, personal, internal rewards to the participant (aside from any applause or from the bills which may mysteriously appear in one's up-turned cap following a particularly self-satisfying routine).

If you use the Jugglebug method, by the time you go to bed tonight you should be able to report with glee, "Look, Ma— I'm Jugglin'." Within a month you should be able to put on a show which actually draws applause, "oohs" and "ahs." Before we begin this adventure, let's toss a few basic points up into the air.

First — If at any time you feel tight, frustrated or klutzy, or if you find yourself repeating the same mistakes over and over, stop at the exact moment of your error. Then close your eyes and think through what you were trying to do. Figure out what went wrong. Try to see it right in your mind's eye. Figure out what you have to do to correct the error, shake your arms and shoulders to loosen up; then reopen your eyes and begin again. Like a springboard diver, the juggler must make all of his or her conscious decisions before going into the air. Unlike diving, the performer remains dry and the balls take the belly flops.

Second — There is a logical progression to this book in general, and to each chapter. Rather than jumping around, proceed page by page from the front to the back of each chapter. Don't move on to the next step until you have full control over what comes before it. This way you can avoid developing or reinforcing bad habits. If you start to get sloppy, go back and perfect the previous step before moving forward again.

Third — Keep your senses fully engaged in what you are doing, but don't depend much on your conscious mind and on the thinking process once the balls start to fly. Thinking takes too much time. Try to feel the pattern that the balls should be making with your body and with your senses. Concentrate the thinking part of your mind on the leading edge, the point at which you made your last error. If step 4 is where you are goofing up, let steps 1, 2 and 3 flow automatically while you concentrate on the movements required in step 4. If you can't do this, you shouldn't be on step 4 yet and should go back and reexperience steps 1 through 3 until they don't tie up your conscious mind.

Fourth — While learning, imagine that you are in a phone booth with a ceiling just a foot over the top of your head. The glass walls and ceiling of this booth are very fragile. Don't let your balls hit the walls or ceiling or the whole building will shatter. Your act takes place entirely within the phone booth until you have gained sufficient control to make longer throws at will. Don't let your friends talk you into testing how high or how far out to the side you can throw until you can juggle in a phone booth.

Carlo, author of "The Juggling Book", uses the term "wall plane" to describe the path the balls should follow. The wall plane is an imaginary surface about a foot in front of you. The balls stay generally in this plane, exept when you consciously try to make them deviate from it. Carlo uses the term "tray plane" to describe the "home" position of your hands. This is the plane formed by your hands held palm up, as if you were carrying a tray. These ideas may be useful for your own practice and will be used occasionally in the book.

Fifth — You will be tempted to rely on your dominant hand, your right if you are right handed, your left if you are left handed. Give your subordinate hand a workout whenever possible. As soon as you have learned a trick with your dominant hand, switch and learn it with the subordinate hand taking the lead. You will find that any effort with your subordinate hand will transfer easily to the dominant hand whereas the reverse is not necessarily true.

Sixth — Finish cleanly. You will shortly learn how to start and stop a juggling routine. The clean finish is essential to learn and to practice. Don't just juggle until the act falls apart. Choose a number of repetitions at which to stop and cut off sharply.

Seventh — Juggle with a friend whenever possible. Use the buddy system to check up on each other's progress. Anyone who uses this book can be a teacher. Help one another to avoid bad habits. For example, if your partner throws too far forward, stand in front of him and act as a living wall. Caution him not to hit you upon pain of punching. You will be surprised how quickly he will get those throws under control!

Eighth — Keep a record of your progress. We provide a form for that purpose in the back of the book. Set a goal for every practice session and set overall goals. Practice is the only key to perfection.

Enough Talk — Now on to the action!

SCARF JUGGLING

HI THERE! I'M PROFESSOR CONFIDENCE. AMY AND I ARE GOING TO TEACH YOU HOW TO JUGGLE WITH SLOW MOVING NYLON SCARVES. YOUR SCARVES ARE SEALED TO THE BACK COVER OF THIS BOOK. GET THEM OUT & LET'S GET STARTED.

THE CASCADE

STEP 1—THROWING 1 SCARF

Hold one scarf in the center like a ghost.

Lift your arm as high as you can across your chest.

Toss the scarf with your palm out, like waving goodbye.

Reach high up with your other hand and catch straight down.

Claw like a lion.

Now raise that arm across in the other direction

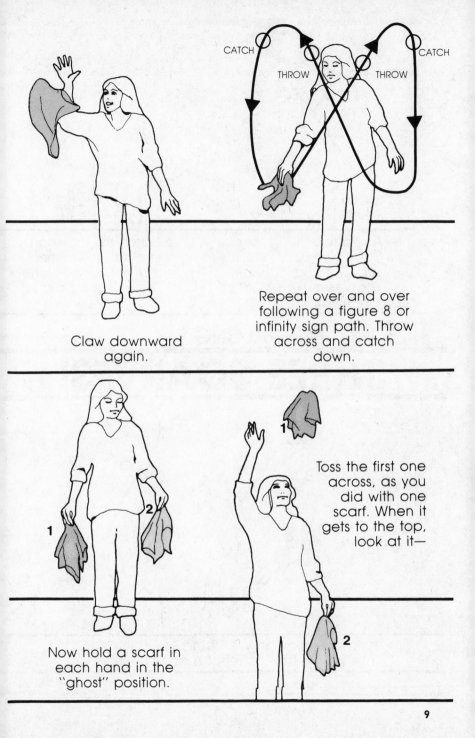

Claw downward again.

CATCH THROW THROW CATCH

Repeat over and over following a figure 8 or infinity sign path. Throw across and catch down.

Now hold a scarf in each hand in the "ghost" position.

Toss the first one across, as you did with one scarf. When it gets to the top, look at it—

And throw the second scarf across in the opposite direction. The scarves make an "X" across your chest.

Catch the first scarf straight down, then catch the second one. Throw-Throw-Catch-Catch.

MOVING RIGHT ALONG.

THREE SCARVES!

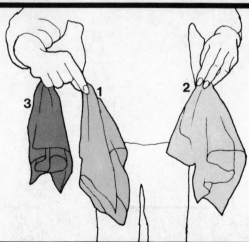

Now hold one scarf on your fingertips in the hand that has two. That's the first scarf you throw.

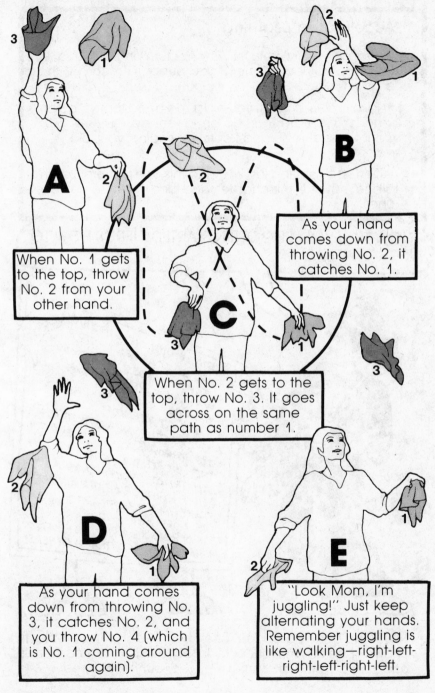

A When No. 1 gets to the top, throw No. 2 from your other hand.

B As your hand comes down from throwing No. 2, it catches No. 1.

C When No. 2 gets to the top, throw No. 3. It goes across on the same path as number 1.

D As your hand comes down from throwing No. 3, it catches No. 2, and you throw No. 4 (which is No. 1 coming around again).

E "Look Mom, I'm juggling!" Just keep alternating your hands. Remember juggling is like walking—right-left-right-left-right-left.

Accelerated Learning

• Juggling is rhythmic, so why not turn on the music. In fact, you will learn faster if you put on a record with a good solid beat.

• Take a challenge. If you did three good throws, go on to four, if you did four, go on to ten, go for 20 or 50. Count your throws and keep exceeding your old record.

• Don't be satisfied just knowing this one pattern. Learn all the moves in this chapter, and then invent some new ones.

NOW THAT YOU'VE GOTTEN STARTED, HERE'S HOW TO KEEP GOING....

1. START WITH THE HAND THAT HAS 2 SCARVES IN IT.
2. THROW ACROSS YOUR BODY WITH AN "X", RELEASING AS HIGH AS POSSIBLE.
3. LOOK AT THE TOP.
4. EVERY TIME ONE GETS TO THE TOP, THROW ANOTHER, THEN CATCH THE ONE THAT'S IN THE AIR
5. ALTERNATE YOUR HANDS AND COUNT "1-2-1-2", OR "LEFT-RIGHT-LEFT."
6. TAKE YOUR TIME, SCARF JUGGLING IS SOFT AND FLOWING.
7. DROPPING IS A SIGN OF PROGRESS
8. HAVE FUN AND TEACH OTHERS!

NOTE: The basic cascade is often perceived as three objects thrown in the air simultaneously. In fact, most of the time there is one object in the air, sometimes two, but never three.

REVERSE CASCADE

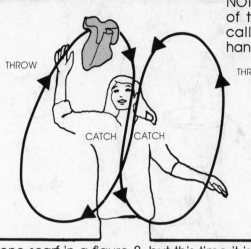

NOTE: For the sake of this book, let's call this an overhand throw.

THROW

THROW

CATCH CATCH

Throw one scarf in a figure 8, but this time it is a throw which goes over the top from the outside of the pattern, and straight down the center.

Start with one in each hand. Throw one scarf overhand. When it begins to come down the center, throw the second with a big overhand movement. Catch the first, catch the second.

NOW TRY 3 SCARVES. Just imagine you have a bucket in front of you at eye level, start with the hand that has two, and toss them in the bucket, one by one.

COLUMNS— THE EASIEST MOVE.

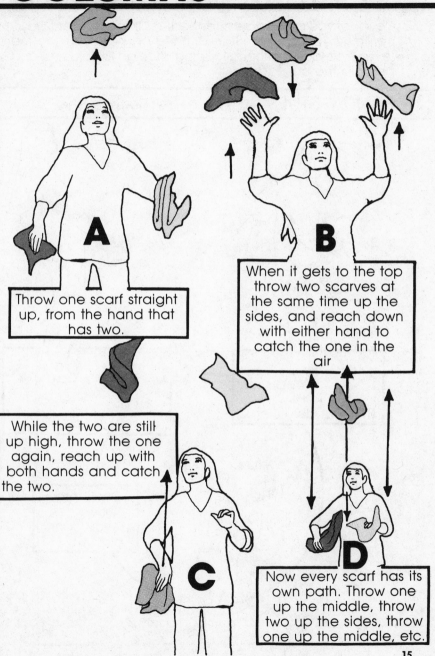

A Throw one scarf straight up, from the hand that has two.

B When it gets to the top throw two scarves at the same time up the sides, and reach down with either hand to catch the one in the air

While the two are still up high, throw the one again, reach up with both hands and catch the two.

C

D Now every scarf has its own path. Throw one up the middle, throw two up the sides, throw one up the middle, etc.

15

COMBINED MOVES

Now that you can juggle three scarves three different ways, combine your moves. Start with the cascade, shift to the reverse cascade without stopping, then go to columns, and back to the cascade.

FANCY STUFF—While juggling the cascade.

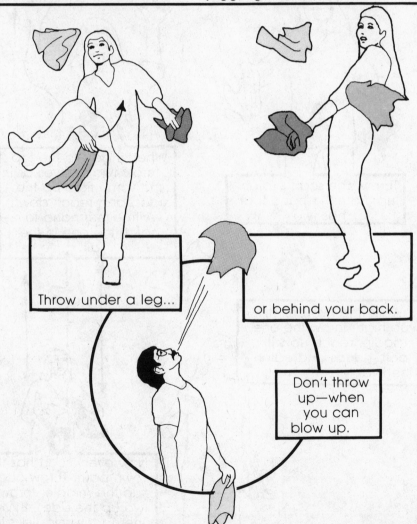

Throw under a leg...

or behind your back.

Don't throw up—when you can blow up.

Or try the black belt of scarf juggling—3 in one hand.

Hint: Move quickly. Catch the scarves one at a time. Go for the lowest one each time. There is no set pattern. Just keep them off the floor. Try cascade, reverse and columns.

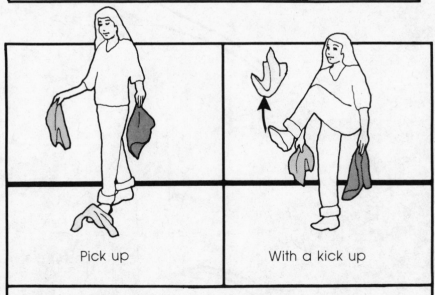

Pick up

With a kick up

Hint: When the kicked scarf gets up, toss one of the others and start juggling.

Pirouette: While doing columns, toss one scarf up, hold the other two, turn and resume juggling.

Hold two scarves.

Toss one up —

do a full pirouette —

and keep juggling.

THE SHOWER

THROW **TWICE** FROM RIGHT

PASS ACROSS FROM LEFT TO RIGHT

CATCH WITH LEFT

To do the "shower" start throwing around in a circle. The right hand does all the throwing. The left hand does all the catching.

Now that you have learned the shower in one direction, learn it in the other also.

Start by throwing the first two scarves from your right hand. Then push the third scarf across from left to right, and throw it along the same path.

Toss one scarf high. As it descends sweep the scarf in your right hand around in a big circle, once, twice or three times. Throw that scarf and keep juggling.

SPLITS

WITH 3

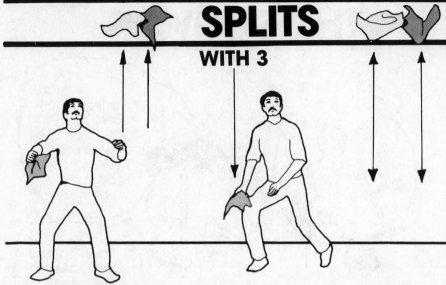

Toss two scarves using both hands. Throw them up one side. When they peak throw a scarf up on the other side. Now go back, catch the two and throw them again. Then the 1, then the 2....etc.

WITH 4

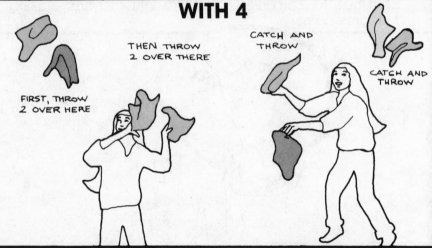

FIRST, THROW 2 OVER HERE

THEN THROW 2 OVER THERE

CATCH AND THROW

CATCH AND THROW

Now do the same with 4 scarves. Lean to the right and throw one from each hand. Then lean to the left and toss the other two straight up. Hurry back to the right, catch the first two and throw them again. Reach quickly to the left, catch those two and throw them again.

4 SCARVES SIMULTANEOUSLY

EACH HAND JUGGLES 2

Throw 2 scarves up the center, so they arc toward the outside. When they peak, throw the next two along the same paths, reach up and catch the first two again.

4 SCARVES STAGGERED

THE SCARVES DON'T CHANGE HANDS

Throw the first right hand scarf and immediately afterward throw the first left hand scarf. As quickly as possible, throw a second right, and catch the first one, throw a second left and catch the first one. Now it is just a matter of alternating. Throw and catch right—throw and catch left.

JUGGLING 3 SCARVES WITH A PARTNER—

Each person is like one hand of a juggler.

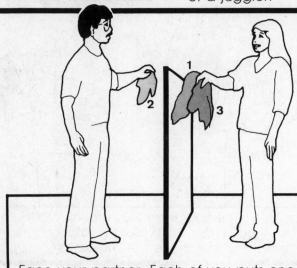

Throw under the scarf in the air, but over an imaginary chest high net.

Face your partner. Each of you puts one hand at your side and leaves it there. One person starts with two scarves and the other starts with one scarf.

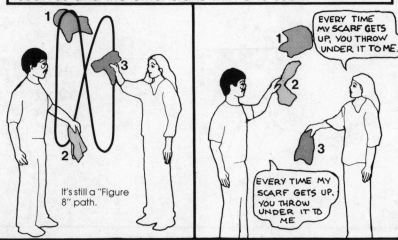

It's still a "Figure 8" path.

EVERY TIME MY SCARF GETS UP, YOU THROW UNDER IT TO ME.

EVERY TIME MY SCARF GETS UP, YOU THROW UNDER IT TO ME

The person with two scarves starts. When their throw gets half way across, the second person throws. Then just keep alternating. No. 1, No. 2, No. 1, No. 2.

SIDE BY SIDE

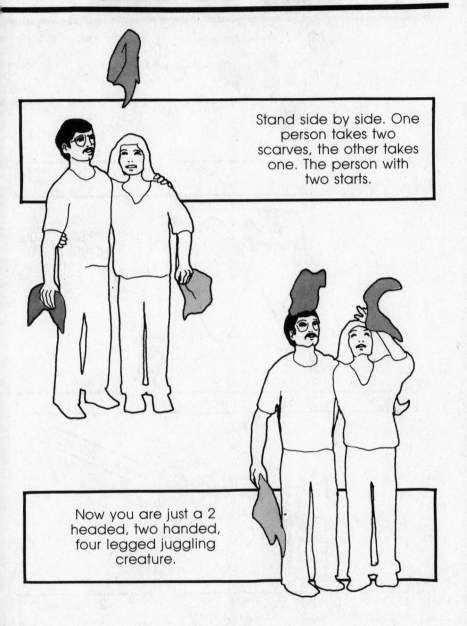

Stand side by side. One person takes two scarves, the other takes one. The person with two starts.

Now you are just a 2 headed, two handed, four legged juggling creature.

JUGGLING 6 SCARVES WITH A PARTNER

Now use both hands. One person holds four scarves, the other holds two.

SURPRISE! IT'S STILL A "FIGURE 8" PATH

The person with 4 scarves goes first. Throw 2.

REMEMBER THE NET

When they get half way the other person throws 2. Just keep alternating. Me-You-Me-You-Me-You.

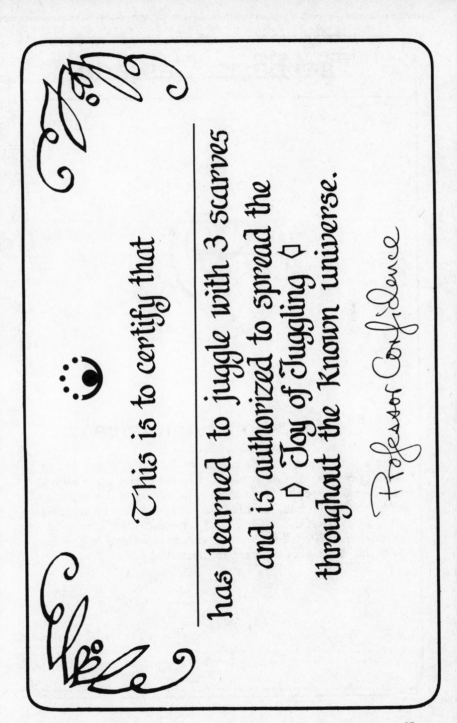

This is to certify that

has learned to juggle with 3 scarves
and is authorized to spread the
◁ Joy of Juggling ▷
throughout the known universe.

Professor Confidence

25

The Basic Cascade

Certification Requirements

Juggle with three balls or beanbags for 20 or more throws without dropping. Finish cleanly. Demonstrate this skill for two or more people. Have them sign a copy of the application form in the back of this book and send that form along with $2 to JUGGLEBUG, 7506 J Olympic View Drive, Edmonds, WA 98020. Your first pin will arrive within 2 to 3 weeks and you will be on the path to mastery.

GETTING STARTED

THE CASCADE

The first juggling move is called the "Cascade." It's as basic and simple as walking, and is a rest position to which the juggler can return at will. Like any new skill, juggling moves are best learned step by step, and the keys are consistency and repetition. Never be afraid to make the next throw, just keep trying until you get it right.

STEP 1 ONE BALL

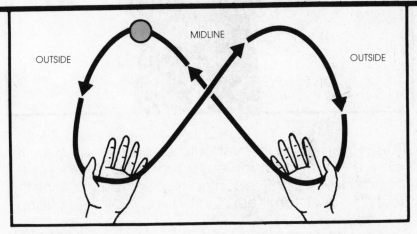

Start with one ball. Throw it from hand to hand in a "Figure 8" or infinity sign pattern, with scooping underhand throws. Let go of the ball toward the midline of your body, and catch it toward the outside, carrying it back to the midline to throw again.

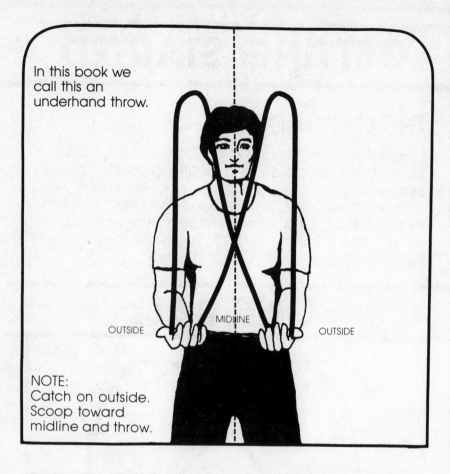

In this book we call this an underhand throw.

OUTSIDE   MIDLINE   OUTSIDE

NOTE:
Catch on outside.
Scoop toward
midline and throw.

This "Figure 8" pattern should extend about a foot above your shoulder on each side. Keep your hands down. Don't reach up higher than your chest to throw or catch. Keep the ball on a plane in front of you.

When you can make a smooth figure 8 without pauses, and without recoiling or cocking your hand before throwing, you have passed the juggler's test. Repeat ten times and move on to Step 2.

STARTING AND STOPPING

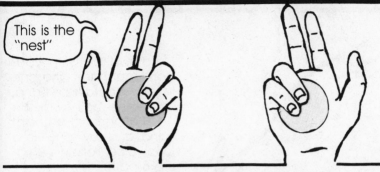

This is the "nest"

Pick up two balls and hold them on the heels of your hands as shown so that you have room in the nest formed by your thumb, forefinger and middle finger for a third ball.

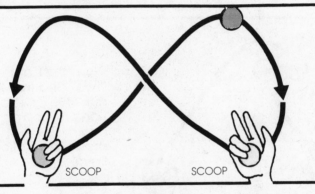

SCOOP   SCOOP

Pick up a third ball and throw it from hand to hand, from nest to nest, following the path described in Step 1.

Remember the figure 8. You are not juggling yet. This is just a warm-up exercise to teach you how to begin and end the juggling routine.

When you can throw one ball from nest to nest ten times in a row without dropping it, move on Step 3.

EXCHANGING TWO BALLS

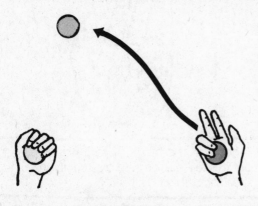

Hold two balls in your dominant hand and one in your subordinate hand. Throw the ball from the nest of your dominant hand, and say "one" in a loud voice. Follow the figure 8 path.

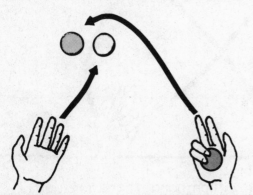

When the ball peaks, say "two" and throw the ball out of your subordinate hand, scooping it underneath the first ball as shown, also following the figure 8 path.

The two balls should cross in the air and change hands.

When you can exchange two balls ten times in a row without a drop, move on to Step 4.

CONTINUING TO JUGGLE

Start again. Throw the first ball from your dominant hand, just as you did in the previous step and say "one."

When Ball 1 peaks, throw the ball from your subordinate hand and say "two."

When Ball 2 peaks, throw the ball from your dominant hand and say "three."

When Ball 3 peaks, throw the ball from your subordinate hand and say "four."

When Ball 4 peaks, throw the ball from your dominant hand and say "five."

Keep throwing and keep counting.

NOTE: Learn to start with two balls in your subordinate hand. You should be able to start with either hand and finish in either hand.

REMEMBER

1. Start with the hand that has two.
2. Every time a ball peaks, throw another one with a scooping underhand throw.
3. Alternate hands left-right-left-right-left-right.
4. Throw to the same height on both sides.
5. Focus on the peaks. Don't look at your hands.
6. Count out loud, or say "right-left-right-left."
7. When you want to stop, stop cleanly by catching the last ball on your three finger nest.
8. Remember every ball follows that same figure 8 path.
9. Keep the balls in a plane in front of you —don't throw them forward.
10. There should always be one ball in the air, and one on the way up.
11. Go slowly, wait for those peaks, don't worry about drops—a dropped ball is a sign of progress.
12. Eventually give up the counting, and bring the whole pattern down below your eyes. That's where more controlled juggling begins.

Now that you have this basic "Cascade" pattern, you have taken the most difficult step in juggling. Don't be complacent; move on to additional tricks.

Three Ball Juggling

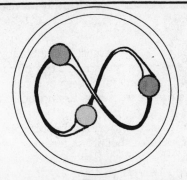

Certification Requirements
(use balls or beanbags)

1. Cascade (20 throws varying your pattern from narrow to wide and high to low)
2. Reverse cascade (20 throws varying pattern from narrow to wide and high to low)
3. Claw (10 throws using both hands continuously)
4. Shower (10 throws from right to left, 10 throws from left to right)
5. Two in one hand, show three different patterns (9 throws in each hand)
6. 3 pauses and 1 fancy start
7. 2 recoveries
8. (with balls) Bounce 10 times on floor and go back to cascade
9. Neck catch and continue
10. Under the leg (both hands throw under each leg)
11. Either
    a. behind the back (both sides) or
    b. over the shoulder (both sides) or
    c. the yo-yo (both sides) or
    d. juggler's tennis (both sides)
12. Either:
    a. Statue of Liberty (11 throws), or
    b. Drop into pattern (12 times), or
    c. Chop (12 times)

ADVANCED 3 BALL JUGGLING

This chapter presents the most essential moves with three balls. Variations are actually endless, but our intention is to give you enough material to build your own complex juggling routines, using these moves as ingredients.

Except for the bouncing tricks, beanbags will be easier to use than balls. Get three that are different colors so you can follow them through the pattern. Soft packed cubes are best for learning since you can catch them by the corner and they stay where they land if dropped. Later you may want to get round beanbags which are a bit more accurate when thrown.

NOTE: LEARNING HOW TO LEARN
In this chapter we will continue to break the complex moves down into their smallest steps and build them up again step by step. However, you must eventually learn to do this for yourself, so start learning the process now. Once you understand this system you become your own best teacher and no juggling move, no matter how complex, is too difficult to master.

Now that you have the basic cascade under control, here are a few pointers to help you clean up your act:

- Teach someone else to juggle. You will learn more through the experience than your student.
- Practice varying your pattern. Juggle high, juggle low, juggle with a wide pattern, juggle with a narrow pattern.
- Practice looking through the pattern while juggling, shifting your focus to a distant object.
- Practice juggling while walking or running.
- Practice juggling while holding a conversation.

REVERSE CASCADE

In the Cascade, you throw underhand, from near the midline, and catch on the outside. In the reverse Cascade, you throw from the outside, and catch near the midline, still following a figure 8 path.

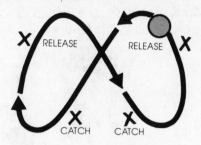

Start by throwing one ball overhand. Release the ball at shoulder height, catch it with your opposite hand at waist height.

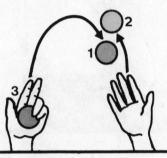

As soon as you can throw one ball hand to hand, try two. Hold one in each hand. Throw the first one. When it peaks, throw the second up over it. The balls cross in the air and change hands.

Now just keep going. Every time a ball peaks, throw another one over it, following the same path. Focus on the peaks.

CLAWING

Clawing means bringing your hand down over the descending ball and throwing backhanded. To learn to claw, start with one ball. Toss it backhanded from hand to hand, bringing your forearm and hand down to meet the ball, palm downward, when it has descended about halfway from the peak of its path to your waist.

Turn your wrist slightly to the inside and throw it back with your palm out. Your throwing hand reaches across your body with your palm out, like waving goodbye.

Once you can toss one ball back and forth fairly uniformly, move right up to three balls.

As you work on this part of the routine, it is vital that you keep your arms and hands down as much as possible and keep the ball in toward your body; don't let it fly away. You will probably find that this is a very rhythmic movement which certainly accentuates the outside catch and the inside throw.

Well, if you've gotten this far, you are starting to feel the effects of juggling. This ancient art is a fine spiritual, mental and physical journey. Keep on juggling. Don't quit now. There are still lots more tricks to learn.

TWO BALLS
IN ONE HAND

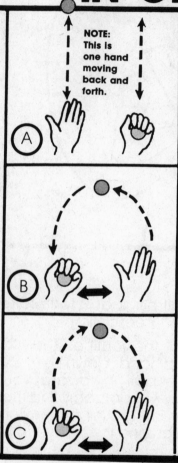

NOTE:
This is one hand moving back and forth.

The timing for this move is the same as for three ball juggling. Every time a ball reaches the peak, you throw the other one; so just focus on the peaks.

You can throw each ball in its own column (A), in a circle toward the outside (B) or in a circle toward the inside (C).

It is important in this move to keep the balls in a plane in front of your body. Work in height and width, not depth. Don't shovel in towards yourself, just go from side to side.

THE SHOWER

In many parts of the world, this move is all there is to juggling. One hand does all the throwing, the other does all the catching, and the balls move in a circle over the juggler's head.

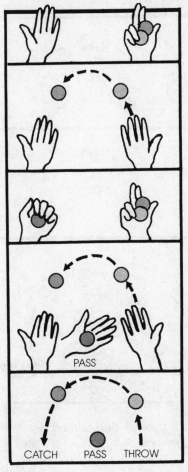

PASS

CATCH   PASS   THROW

Start with two balls in your dominant hand. Throw them one at a time in a high arc so rapidly that the second ball is well on its way when the first lands. Repeat ten times.

Put one ball in your subordinate hand. Throw the two from your dominant in rapid succession, and just before the first ball lands, pass the third ball across and throw it with your dominant hand.

Then every time a ball lands in your subordinate hand, immediately pass it across and throw it in that same high arc from the dominant hand.

Accuracy and speed are the keys to a successful shower. Just keep throwing as fast as possible and keep catching with your subordinate hand and passing across.

JUGGLERS' TENNIS

Now that you can juggle with underhand throws (cascade) and overhand throws (reverse cascade), you can combine the two.

Toss over with the right and under with the left, or

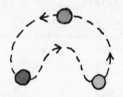

Toss under with the right and over with the left.

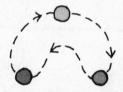

Now juggle with three balls, one of which is distinctly different. The trick is to juggle a cascade with the other two (number 1 and number 2), but to toss that "odd" ball (number 3) back and forth over the top. You can shoot lobs or smashes with this tennis ball.

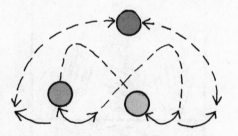

Number 1 and number 2 are the net; number 3 is the tennis ball.

Some Practice Points

- Remember to set a goal for each practice session.
- Stretch and limber up before practicing.
- Pay attention to your posture. Keep your back straight and chest out.
- Juggle over mats or sand if available to minimize wear and tear on equipment.
- Practice to non-obtrusive music with a solid beat.
- Whenever you start a practice session go through a routine of the tricks you already know. Then work on something new until you get it.
- If possible, occasionally videotape a practice session. Whenever possible, practice in front of a mirror.
- Keep these slogans in mind:
  "A drop is a sign of progress."
  "A touch is as good as a catch—because you knew where it was headed."
  "End every practice session with an accomplishment."
  "Anything is possible with a good plan, practice and commitment."

THE YO-YO (AND THE OY-OY)

Once you can juggle two in one hand a series of entertaining tricks is possible.

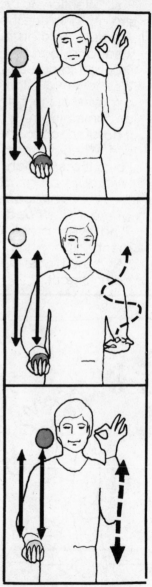

1. Juggle 2 balls in columns in your dominant hand, each one in its own pathway. Hold your other hand out where you can see it, but don't move it yet, just get used to seeing it there.

2. Now begin to move that other hand around. Start with random movements.

3. Now keep one of the balls you are juggling in mind. Every time you throw it, raise your other hand. Parallel the movement of this one ball with your empty hand.

4. Now do this same step, but hold a ball in the subordinate hand. (You could call this move the "bar-bell" since the two balls appear to be connected by an invisible rod.)

5. Now move the subordinate hand up and down above that one ball. Keep the same distance between the ball in your subordinate hand and the one you seem to be pulling up and pushing down with an invisible string.

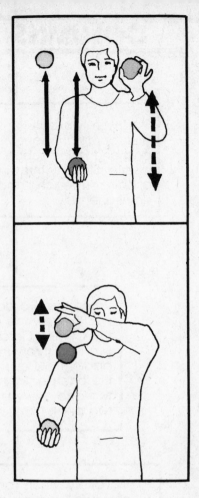

Although these variations of one handed juggling are relatively simple, people don't know it; and kids especially will giggle and "ooh" and "ah" at this part of your routine.

COLUMNS

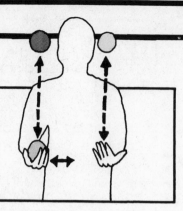

Start with two balls in your dominant hand and one in the subordinate. Start by throwing a ball from each hand simultaneously.

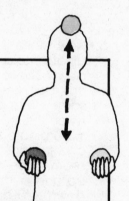

When the two balls peak, throw the third up the Center. Catch the two and throw them again. Now every time the one peaks, throw two and every time the two peak throw one.

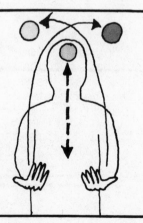

For variety, when you throw the two balls arc them in toward the center so they cross in the air and change hands. If you keep one hand forward and one hand back a bit, the two balls won't hit. Or else you can throw one high and one low every time.

Now that you can throw straight up and down and cross the balls at will, try a few variations.

Toss two balls as if to cross them, but throw them with equal and identical force. They will bump into one another and fall back into their respective throwing hands.

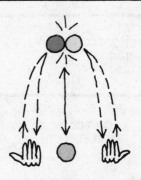

Toss two balls straight up and throw the third ball back and forth over the top of the two. This is a variation of jugglers' tennis.

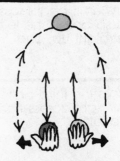

A simpler method of kissing is a planned collision on the way up. Use two balls to practice, throw them in toward one another and slightly upward.

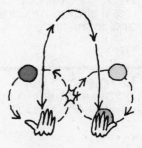

THE SEE SAW

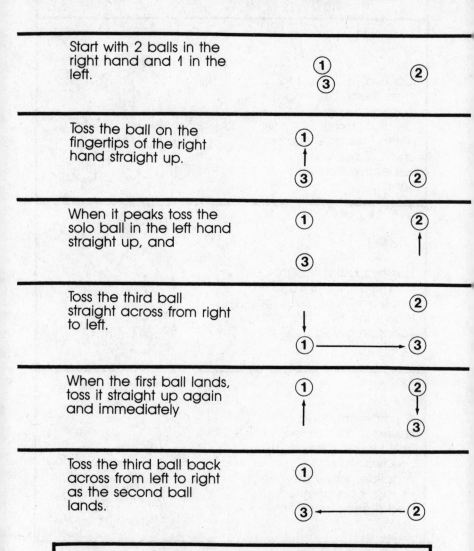

Start with 2 balls in the right hand and 1 in the left.

Toss the ball on the fingertips of the right hand straight up.

When it peaks toss the solo ball in the left hand straight up, and

Toss the third ball straight across from right to left.

When the first ball lands, toss it straight up again and immediately

Toss the third ball back across from left to right as the second ball lands.

Now number 1 and number 2 go straight up and down, and number 3 goes back and forth from hand to hand.

Now let's put the see saw together with the shower and see what we come up with.

1 Start showering from right to left

2 Throw your last ball straight up

3 Shift suddenly to a shower from left to right

Now you can create a nice move out of these several pieces. Start by showering 4 times to the right. Then shower 4 times to the left. Next shower twice to the right. And shower twice to the left. Then do the see saw about 3 times on each side — up right — up left — across — up right — across — up left — across — up right across — up left

CARRYING AND PLACING

Instead of tossing a ball to a particular point you can carry it there and either drop it, pass it or throw it to the other hand. Four examples follow—

- Carry the ball under your opposite arm and toss it straight up into the pattern.

- Carry the ball across the top of your pattern and drop it straight down to a juggle.

As soon as you drop #1, reach to your right and catch #2, palm down. Meanwhile, you have thrown #3 and caught #1. Now carry #2 across and drop it, then reach quickly over and catch #3.

Every ball will follow this path.

- Place the ball on your head and let it drop into the pattern.

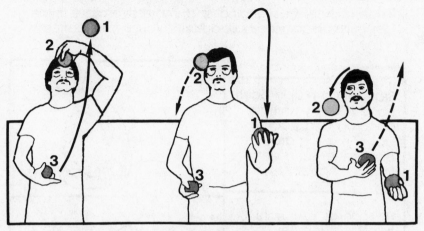

Throw #1 with your right hand. Reach up and put #2 on your head with your left hand and reach back over to catch #1 with your left. When #2 falls, throw #3 up under it, following #1.

- Create the Statue of Liberty by throwing up to your extended arm and letting the balls drop straight down to be caught and thrown again.

You learn the Statue of Liberty the way you learned the Shower. Start with two in your right hand. Throw them quickly. After you have thrown them both, drop the ball out of your left. Now every time a ball comes to the right, throw; and every time a ball comes to the left, drop it immediately.

CHOPS

An especially challenging and impressive move that depends on carrying balls quickly through your pattern is the chop.

Start with a ball in each hand. Carry your right hand up and back down in a big arc ending up just next to your left hand.

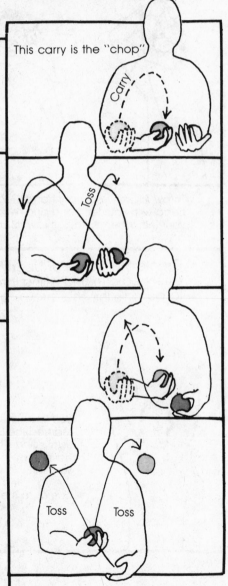

This carry is the "chop"

Carry

As soon as your right hand is in this new position toss the ball from that hand in a short cascade pattern toward the left. Then toss the ball from the left hand in the cascade. The balls cross.

Toss

Now use three balls, two in the right, one in the left. Chop the right hand over as you did above, and as it descends toward the throwing position toss the fingertip ball from the right hand, and start the cascade.

Toss   Toss

Now try the move while continuously juggling. Chop with the right hand in a big arc, then throw right, left, right, left, and keep juggling.

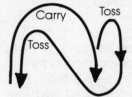

Each ball follows this path.

Carry

Toss

Toss

Start juggling. Now every time you catch with the right, chop, throw, return, pick up the next ball, chop, throw and return.

- All right hand throws are first carried over from right to left, then thrown straight up.
- All left hand throws go in a normal cascade pattern.

Got it? It's time to learn the whole series from the other side now.

O.K., now you can do one chop on each side. It's time to learn to do a series, first on one side, then on the other, then on both sides, chopping every ball before it is thrown.

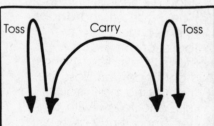

Toss

Carry

Toss

And now for the moment of truth. As soon as you have completed the chop with the right hand, toss with the right and chop with the left, then toss with the left and chop with the right.

- Every ball that crosses your chest is carried.
- All throws are straight up and come straight down.

CROSSED ARMS

Cross your arms and practice juggling. Start by throwing one ball from hand to hand. Use the reverse cascade. Move on to two and to three. Although this can be an impressive trick by itself, it is best presented as a series of moves where you cross and uncross your arms.

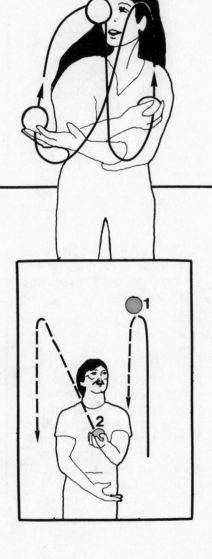

One of the easiest of these moves is like jugglers' tennis, with the "odd ball" going **under** the net. Start with two balls, one in each hand. Cross your hands, right under left. Toss the right hand ball straight up, and follow with a left hand throw as shown. Uncross your hands and catch the ball you threw from the right in the left, and the ball you threw from the left in the right.

Now hold two balls in your right hand, and one in the left. Cross your right hand under your left arm, toss the first ball straight up, and the second in the cascade just as you did in the last step. As the second ball peaks, throw the third and start juggling.

Now learn this same series on the opposite side, crossing your left hand under your right.

Now you should be able to play "upside down tennis." the odd ball (number 3) is carried under in one direction, thrown straight up, and caught in the opposite hand, then it is carried under, thrown straight up on the other side and caught in the opposite hand.

One ball makes a "U" under the pattern, while the other two dance above.

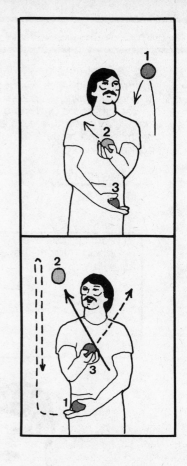

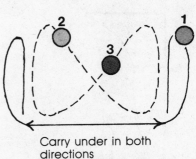

Carry under in both directions

PAUSES

You can create your own applause points by pausing in the midst of your routine. It helps if your pause comes as a "shock" in the middle of furious juggling. Surprise is your ally. The audience builds up a tension as you get more and more creative, take chances and do amazing tricks. They need to release this tension, so you pause, look at them, wink or smile, and resume the activity. Places to catch a beanbag for a pause include:

The arm

To practice, use one beanbag. Absorb the fall with your forearm.

The shoulder

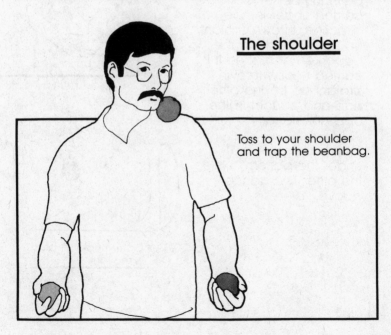

Toss to your shoulder and trap the beanbag.

The foot

Raise your toe slightly and absorb the shock with your knee.

The back of the hand

Catch the beanbag at the peak of its flight by inserting your hand under it.

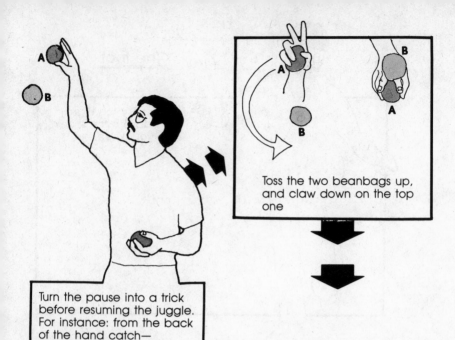

Toss the two beanbags up, and claw down on the top one

Turn the pause into a trick before resuming the juggle. For instance: from the back of the hand catch—

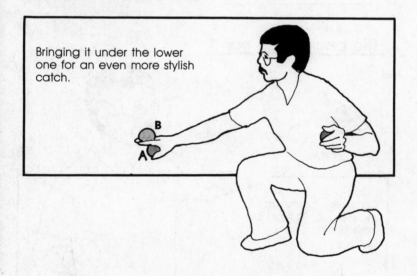

Bringing it under the lower one for an even more stylish catch.

Catch on your hat

Roll your eyes upward, and look surprised!

Or on the back of your neck—

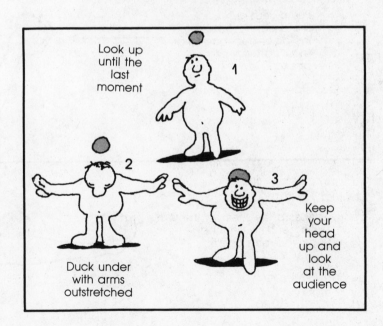

Look up until the last moment

1

Duck under with arms outstretched

2

3

Keep your head up and look at the audience

Additional difficult variations of pauses include:

From the arm catch, exchange the ball in the hand with the one on the arm in one fast move.

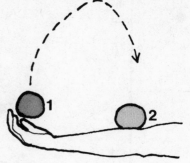

Toss the beanbag in the hand in a high arc.

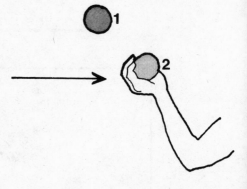

Pump your arm back like a piston, grabbing the other beanbag and shooting back into position.

Absorb the shock of the descending beanbag on your arm again.

Toss from one foot

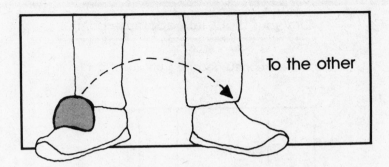

To the other

Or make a shoulder catch from the rear, throwing across the back.

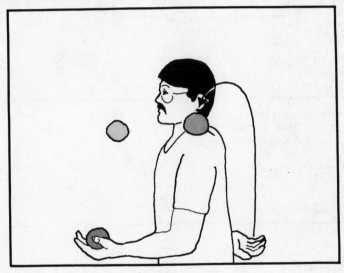

Or put your pauses together. For instance, you could toss from the back of the hand to the wrist to the foot, the knee, the other foot and end up with an automatic bow and neck catch.

RECOVERIES

Turn your drops into applause points.

Clasp the dropped beanbag between your heels—

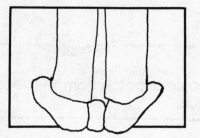

Kick up and bring your feet to one side, so the beanbag goes over one shoulder—

And resume juggling!

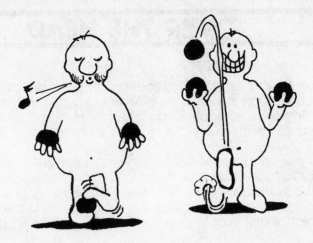

Or roll the beanbag onto your toe with your other foot and kick it up, into the pattern.

Or drop the other two beanbags and make a "shell game" out of it by hopping the beanbags over one another on the ground, in a cascade pattern.

OVER THE HEAD

Lie on your back on the floor holding 3 beanbags. Now go through the process of learning the cascade while lying on your back. Throw one beanbag from hand to hand. Learn to cross two. Then learn to juggle three.

Now stand up and start juggling. Toss one beanbag extra high. Lean your head back and start juggling just the same way you did when you were lying on your back. To go back to regular juggling toss a beanbag high, point your fingers to the front, and keep going.

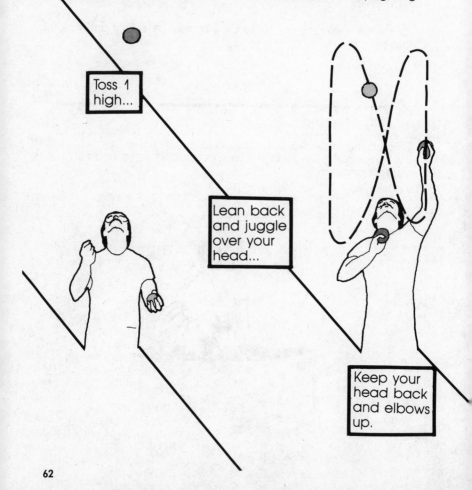

Toss 1 high...

Lean back and juggle over your head...

Keep your head back and elbows up.

JUGGLING WITH HANDS REVERSED

This special catch and tricky throw can be used as a one shot surprise or as an amazing set in a longer routine. The steps in learning this difficult move are:

Learn to catch one ball with hands reversed.

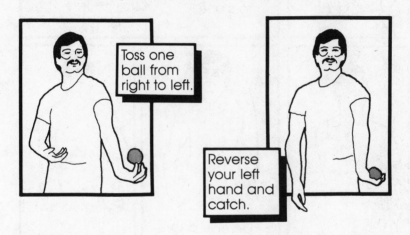

Toss one ball from right to left.

Reverse your left hand and catch.

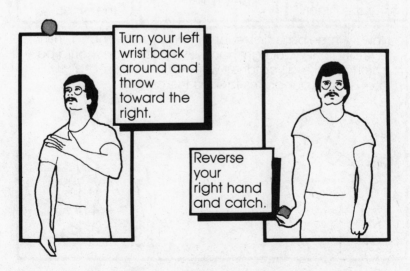

Turn your left wrist back around and throw toward the right.

Reverse your right hand and catch.

Now learn the variations with two balls.

Hold a ball in each hand. With hands reversed. Turn your wrist and toss one.

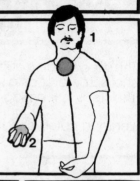

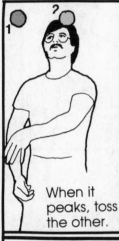

When it peaks, toss the other.

Reverse and catch with one hand.

Reverse and catch with the other.

Now try three balls, first reversing only your left hand, then reversing only your right hand. Eventually you should be able to make all catches with hands reversed and all throws with your palms toward the center.

64

BODY SHOTS

You can throw an occasional ball or a series of balls under or behind some part of your body. Some of the most common of these moves are:

UNDER THE LEG

To learn easily, raise your knee and throw your first ball under that leg to start juggling.

Raise your knee

Toss the first ball under to start

Now you can go under your leg in the middle of the juggling pattern. As soon as you have thrown with your right hand, raise your knee and toss the next right hand throw under your knee. Lower your leg and keep juggling.

BEHIND THE BACK

Practice with one ball. Toss it from your right hand behind your back across and up over your left shoulder. Catch it in front in the left hand. Then toss it behind your back across and up over your right shoulder and catch it in yor right hand.

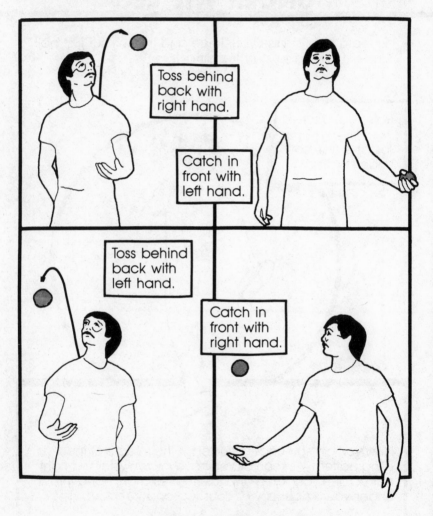

Toss behind back with right hand.

Catch in front with left hand.

Toss behind back with left hand.

Catch in front with right hand.

Now move on to two balls.

With one ball in each hand, toss behind the back with the right, and as that ball comes into view over your left shoulder, toss the ball from your left hand across to the right in a normal cascade.

Toss with right hand behind back and over left shoulder...

Look to left and as the ball comes into view...

Throw the one in your left hand up and across.

Now try the same move while juggling. Concentrate on one ball. When that ball comes to your right hand reach behind your back and throw up and across your back so it comes over your left shoulder.

While juggling, reach back and throw with the right hand.

Now reach out and catch the ball that is coming toward your right hand. Pause.

As the ball comes into view throw from the left and continue.

Once you can throw over either shoulder consistently you can throw over both shoulders sequentially. This is a BACKCROSS.

Toss with the right, look to the left.

Toss with the left, look to the right.

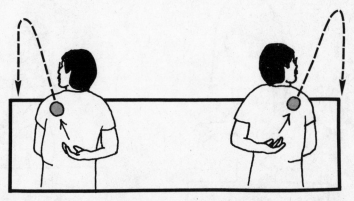

Now that you can do two throws in succession, try three balls and three throws. Then do four throws, five, six and seven. Work your way up, one throw at a time, until you can just keep going.

POINTERS:
- Reach high to throw and practice with one ball and two balls until smooth and precise.
- Practice turning your head from side to side, moving your arms but not throwing.
- Throw higher than usual to give yourself more time.
- Your catches are all in front and are blind since your head is turned the opposite way when you catch.
- Your throws are all from the back and must be precise to make catching easier.

OVER THE SHOULDER

Learn this move one ball at a time as you did with the previous one. The only differences are:

1. The ball comes over the shoulder of the hand that threw it;
2. The next throw is from that same hand.

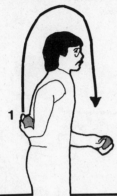

Toss up and over the same shoulder. (This will feel like a contortion at first.)

When the ball comes into view toss the next throw from that same hand. Keep juggling.

Of course you can go in the opposite direction. Toss over the shoulder toward the back. The next throw is across the chest with the same hand; then reach back and catch. Bring that hand back to the front. Resume juggling.

UNDER THE ARM

Go through the steps to learn how to juggle, but with one arm behind your back as shown. Once you can throw one ball from hand to hand, learn to switch two. Once you can switch two, learn to juggle three. You will have to use a very small pattern to do this.

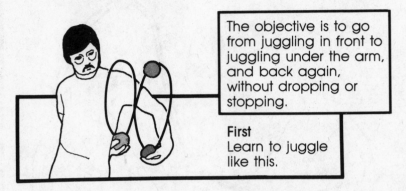

The objective is to go from juggling in front to juggling under the arm, and back again, without dropping or stopping.

First
Learn to juggle like this.

Next, while juggling under the arm toss a left hand throw high, pull your right arm out in front, and resume normal juggling. (It is easier to get out of this position than into it.)

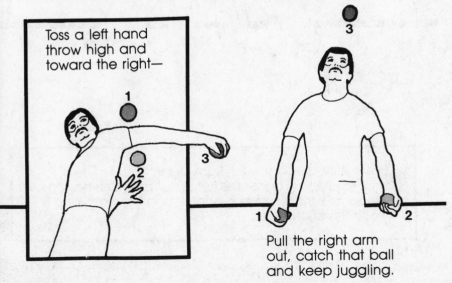

Toss a left hand throw high and toward the right—

Pull the right arm out, catch that ball and keep juggling.

Now use two balls, one in each hand. Toss the left hand ball (number 1) short and quickly reach behind the back into the underarm position, tossing the right hand ball (number 2) toward the left. Catch number 1 in the right hand and number 2 in the left. Now while juggling in front toss a left hand throw shorter than usual. Reach back and through with your right hand and start juggling under the arm.

Eventually you can switch from juggling under the right arm, to juggling under the left arm. Yes, it is as hard as it looks, but this is a major league juggling move and is worth the effort to learn.

BOUNCING ON THE FLOOR

Learn to bounce just as you learned the cascade. Bounce one ball back and forth in front of you. Once you can do this successfully, throw one ball down, as soon as it hits the ground, throw the second ball so that it goes outside of the first, hits the same spot, and bounces to the other hand. Now try three.

Now work on putting your leg through the bouncing pattern so one ball goes under your leg.

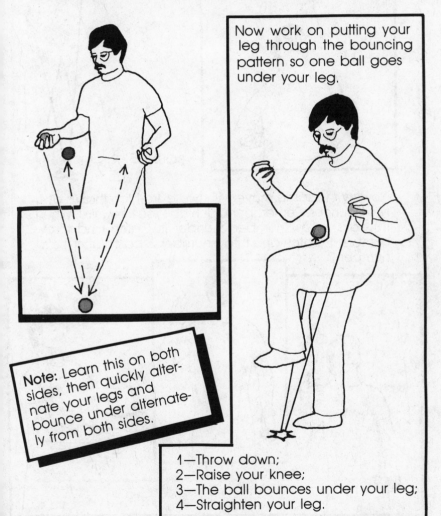

Note: Learn this on both sides, then quickly alternate your legs and bounce under alternately from both sides.

1—Throw down;
2—Raise your knee;
3—The ball bounces under your leg;
4—Straighten your leg.

While juggling, toss one ball extra high and let it bounce. Pause. When it comes back up past your hands, imagine it is the first ball in a cascade pattern, and start juggling.

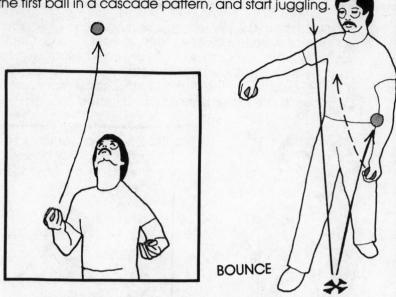

BOUNCE

Now try the same move with two extra-high throws and two bounces. Remember which ball you threw first. When it peaks, throw number 3 under it. Catch and throw number 1, catch and throw number 2, catch and throw number 3.

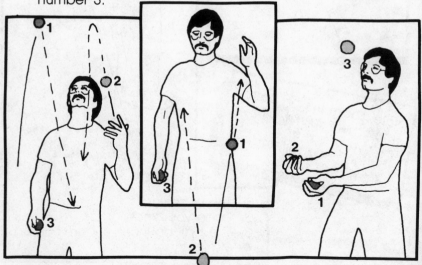

Now you can throw and catch all three balls in turn. Just remember the colors of the balls. If you throw red, yellow, blue, catch red, yellow, blue, and start juggling again. Just throw, throw, throw, bounce, bounce, bounce, catch, catch, toss and catch.

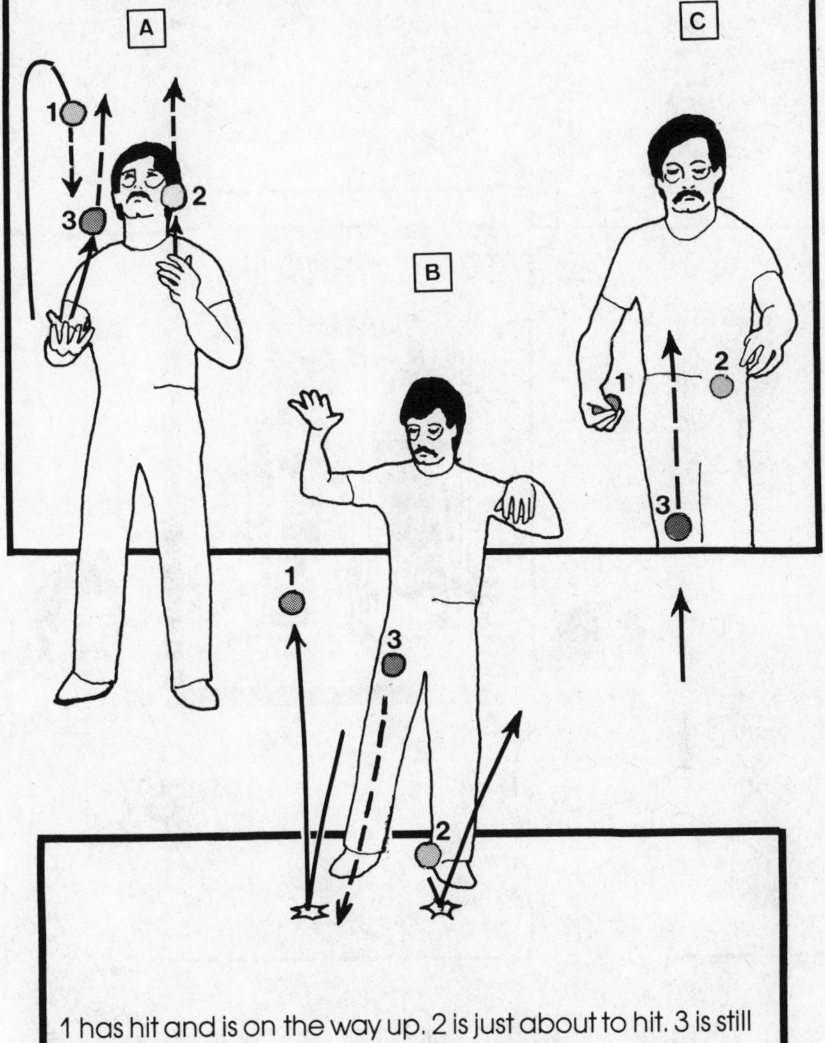

A

C

B

1 has hit and is on the way up. 2 is just about to hit. 3 is still going down.

Toss all 3 balls into the air in a triangle, keeping them separated and at the same height.

Let them fall onto a bouncy wooden floor.

When they come back up, claw downward on the outer two before they peak. The center ball bounces up high and you start juggling as if it were the first ball in a cascade.

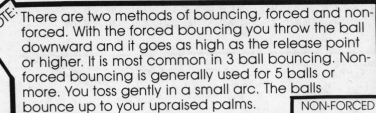

There are two methods of bouncing, forced and non-forced. With the forced bouncing you throw the ball downward and it goes as high as the release point or higher. It is most common in 3 ball bouncing. Non-forced bouncing is generally used for 5 balls or more. You toss gently in a small arc. The balls bounce up to your upraised palms.

FORCED
Palms down
Toss down
  hard
Every ball
  goes to
  same point
Balls go down
  the outside
They come up
  the inside

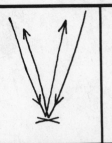

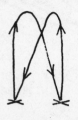

NON-FORCED
Palms up
Toss up to
  throw
There are two
  bounce
  points.
Balls cross on
  way down
Balls go down
  the inside
Balls come up
  the outside

"ENGLISH"

Usually the angle at which the ball goes down is about the same as the angle at which it comes up. For a special bouncing effort you can put "English" (forward spin or back spin) on the ball. This makes the ball bounce erratically. With English you can toss the ball away and make it bounce back to you.

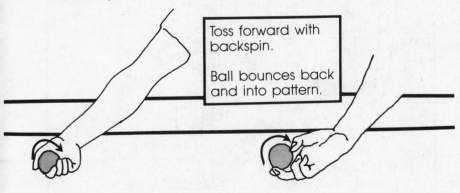

Toss forward with backspin.

Ball bounces back and into pattern.

To put backspin on the ball, as you throw it pull down with your thumb over the top.

To put forward spin on the ball, simply pull your hand out from under and rotate the ball as you throw.

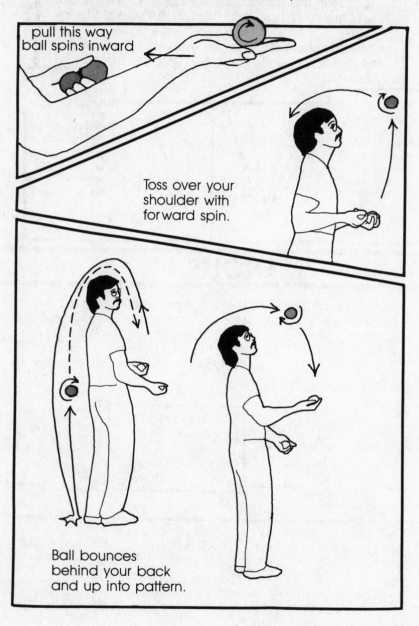

pull this way
ball spins inward

Toss over your shoulder with forward spin.

Ball bounces behind your back and up into pattern.

BODY BOUNCES

Just think of all the parts of your body where a ball or beanbag can be bounced. Toss one ball to that spot, bounce it and catch it. Then toss one, bounce it off and start juggling. Finally, toss out of the juggle, bounce, and keep going.

You can bounce off your

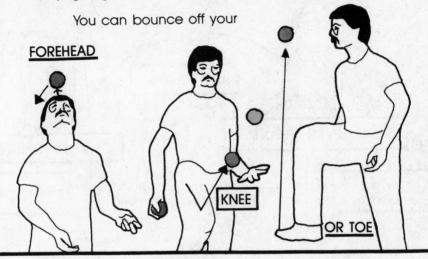

FOREHEAD

KNEE

OR TOE

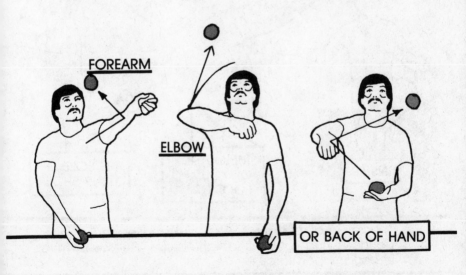

FOREARM

ELBOW

OR BACK OF HAND

If you spend some time in practice you can bounce a ball repeatedly from...

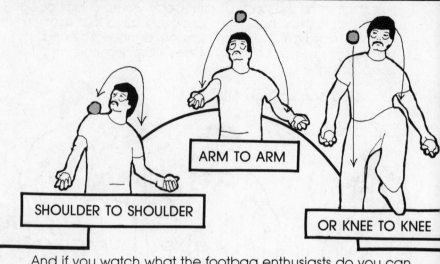

ARM TO ARM

SHOULDER TO SHOULDER

OR KNEE TO KNEE

And if you watch what the footbag enthusiasts do you can also kick back into your pattern using your

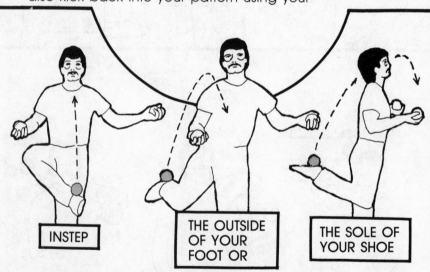

INSTEP

THE OUTSIDE OF YOUR FOOT OR

THE SOLE OF YOUR SHOE

The key in all of this is to practice smaller and smaller bounces and lighter and lighter taps. Finesse is more important than force.

FLASHY STARTS

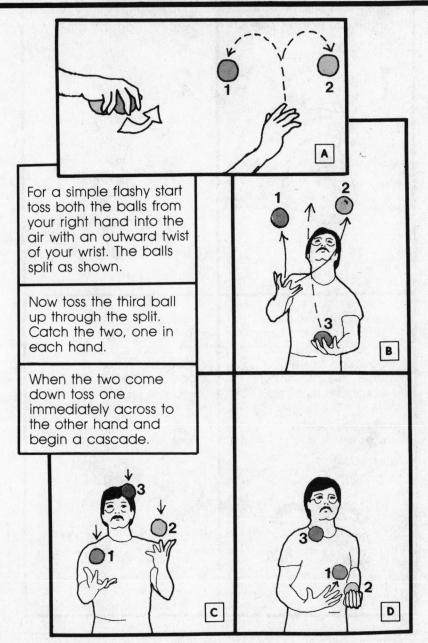

For a simple flashy start toss both the balls from your right hand into the air with an outward twist of your wrist. The balls split as shown.

Now toss the third ball up through the split. Catch the two, one in each hand.

When the two come down toss one immediately across to the other hand and begin a cascade.

Even fancier is to hold all three balls in your dominant hand (Step 1).

Toss all three at once. The center ball goes higher than the other two (Step 2).

1

2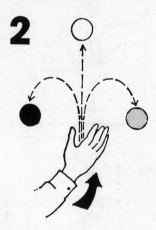

When the two outer balls are at their peaks, reach up and claw down on them (Step 3) while the center ball continues to climb.

As the center ball starts to fall, toss the right hand ball up and across in a cascade pattern (Step 4). Now you are juggling.

3

4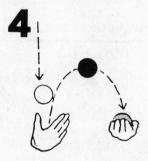

THE KICK BACK

When juggling bouncy balls you can retrieve a drop by stepping hard on the ball as it bounces away, pulling your foot in toward you at the same time. The errant ball will bounce up and back, high enough to work it into your routine. As it comes to you, toss the ball from the hand that is about to receive the runaway ball, and begin your routine again.

If you lose a ball and it goes so far away that you can't retrieve it, you can still salvage the act. As soon as an audience member touches it point straight at them and exclaim, "My first volunteer." Direct them to lob the ball to you. As it comes in resume juggling.

Whatever you do, never act flustered if you drop. It's part of the act. Keep going!

EATING AN APPLE

This trick is the most requested in the juggler's repertoire, and one of the easiest. Like everything in this book you learn it step by step.

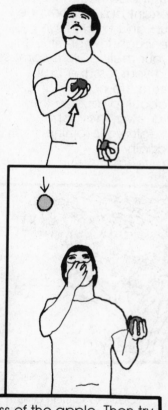

First wash a juggling ball and use it as an imaginary apple. Every third time that this ball comes to your dominant hand throw the following ball extra high to give yourself a bit of extra time, lift this ball to your mouth, and kiss it.

As soon as you have kissed the ball quickly lower your hand and throw that ball along the usual cascade path.

As you practice, throw the following ball lower until it is no higher than an ordinary toss. Once you can kiss a ball repeatedly on every pass, use an apple and start taking bites.

NOTE: Start with every third pass of the apple. Then try every second pass and eventually bite it every time it comes to the right hand. Once you can do the right, learn the left. The ultimate apple trick is to eat three apples with both hands. Every throw is preceded by a bite. Remember, there are lots of things to eat besides apples, and some of them can be pretty comical.

THREE IN ONE HAND

NOTE: Most people are amazed by three in two hands. Make certain that you tell them that three in one hand is twice as hard. It is.

THE SHOWER

There are 3 relatively easy patterns for 3 in one hand. The fastest of these is the shower. The trick is to toss very fast and keep your three balls going in a circle. The second ball must leave your hand before the first one peaks. Toss from the midline of your body toward the outside. Throw as quickly as possible and still maintain the arc.

Before number 2 gets up throw number 3. Then throw high and fast. Keep going.

Now try the shower from outside to inside.

THE CASCADE

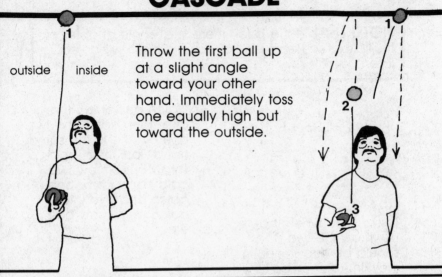

outside   inside

Throw the first ball up at a slight angle toward your other hand. Immediately toss one equally high but toward the outside.

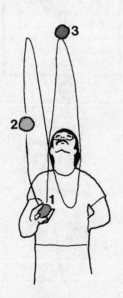

Before number 2 peaks, throw number 3 up along the same path as number 1. Now keep going. Toss inside — outside — inside — outside. The balls pop up the center and alternate going right and left. As you gain control and speed bring your pattern down until it is tight and fast.

Your hand moves back and forth quickly. It is taking the place of two hands. Catch on the outside throw from the center. Then catch on the other side and throw the other way.

Now try the reverse cascade and columns.

MULTIPLEX (THREE IN ONE HAND)

NOTE: Later in the book there is a whole chapter on multiplex. If you learn this trick now, multiplex will be easier later.

Hold 3 balls in 1 hand.

Catch and throw the one. Then catch the two one by one in the same hand. Toss them again. Throw one, throw two, catch and throw one, catch and throw two, catch and throw one, etc.

Toss 1, and when it gets up throw the two. They should be thrown so they line up vertically.

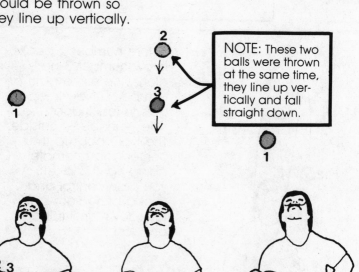

2

3

1

NOTE: These two balls were thrown at the same time, they line up vertically and fall straight down.

1

2 3

Juggling 4 & 5 Balls

Certification Requirements

1. Demonstrate four balls with simultaneous and alternating throws (20 each)
2. Complete a 4 ball series including:
   a. 10 or more throws in an outside circle, and
   b. 10 or more throws in an inside circle, and
   c. 10 or more throws in columns
3. Demonstrate a crossing pattern with four balls (10 throws)
4. Go from a three ball pattern to four balls and back to three
5. Either:
   a. Throw under both legs in a four ball pattern, or
   b. Throw over the shoulder on both sides in a four ball pattern
6. Get into and out of a four ball split (10 throws)
7. Complete 20 throws in cascade pattern with 5 balls ending in a neck catch
8. Go from cascade with 5 to half shower (10 throws) and back to cascade
9. Do 20 throws reverse cascade with five balls
10. Shower 4 balls for 20 throws (one direction only)
11. While juggling five balls in cascade either:
    a. Throw one or more under a leg, or
    b. Throw one or more behind the back, or
    c. Throw one ball back and forth over the pattern (Jugglers' tennis)

4 BALLS

Four balls are just two in each hand, so first, practice the following moves in each hand separately:

1. Two in a circle from the center toward the outside.

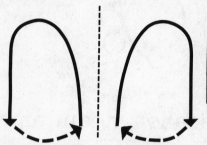

NOTE: Your hand catches on the outside, scoops toward the center and throws.

OUTSIDE CIRCLES

2. Two in a circle from the outside toward the center.

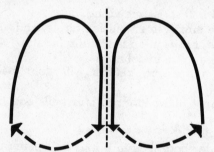

NOTE: Your hand catches toward the midline or center, scoops, toward the outside, and throws in toward the center.

INSIDE CIRCLES

3. Two straight up and down in their own pathways.

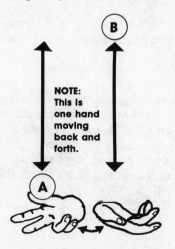

NOTE: This is one hand moving back and forth.

NOTE: Each ball has its own pathway. Your hand shifts back and forth. Throw A Throw B Catch and throw A Catch and throw B Catch and throw A Catch and throw B

COLUMNS

SIMULTANEOUS THROWS

OUTSIDE CIRCLES

Throw 2 beanbags, one from each hand. Circle them toward the outside. When they peak, throw the next two. Keep going. Every time two get up, throw another two.

HINT: Don't scoop in toward yourself. Keep all 4 balls in a plane in front of your body.

INSIDE CIRCLES

Throw 2 beanbags, one from each hand. Circle them in toward the midline. When they peak, throw the next two. Keep going.

WARNING: Collisions and crossed beanbags are common at this point. Use two beanbags of one color in each hand. Don't let the colors change hands.

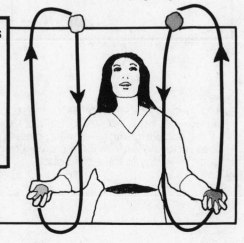

ALTERNATING THROWS

By alternating your hands you can make four balls look very complex. Amy has started with her left hand in this picture.

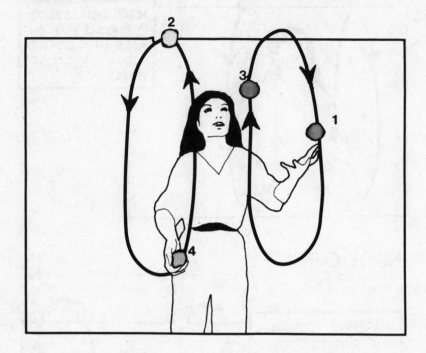

Throw left, right, left, right. Stop and try again, but go for 2 more throws—left, right, left, right, left, right. The throws come in quick succession. **Remember**—nothing crosses your midline. Each hand does **separate** work. In the picture −1 and −3 stay in the left hand. −2 and −4 stay in the right hand.

COLUMNS AND SPLITS

A great 4 ball effect is to throw two simultaneously on one side, then throw two up on the other side. Once they are going up and down in their own elevator shafts you can switch back and forth, widening the split each time.

Here is what a wide split looks like.

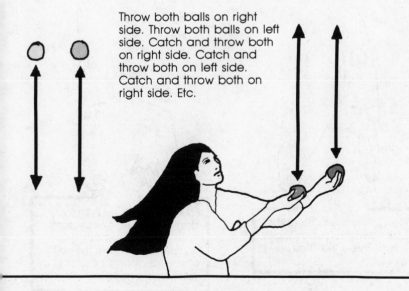

Throw both balls on right side. Throw both balls on left side. Catch and throw both on right side. Catch and throw both on left side. Catch and throw both on right side. Etc.

CROSSING PATTERNS WITH 4

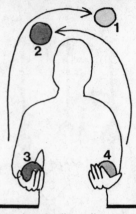

Throw two balls so they cross. Your dominant hand should throw a bit higher. Throws are simultaneous.

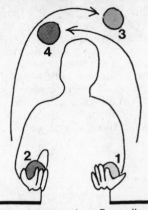

Now keep going. Every time two cross, throw the next two. All throws are simultaneous.

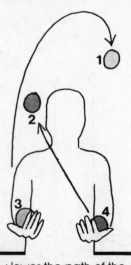

Now lower the path of the ball from your subordinate hand. This is the "half-shower."

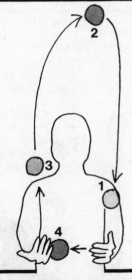

To learn a shower with four, start with three in your dominant hand. Throw those 3 rapidly. Just before the first one lands, hand #4 across to your empty hand.

TRICKS WITH FOUR BALLS

While juggling with four in alternating pattern, raise one leg and toss under. Three counts later, raise the other and toss under.

Over the Shoulder

You can learn to throw simultaneous throws from back to front. (Even harder, but possible, is to throw over the shoulder from front to back.)

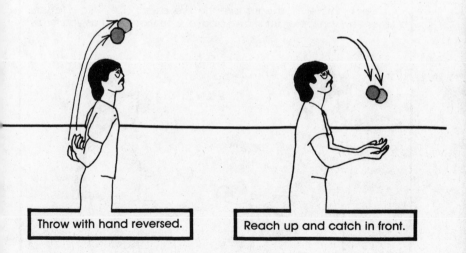

Throw with hand reversed.

Reach up and catch in front.

5 BALLS (the easy way)

Thanks to Roger Dollarhide who showed me this method for painlessly teaching five balls.

FIRST—Get a partner who can juggle 3.

Start with five beanbags held as shown.

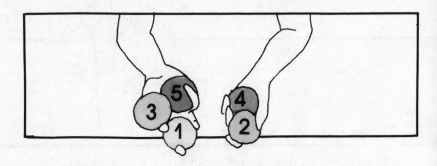

Face your partner. You will share the five beanbags. Throw to your partner slowly in the order shown above. Count out loud as you throw.

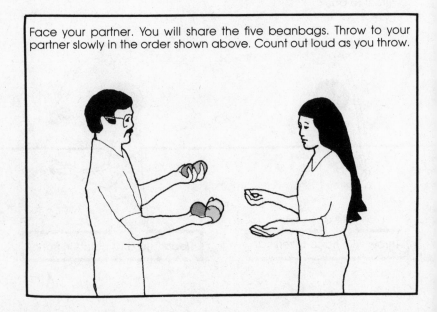

The beanbags all cross, just as with the cascade. This means that the three which start in my right hand end up in my partner's right.

Your partner simply catches the beanbags one by one.

She then throws them back to you in the same manner.

Build up your speed. This is a process of increasing speed without losing the nice high-peaked "figure 8" pattern or changing the peaks.

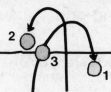

Once you can throw all five beanbags before your partner catches the first one, you are ready to solo. Now toss all five as fast as you can.

Listen to the "plops", and note where they fall—

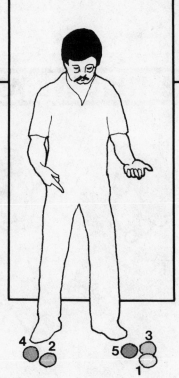

NOTE 1: A good tempo means equal time between the "plops."

NOTE 2: A good pattern means the beanbags are close to each other on the floor, in the pattern shown.

Now you can start throwing **and** catching!

★ Get 5 beanbags that are all different colors.
★ Toss all 5 quickly in order and catch number 1, but let numbers 2, 3, 4 and 5 crash.
★ Start again, but this time catch numbers 1 and 2.
★ Start again, now catch numbers 1, 2 and 3 in order.
★ Start again, and catch numbers 1, 2, 3 and 4, letting only number 5 crash.
★ Start again and catch them all in order. Now you can throw, catch, and throw again.
★ Remember number 1. Start throwing and catching and as number 1 is caught, throw it again. It should end up just where it started, on the fingertip nest of the right hand.

6 THROWS AND 6 CATCHES

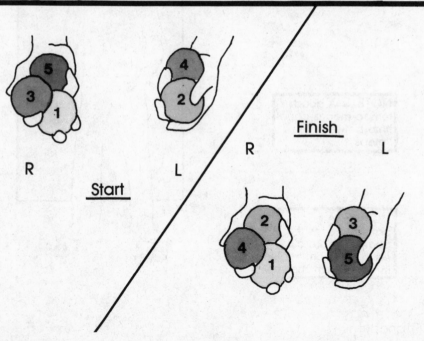

R   L

<u>Start</u>

<u>Finish</u>

R   L

Now just go for one more throw each time, and follow number 1 through the pattern. Here is how you end up each time:

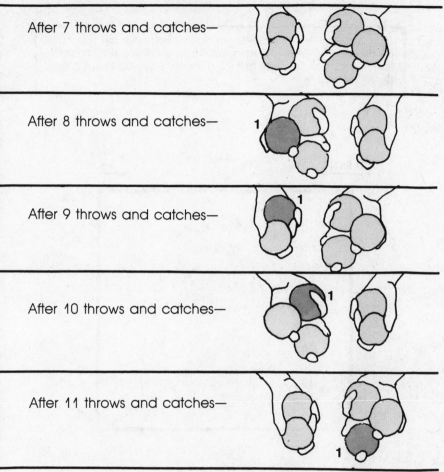

After 7 throws and catches—

After 8 throws and catches—

After 9 throws and catches—

After 10 throws and catches—

After 11 throws and catches—

You don't need to notice where any beanbag but number 1 goes. Just follow it through your pattern, adding one more throw every time.

Now you are ready to keep going, and the method is quite straightforward—just count every right hand throw. Once you get to 20 right hand throws you can continue almost indefinitely. Additional hints on learning to keep five going can be found in the ring chapter.

HALF SHOWER WITH 5 BALLS

Start with 3 balls in the dominant hand and two in the subordinate. For the first five throws, alternate quickly: right, left, right, left, right. Once you start catching, as soon as you touch a ball, throw it along its path.

5 balls

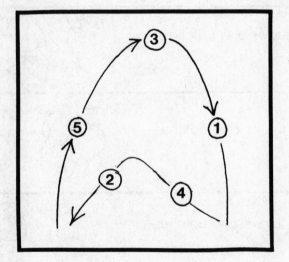

Now, learn the same move from your subordinate to dominant hand.

REVERSE CASCADE WITH 5 BALLS

Once you can do a half shower from each side, the reverse cascade or "reverse" is relatively easy to learn. The problem is keeping track of the beanbags as they fall down the center.

Reverse Cascade

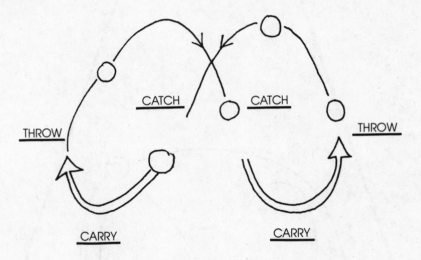

THROW   CATCH   CATCH   THROW

CARRY   CARRY

Use five different colors to learn this move. Keep track of the colors and you can keep your catches in order.

TENNIS WITH FIVE

Once you have a half shower from both sides, tennis is possible. Start with a 5 ball cascade. Then toss one ball back and forth over the top.

You have to keep a space.

It's like juggling 4 in a 5 ball pattern.

FULL SHOWER WITH FIVE

Start with 4 in your dominant hand, nothing in the subordinate. Toss the 4 quickly along the same path and catch them all in the subordinate hand. Throw, throw, throw, throw, catch, catch, catch, catch.

Now try the same move, but this time every time you catch in the subordinate hand, quickly pass the ball to your dominant hand, and throw.

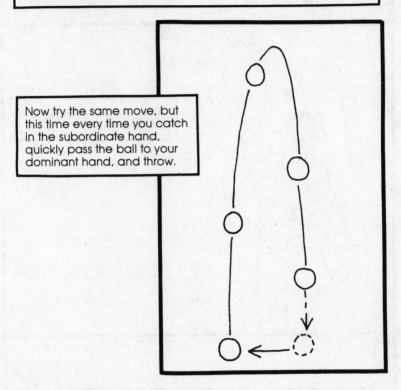

Finally start with 4 in the dominant and 1 in the subordinate. Now as soon as your dominant hand is empty, pass #5 across. From now on, as soon as anything hits your dominant hand, throw it. As soon as anything hits your subordinate hand, pass it!

UNDER THE LEG

The key to this move is to not allow your leg movement to disturb the stable five ball cascade. Your timing and pattern should not change.

HINT — Loose fitting trousers are essential.

FIRST — Start by throwing under your leg. This helps you to feel the move. Your leg has to go high.

SECOND — Toss under in the middle of a sustained juggle, get your leg down and the next 2 throws off. Then fall apart.

THIRD — Go for it!

BEHIND THE BACK

In the midst of a sustained juggle you throw one ball over the opposite shoulder and keep juggling.

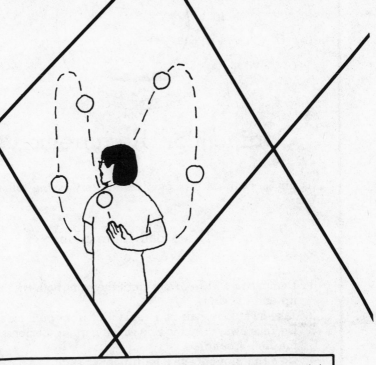

The key here is to practice with one ball first, so that the special throw won't disturb your pattern. If you juggle higher and slower than normal you will have more time for the move which requires a lot of **precise** arm motion in a very short time.

Ball Mastery

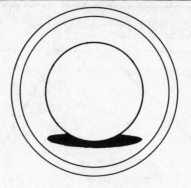

Certification Requirements

This pin is awarded for complete mastery in the following areas:

I Three Ball Interaction

1. Demonstrate Take-aways from the front both with palms up and clawing—
2. Take-away one ball and replace it from both sides—
3. Do Take-away from the side with a partner, demonstrating the Run-around—
4. Do a run-around with a fourth object such as a hat, towel or carrot—
5. Pass three balls over your head with a "flash" to your partner—
6. Do take-away either by coming between your partner's legs or leap-frogging over—
7. Juggle three balls side-by-side and demonstrate 5 tricks—
8. Using a volunteer who does not know how to juggle, demonstrate "half juggling"—
9. Demonstrate six ball passing pattern with three balls ("running three")

II Passing Six Balls

1. Demonstrate cross passing with five balls—
2. Complete 3-3-10 with 6 balls—
3. Either:
   a. Do 3-3-10 "backwards", with left hand passes, or
   b. Do 3-3-10 clawing every catch—
4. Pass every other throw with your partner either
   a. back to front (10 throws) or
   b. back to back (10 throws) or
   c. side to side (10 throws)—
5. Pass 6 "solids" (both hands, every throw)—
6. Either:
   a. Bounce pass 6 balls for 10 throws, or
   b. Pass 6 mixed objects for 12 throws, or
   c. Eat an apple while passing—
7. While passing 5, demonstrate ability to keep a space and pick up 6th ball into pattern—
8. Either
   a. Pass 7 balls (20 throws and clean finish) or
   b. Pass 5 balls and one hat, placing hat on head, or
   c. Pass 6 under both legs or over right shoulder for 10 continuous throws.

III Multiplex

1. Demonstrate four and five ball multiplex for 20 throws each—
2. Go from three and four ball non-multiplex patterns to multiplex, and back again—
3. Demonstrate vertical and diagonal splits of two in a five ball multiplex—
4. Incorporate splits of 3 in a 5 or 6 ball pattern—
5. Toss splits of two under the leg or over the back (both sides) while juggling—
6. Juggle 6 in a three object cascade pattern (10 throws)—
7. Either:
   a. Multiplex 3 in one hand in both hands simultaneously, or
   b. Multiplex 7 in a cascade pattern for 10 throws, or
   c. Teach someone to multiplex 5 balls.

THREE BALL INTERACTION

Once you can juggle three balls or beanbags it is time to find or develop a partner. Working together takes patience, but develops it as well. Remember to laugh occasionally, and **never** blame yourself or your partner for drops. Nobody's perfect.

THE TAKE-AWAY

Face your partner and get close, so you could share a juggling space. Your partner starts juggling slowly with three balls, one of which is a different color. Just watch that different colored ball, and when your partner throws it from her right to her left reach up with your right hand and take it at the moment when it peaks.

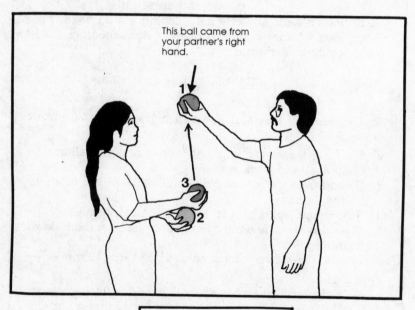

This ball came from your partner's right hand.

Get a nice high pattern to start.

Now you are committed to take all three. Immediately after taking the first ball, reach up with your left hand and take the second ball, the next one to come from your partner's left hand, headed toward her right. Take it at the peak also.

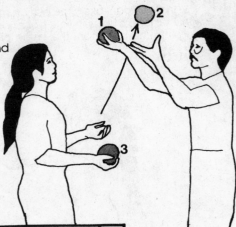

Every time one peaks, reach in and take it.

Remember, you alternate your hands. Take right, take left, take right.

Now you have one ball in each hand. Wait until your partner's third ball peaks, then throw the first one you caught underneath into a cascade pattern, and take over the juggling equipment. You can keep the balls for a while, or your partner can take them right back on the next throw.

Now that you can take three balls from the front you can grab them with your palms up, with your palms down (clawing), and by chopping into the balls from the inside or outside.

Once you feel comfortable taking all 3 balls, just take out one, and replace it in the pattern. Your partner keeps juggling the remaining 2 balls at a normal cadence, with an empty space for the missing ball. As soon as possible find this space, and toss or drop the stolen ball back into the pattern.

THE RUN-AROUND

When you and your partner can both come in from the side and take over the juggle you can run around and around one another, sharing three objects.

First learn to step in boldly and take over the pattern. Your partner juggles three. You come in from her left, reaching up with your left hand to take a ball intended for her left hand. Reach high and take it at its peak.

As soon as you have the ball in your left hand reach rudely across with the right hand and catch the next ball, the one intended for her right hand.

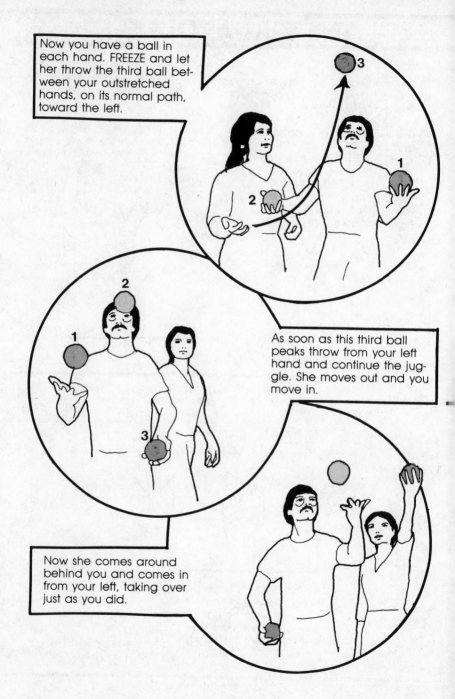

Now you have a ball in each hand. FREEZE and let her throw the third ball between your outstretched hands, on its normal path, toward the left.

As soon as this third ball peaks throw from your left hand and continue the juggle. She moves out and you move in.

Now she comes around behind you and comes in from your left, taking over just as you did.

Once you can complete a run—around you can go faster and faster until your last throw is the first one you catch. Once you have control of this move you can slow down the pace and add other elements, for instance:

You can take your partner's hat

Take his scarf and his carrot.

And then take the balls.

Now you can create a story complete with character development and a dramatic ending. Give it a try.

SIDE BY SIDE

You can stand side by side and put your arms over one another's shoulders. Your arms can act as the two hands of a single juggler.

Once you can do juggling tricks as a side by side team, you can also use your free hands to move a hat or a cigar back and forth between you.

FLASH PASSING

There are many ways to get three objects to your partner. A speedy method is the "flash pass." A flash means all the objects are in the air before anything has been caught.

Face your partner and juggle three balls. As fast as you can toss the three balls across to your partner right-left-right.

Your partner catches the incoming balls, right-left-right, and starts juggling immediately.

Once you can complete a flash pass to the front, you can pass to your partner standing behind you. A handclap can be your signal that she is ready.

Now that you are comfortable both taking the objects away and giving them up it is time to experiment.

Your partner can come through your legs from behind, stand up, and take the balls—

The key here is for the person on the bottom to toss the last ball up between the legs of the leaper at the last moment.

And you can leap frog over her, taking control on the way down.

Leaper: Use her shoulders for an initial push, then she ducks away as you go over.

RUNNING THREE

This is a lead-in to passing six objects and is a great way to practice passing tricks without having to worry about drops.

Start juggling three balls, facing your partner, about 6 feet apart. After you are stabilized, toss one of your right-hand throws across to your partner's left.

Now every right-hand throw goes across to your partner's left. All your left-hand throws go across your chest from left to right in the usual pattern. Remember to alternate your throws as usual.

Your partner catches the incoming balls in the left-hand one by one, and throws across her chest to her right in the usual manner.

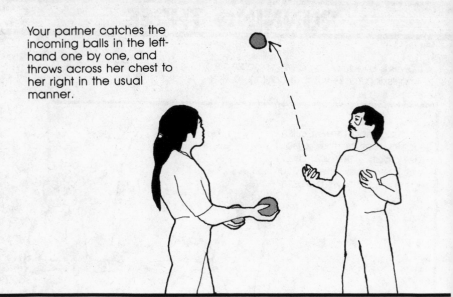

As soon as she is stabilized she can throw across to you again from her right.

The balls make a rectangle, from your left, to your right, to her left, to her right, and back to your left. Remember to alternate your hands and to throw across your chest with your left hand.

PASSING 5, 6, 7 AND MORE BALLS

Now that you can share three balls with a partner, you are beginning to appreciate the joy of interactive juggling. You can probably see how learning to pass six balls will lead inevitably to passing six or more clubs. In terms of audience appeal, working with a partner is usually far more impressive than a solo routine.

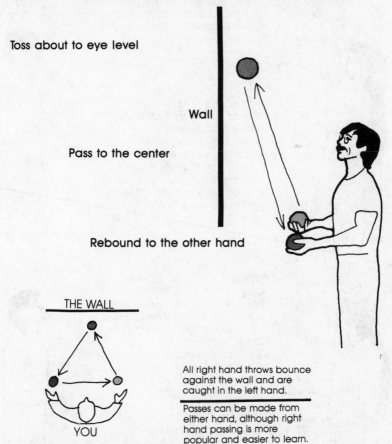

Toss about to eye level

Wall

Pass to the center

Rebound to the other hand

THE WALL

All right hand throws bounce against the wall and are caught in the left hand.

Passes can be made from either hand, although right hand passing is more popular and easier to learn.

YOU

You can begin to learn ball passing by bouncing against a wall. Although the motion of throwing to a wall is diagonal rather than straight across as in real partnership juggling, the wall is a great way to learn when practicing alone.

3-3-10

The most common 6-object passing pattern is one called "3-3-10" in which every third ball leaving your right hand is passed across to your partner three times; every second right hand ball is then passed three times; and finally every right hand ball is passed 10 times, in a flurry of activity.

←   6 ft.   →

To begin any passing routine, stand facing your partner about six feet away. Hold the balls just as you did for the beginning of the basic cascade, except that both of you start as if you were right handed. In other words, put two balls in the right hand and one in the left hand.

Both you and your partner should raise your hands shoulder high and when the one of you designated as leader says "go" lower your hands together and begin juggling. If you don't juggle at the same speed and to the same height, you will get out of synchronization; so try to stay together.

Before you begin throwing, juggle together and say the rhythm together. The first "3" goes like this (every number or the words "go" and "halt" signifies a ball leaving the right hand, the "ands" are balls leaving the left hand):

"Go, one, and, two, and, throw; and, one, and, two, and, throw; and, one, and, two, and, throw; and, halt."

Now it is best if you and your partner each have an "odd ball." Start with it in your left hand, and your hands held high. Bring them down, and begin.

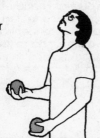

YOUR THROWS SHOULD FOLLOW A DISTINCT RECTANGLE

Use the same count, but throw the "odd" ball every time you say "throw" in a clean, eye-high, arc across from your right to your partner's left hand. This throw should be right in with the timing of the rest of the routine, your odd ball goes from your right hand to your partner's left, and his odd ball comes to your left (just as your own odd ball would have if you had thrown it across your own body from right to left, instead of tossing it to your partner).

For this first piece of the routine, your odd balls will be the ones that move. In the next segment every second ball goes across. The count picks up from the third "throw" of the first segment: ". . ., and, one, and, throw; and, one, and, throw; and, one, and, throw; and, halt."

Practice this second segment right after the first, without a break. You may find that your left hand throws are trying to mimic your right hand throws and are going out from your body, causing you to move your right hand and shoulder farther and farther forward. This error can be corrected by practicing alone, close to and facing a wall, and by concentrating on not letting your throws from the left hand (or your right hand itself) touch the wall. Only your right hand throws should go out in front of you, left hand throws should simply cross your body from the left to the right hand.

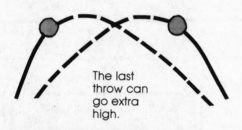

The last throw can go extra high.

You may want to throw the ball from your right hand high in the air on "HALT" and catch it together with your partner to signal that you are finished.

Now for the third segment. Start off with your sixth "throw" and count: "..., and, throw; and, throw; and, throw; and, throw; and, throw; and, throw; and, throw; and, throw; and, throw; and, throw; and, throw; and, throw; and, HALT."

The full count for "3-3-10" is: "Go, one, and two, and throw; and, two, and, two, and, throw; and three, and, two, and, throw; and, one, and throw; and, two, and, throw; and three, and, throw; and, throw; and, throw; and, throw; and, throw; and, throw; and, throw; and, throw; and, throw; and, throw; and, throw; and, throw; and, throw; and HALT."

Catch that last ball together for a fancy finish,

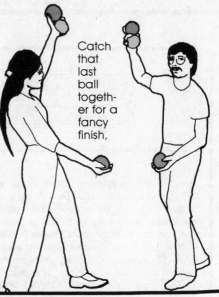

In this illustration we have each switched a ball to our far hand and caught our final self throw with our near hand for a fancy finish.

Of course you can try variations of the "3-3-10" routine. However, you may find that "3-3-3" is about all you can handle at first. The simplest variation is to have a skinny friend stand in between you and your partner as you pass, doing a regular cascade pattern. Or, you can claw every catch, tossing high, hard throws to your partner. Another, far more difficult, but good for humbling the soul, is to do all throws with your left hand and catches with your right, reversing all your habits completely.

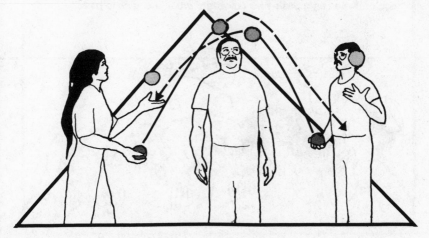

COUNTING

Now that we are entering the wonderful world of passing, it's time to learn to count. The count is the beat or rhythm of the pattern. It tells you when to throw, and is a precise way of communicating with other jugglers. The count of a particular pattern is determined by counting every throw, starting from the previous pass. For example, in the 3-3-10 pattern described above, there are three separate counts. The first of these is called a 6 COUNT, meaning the pass comes every sixth toss. Just count the words. Each word is either a throw, or a pass. This count is also called EVERY THIRDS, meaning every third right-hand throw goes across. The second count is a 4 COUNT, meaning that every fourth toss is a pass. This is also called EVERY OTHERS. The last segment of a 3-3-10, when every right-hand toss goes across to your partner, is called a 2 count. This is often called "SHOWER PASSING," or "EVERY RIGHT HAND." Using the counting system described above, throwing every ball to your partner with both hands would be a 1 COUNT, and if you toss first with one hand, then three beats later toss across with the other hand, it would be a 3 COUNT. Knowing the common counting systems makes passing with stranger possible. In fact, wherever you go in the world you will find jugglers who can "speak your language" when it comes to passing.

DIAGONAL PASSES WITH 5 BALLS

This is a great way to develop confidence and work on passing and catching skills. It is a good deal easier than the 3-3-10 routine outlined above, and can be carried out between one experienced juggler and one novice.

The experienced juggler tosses one ball from her right hand to her partner's left with a high arc. As that ball peaks the novice tosses number 2 diagonally from his left to hers.

As number 2 peaks the first juggler tosses number 3 straight across from her left to her partner's right, and as it peaks the novice passes diagonally again.

In other words, the person who starts always passes straight across, and the second person always passes diagonally. Only one ball is passed at a time, first me, then you, then me, then you. The next ball is always thrown when the previous one peaks. Try this with soccer balls or basketballs if you want to take a challenge.

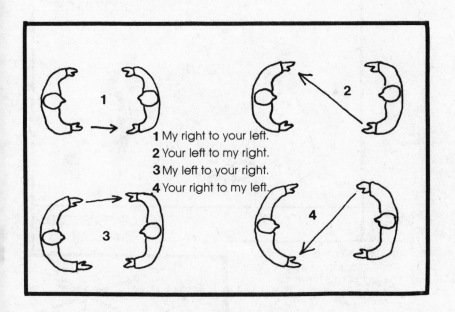

1 My right to your left.
2 Your left to my right.
3 My left to your right.
4 Your right to my left.

CONFIGURATIONS

How jugglers are physically arranged while juggling is the configuration. There are a number of positions two jugglers may take with relation to one another while passing, for instance—

HINT: To make it easier on yourselves, try using a 4 count (every others) when learning these configurations.

BACK TO FRONT

Here you get to practice two common throws, the drop-up and the drop-back. Usually the drop-back and drop-up are thrown across in this configuration as shown below:

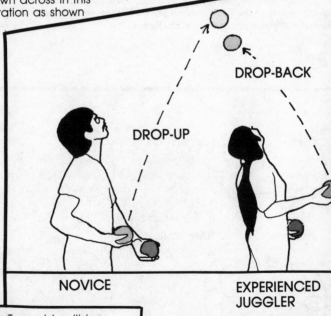

DROP-BACK

DROP-UP

NOVICE

EXPERIENCED JUGGLER

NOTE: To avoid collisions when passing in this manner, the juggler to the rear should pass higher than the one in front.

BACK TO BACK

This configuration is actually easier than it looks, but first you must learn to catch an incoming object by looking up and to the left. Start by throwing one ball around the pattern. Then move to two, tossing simultaneously with your partner.

Next go on to three, and run them back to back like you did front to front. Finally go on to six balls. Start back to back with your hands high and backs just touching. Count and throw together. Look over your shoulder for those incoming passes.

NOTE: High, slow juggling and high passes with larger balls makes this easier.

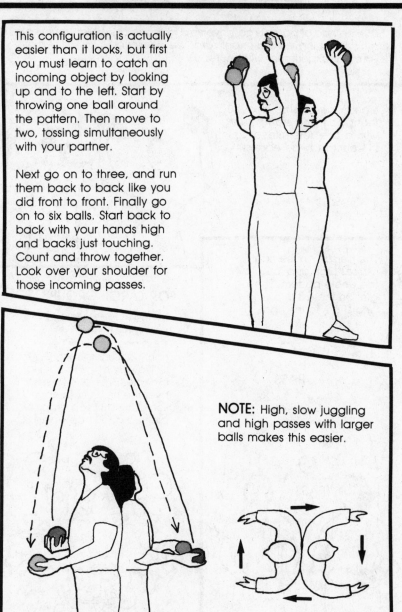

SIDE BY SIDE

This method of passing can involve a long line of jugglers, or even a circle facing inward or outward. We'll describe it for just two of you, but experiment with more.

Stand side by side about 3 feet apart and start passing with a pre-determined count (4 count may be easiest).

The person on the right passes high and long, over the whole pattern. The juggler on the left throws low and short, to the right.

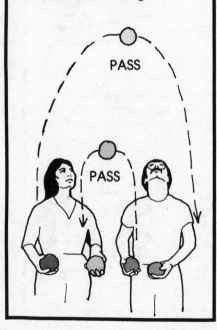

PASS

PASS

FOR LARGE GROUPS

Try this in a circle. Now **everyone** tosses the low short pass to his or her right-hand neighbor. Got it? Now try back to front in a circle. Everyone tosses over the head to the person behind. If you drop, pick up and keep going.

STARTS

There are certain conventions to starting a passing pattern. For instance, you generally are facing your partner, so look at them and smile. Agree on your start and your count. Also, decide what to do if you drop. Do you keep going or stop and start again? Now you are ready for either a slow start or a fast start.

SLOW START

This is also called a 5 count, or lead, start. It is the one you previously practiced in the 3—3—10. The ball that starts in your left hand is the first one that gets passed to your partner.

FAST START

This is also called a "Live Start" since you don't juggle to yourself at all before you start passing. The first throw is from your right hand which has two balls in it.

You pass straight across to your partner's left, and the action begins.

When you first start passing, the slow start is easier. It is also a great way to synchronize your juggling with your partner. It is a good lead-in to slow and relaxed passing.

Later, when you are more accomplished (or if you are doing a show and want to cover up your drops), the live or fast start is useful. When you pass 7 or more objects most jugglers use a fast start, so get used to it.

SOLIDS OR 1 COUNT

Passing every throw across to your partner is fast, but not impossible. Your right hand and your partner's left hand cooperate just like one person. Your left hand and your partner's right are another person. So you learn one side at a time.

Face your partner. One hand is behind your back. You have 2 balls, he has one. Use your left and his right. You start. When your first ball gets to the top, he throws. Just alternate.

Now put your right hand behind your back and let him start with two in his right hand. Once you can do either hand, try both hands.

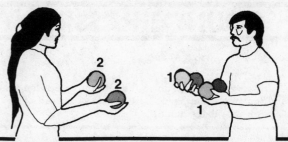

If you throw simultaneously with right and left hands, it is best if one of you starts with four and the other with two.

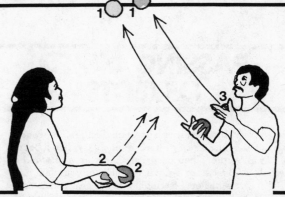

I throw 2, you throw 2, I throw 2, etc. (This is slower and easier).

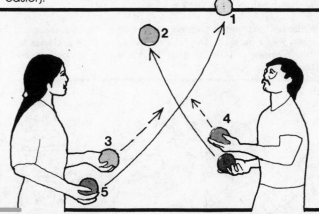

But if you alternate hands it is easier if each of you starts with two in your right hand.

I throw right—you throw right—I throw left—you throw left.

(This is faster and harder and is called the "Thunder Shower.")

BOUNCE PASSING

Of course, whatever you do in the air you can do on the ground (or on a drum head). Just toss down instead of up. (Balls work, beanbags don't!)

PASSING MIXED OBJECTS

Passing mixed objects can be a great challenge. Simply add one object at a time. Start with something easy, like 5 beanbags and an apple. Then try 4 beanbags, an apple and a basketball. Add a hat, or a glove, or a shoe or your imagination. If you give each item a test flight with five beanbags before adding it to the mix, the trick is far easier. For a real challenge, try some "impossible" items like a water balloon, a flounder or a lit dynamite stick (just kidding).

While on the topic of passing strange stuff, why not share an apple while passing. You take a bite every time it comes to you. Working out the count and some snappy dialog can be fun.

KEEPING A SPACE

Eventually you will want to be able to pass continuously, even if you drop. To do this, you will need to learn to pass five in a six pattern.

Start by passing 6 balls with a 2 count, but drop one ball and keep going with the same rhythm. This means that the space will move through the pattern just as the missing ball would.

HERE IS THE SPACE!

One way to note the space is to snap your fingers when it comes to your right hand, then snap them when it gets to your left hand.

PICK UP TO SIX

Once you can keep a space, you can pick up a dropped ball. At first this seems fast, but eventually it becomes automatic.

As soon as the space gets to your left hand, look down quickly and find the dropped ball. Look up again and move into position with the dropped ball by your right foot.

This time when the space is one count away from your right hand squat quickly as you throw with the left, grab, pass, stand and catch the pass from your partner.

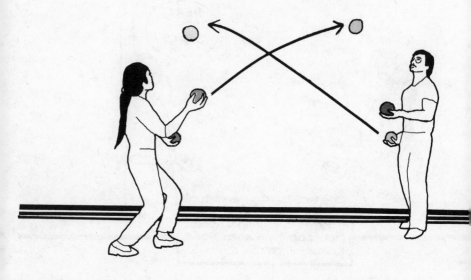

PASSING THE HAT

Once you can keep a space, there are lots of things you can do in that space such as waving at the audience, slapping your thigh or cheek, adjusting your hat or eyeglasses. Why not leave the sixth ball on the ground, reach up, remove and pass your hat.

When the space comes around reach up and remove your hat, and...

Toss it to your partner who can put it on, or throw it back to you.

NOTE: You toss a hat like a ring.

PASSING 7 (OR MORE)

Ambitious, aren't we? Well, you can pass 7 if you can pass 6. Your individual juggling rhythm is the same, it's just a bit faster. When you pass 6 (or 8 or 10) you and your partner throw at the same time, and the objects you threw cross in mid-air and come in to your waiting hands at the same time. That means you can listen to the rhythm, and you will both be doing the same thing at the same time. When you pass 7 or 9 you alternate throws with your partner. When you are throwing with your right, she is throwing with the left.

You start with four, two in each hand. Your partner starts with three—two in the right and one in the left. You needn't raise your hands to start since you don't start at the same time.

The person with 4 starts by throwing a beanbag directly across in a high arc from his right to his partner's left. Throw a foot or two higher than usual.

The other juggler starts ½ beat later with a similar throw. As soon as each of you tosses this first throw, start juggling and passing. Every right hand throw goes to your partner.

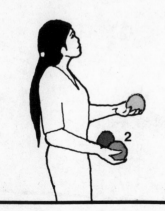

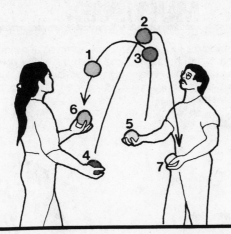

NOTE: Here is what our 9 ball pattern looked like for the first 9 throws. After that, chaos, but we're still trying.

MULTIPLEX

Multiplex is a method for juggling a larger number of objects by throwing two, three or more at the same time. With multiplex you can juggle 4 or 5 beanbags or balls very soon after doing 3. First Amy will demonstrate the basics. Then we'll discuss the infinite variations of this unique juggling system.

Start with 2 beanbags in your right hand.

NOTE: Point your fingers toward the midline.

Toss the two balls at the same time. The one from the fingertips goes higher and farther.

NOTE: The balls split in the air.

Catch one in each hand.

NOTE: Catch the right, then the left.

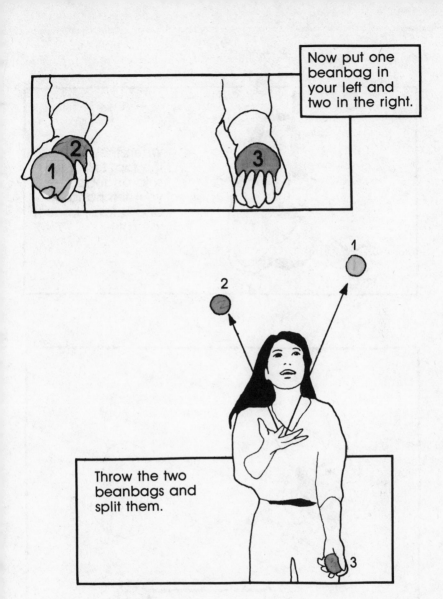

Now put one beanbag in your left and two in the right.

Throw the two beanbags and split them.

When they get to the top, toss the solo beanbag from your left hand up and across, through the split.

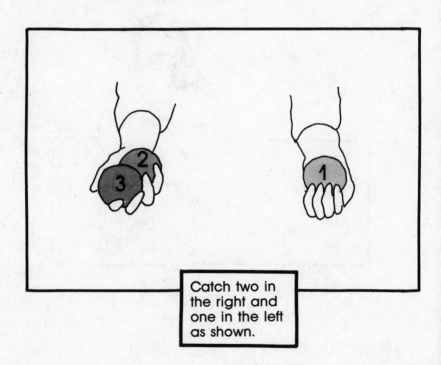

Catch two in the right and one in the left as shown.

Now do this same series from the opposite side.

1. Start with two in the left hand.
2. Toss and split them, catching one in each hand.
3. Put two in your left hand and one in the right.
4. Toss and split the two, when they peak throw the solo beanbag from the right hand through the split.
5. Catch two in the left and one in the right.
6. Repeat.

Now it's time for four. Start with two in each hand.

Throw and split the two from the left hand.

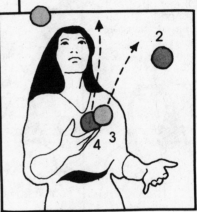

When they peak, toss and split the two from the right hand. They go between the two in the air.

NOW catch left-right, pause, right-left.

NOTE: The rhythm is throw left, pause. Throw right. Catch (left)—catch (right), pause. Catch (right)—catch (left).

A HELPFUL HINT: Don't try to understand this, **JUST DO IT!**

ON TO FIVE BALLS

Hold five balls as shown.

Throw number 1. When it peaks, throw and split 2 and 3.

When 2 and 3 peak, throw and split 4 and 5.

Catch number 1.

Catch 2 and 3. Catch 4 and 5.

You end up like this

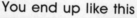

NOTE: #1, #2, #4 cross. #3 and #5 go straight up and straight down.

CONFUSED? Don't try to figure this out yet, **JUST DO IT!**

Now you can keep going with five beanbags.

- Throw #1.
- When #1 peaks, throw #2 and #3.
- When #2 and #3 peak, throw #4 and #5.
- Just keep going, alternate your hands.
- Every time two balls peak, throw and split the two from the other hand.
- There are always 2 in the air, and 2 on the way up.
- Remember to throw through the split.

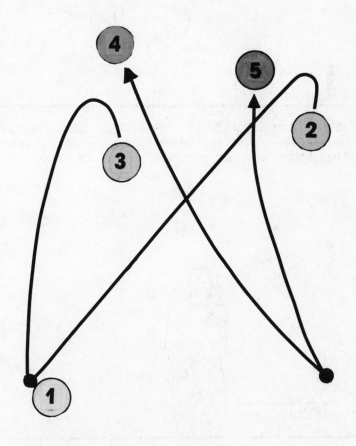

Vertical stacking

Instead of splitting two balls, stack them. Toss two from the right hand so they line up vertically, and catch them in the left hand. Then toss two from the left and catch them in the right.

Now you can juggle 5 with vertical stacks. Toss one from the right, then toss two from the left hand, then two from the right, then one from the left, two from the right, etc.

6 in a 3 ball pattern

Start with 4 in the right hand, and two in the left. Toss two from the right, stacked. Now every throw from either hand is two balls stacked.

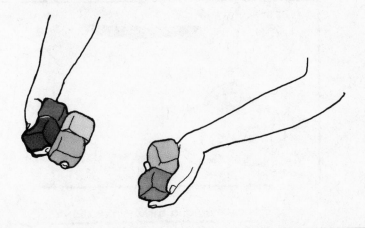

Just juggle in a cascade; but every catch is two balls in quick succession, and every throw is a stack of two.

Just one more concept, and you are on your own to play and create with multiplex!

SPLITTING THREE

Start with 3 beanbags in your right hand as shown.

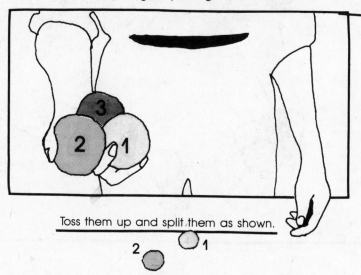

Toss them up and split them as shown.

NOTE: Number 1 goes high and crosses to the left hand. Number 2 and 3 go straight up and come straight down.

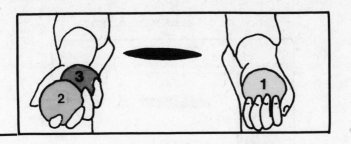

Catch as shown.

Now do the same throw from the other side—

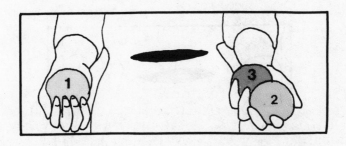

And the same catch.

Now hold 4 beanbags as shown.

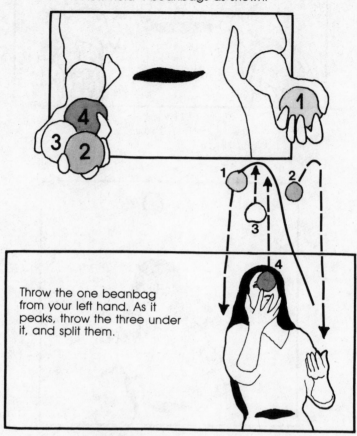

Throw the one beanbag from your left hand. As it peaks, throw the three under it, and split them.

Catch number 1. Then catch #4, #3 and #2 in quick succession.

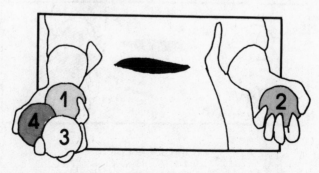

Once again hold 4 beanbags as shown.

Throw the three beanbags from your right hand, and split them.

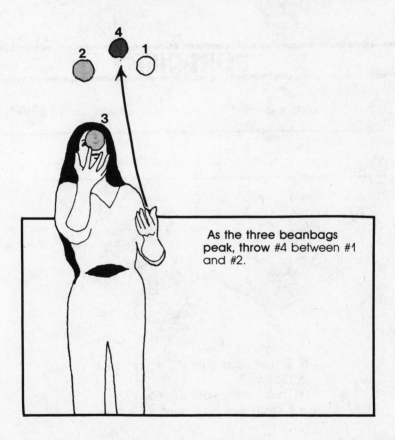

As the three beanbags peak, throw #4 between #1 and #2.

Catch in this order:

Three, Two, One—pause—Four.
They end up as shown.

SURPRISE

Now that you can throw and catch a split of 3, you can juggle **SEVEN** beanbags.

Surprised? Start as shown.

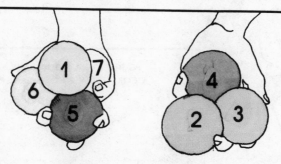

- Throw #1.
- Throw and split #2, #3 and #4.
- Catch #1.
- Throw and split #5, #6, #7.
- Catch 4, 3, 2, 7, 6, 5.

Now the sequence is the same as juggling 5 in a multiplex pattern.

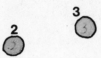

☆ Throw 1 from the right hand
☆ Throw a split of 3 from the left hand.
☆ Catch the 1 in the left hand.
☆ Throw a split of 3 from the right hand.
☆ Throw a split of 3 from the left hand and as soon as the right hand has 3, throw and split them.
☆ As soon as the left hand has 3, throw and split them.

Hey, I know this sounds crazy, but:

A HELPFUL HINT: Don't try to understand this, **JUST DO IT!**

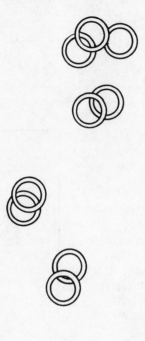

ALBERT LUCAS

Juggling Rings

Certification Requirements

1. Cascade
2. Reverse cascade (12 throws)
3. Pancake flips (6 throws)
4. Spin a ring on a ring and return to the cascade
5. Juggle flat to the audience
6. Throw under the leg on both sides
7. Juggle 2 rings in each hand
8. Do a split with 3 rings
9. Throw 3 rings in a shower pattern
10. Throw one ring around your collar
11. Finish with three rings around the collar
12. Complete one additional 3 ring move:
    a. Color change
    b. Flash and half-turn
    c. Finger spin
    d. Toss a ball through a ring.

GETTING STARTED

★Juggling rings is like juggling balls only you can throw higher.

ONE RING

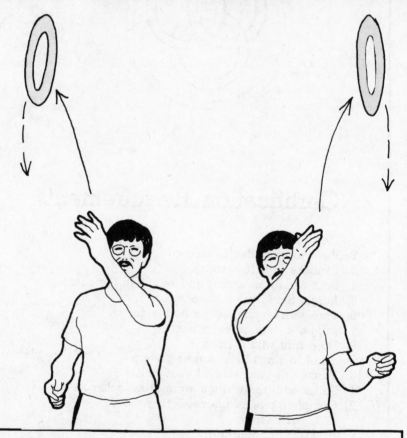

Throw one ring from hand to hand—the sky's the limit—rings can go higher than balls.

★Give the ring a spin as you throw, this will stabilize it.
★You can reach up to throw and catch with rings.
★Tilt your head back and look up.

REMEMBER
THROW NICE AND HIGH WITH TWO PEAKS

TWO RINGS

ONE IN EACH HAND   READY?

Throw the first ring. When it reaches its peak, throw the second.

HOLDING THREE RINGS

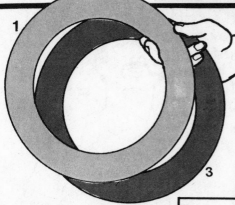

Hold two rings in your dominant hand, The one on your finger tips is the one you throw first.

Hold it loosely. Your second ring is in your other hand.

NOW GO FOR IT! EVERY TIME ONE PEAKS, THROW ANOTHER!

Throw #1;

When #1 gets to the top, throw #2;

When #2 gets to the top, throw #3

COLOR CHANGE

If you have rings with a different color on each side, and want to change the side seen by the audience, there are at least two ways to change it. One is described here, and one in the section on five rings.

While juggling, catch with your palm up and thumb out.

Twist the ring inward and throw again. Keep juggling.

This changes the sides of the ring.

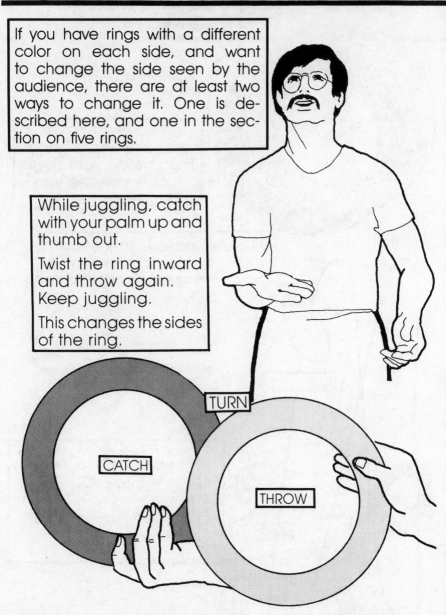

CATCH

TURN

THROW

SPINNING THE RING

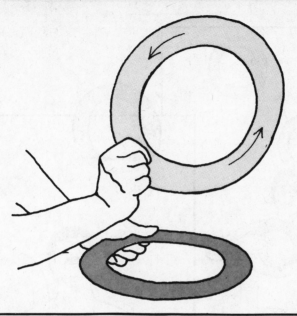

To spin a ring on a ring, pinch the spinner ring with the fingers of your dominant hand.

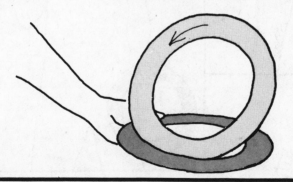

TIP
Don't throw high—instead, "Snap" your wrist.

If you are facing the audience, you can turn the rings so they are flat in front of you.

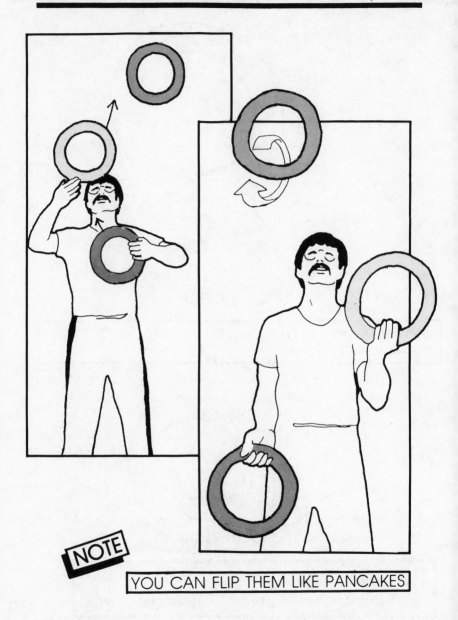

NOTE

YOU CAN FLIP THEM LIKE PANCAKES

JUGGLING FOUR

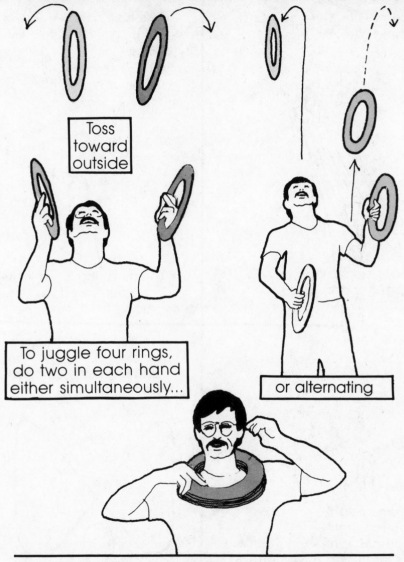

Toss toward outside

To juggle four rings, do two in each hand either simultaneously...

or alternating

My favorite finale is to stack the rings around my neck and end up with ring around the collar.

JUGGLING 5 RINGS

Start with 3 in one hand held like this.

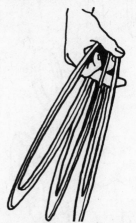

Now keep 3 rings moving from hand to hand.

Toss them quickly to the other hand with high peaks.

The third ring is just leaving your hand as you catch #1.

Now you have the speed for 5. Hold 3 in one hand and two in the other and go for it!

Throw right—
Throw right—
Throw right—
Catch and throw left—
Catch and throw left—
Catch and throw left—
Catch and throw right—
etc.

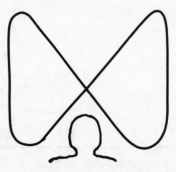

Keep the pattern high and angle the rings out slightly as you throw.

COLOR CHANGE WITH 5

You need 2 color rings for this trick.

Once you can keep 5 rings going, you can do a color change. Simply reach inside every ring as you catch it, let the ring drop over, and throw again.

(A) Juggle sideways to the audience.

(C) Let ring drop. At the same time, turning it over.

Throw again.

(B) Reach inside.

(D) Opposite side now faces the audience.

(E) Try with 1 ring, then every right hand catch, then every left hand catch. Finally, turn every ring with each hand.

BALANCE ON FOREHEAD TO 5

Juggle 4 rings with an alternating pattern and outside circles. Next practice balancing a ring on your forehead. Then put the two together.

Start with one ring balanced on your forehead, while juggling 4.

Shift to a five ring pattern. Toss a little higher and a little faster. Start with a right hand throw.

Your fifth throw is the ring that was on your forehead.

FLASH AND TURN

STEP 1 — Juggle 3 rings. Throw them up with a flash and clap, catch and keep juggling.

STEP 2 — Juggle 3 rings. Flash, turn a pirouette, catch and keep juggling.

STEP 3 — Juggle 5 rings. Throw 3 of the 5 high, hold 2, turn, toss the 2 you held and keep juggling. (Try 1/2 and full turns.)

STEP 4 — Juggle 5 rings. Flash all 5, clap, catch and keep juggling.

STEP 5 — Juggle 5 rings. Flash all 5, turn 1/2 way, catch and keep juggling.

STEP 6 — Juggle 5 rings. Flash all 5, turn all the way around, catch and keep juggling.

POINTERS:
- When you do a 1/2 turn, you start again with the last hand that threw.
- To give yourself time to make the turn you will have to throw higher and faster than usual. You will find that throwing twice as high only increases the time aloft by 40%.

A SUPER FINALE

While juggling 5 rings, throw one extra high with a slow pancake flip. Bring the other 4 down around your neck one at a time as you catch them, and let that last ring flip right onto your neck.

6 AND 7 RINGS (OR MORE)

6 RINGS — The rings do not cross. Practice 3 in one hand. Practice 3 in the other hand. Use all three patterns, inside circles, outside circles and columns, where each has its own pathway. Knowing all 3 patterns will help you to adjust bad throws later. Now try the trick with both hands throwing simultaneously. Use outside circles. Then try staggered throws which seem faster, but are easier to control.

7 RINGS—Practice 5 with an extra high cascade pattern. Practice flashing 5 to this height, and clapping below the flash before you catch and resume. This should require throws of 20 feet or more in height. Throw 4 from one hand and catch them in the other hand. Then throw them back. Now hold 4 as shown in your starting hand.

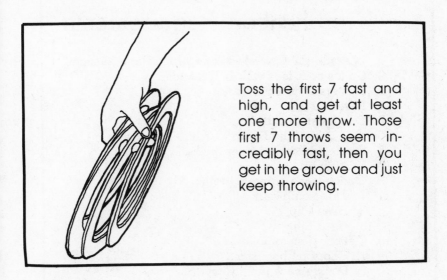

Toss the first 7 fast and high, and get at least one more throw. Those first 7 throws seem incredibly fast, then you get in the groove and just keep throwing.

OR MORE — Even numbers do not cross. Each hand does its own work. Odd numbers cross and may be harder to sustain at the higher limits of ability.

Juggling 3 Clubs

Certification Requirements

1. Cascade (12 throws) looking around at audience
2. Under both legs with both hands
3. Floaters from both sides
4. Reverse spin
5. One balance trick
6. One behind the back move on each side
7. Single and double over the head
8. Kick up on one side
9. Option—one of the following
   1. Three club start
   2. Head Flip
   3. Head Spin
10. Option—One of following
    1. Chops on both sides
    2. Double back crosses on both sides
    3. Between the legs on both sides

CLUB JUGGLING

BARRETT FELKER

GETTING STARTED

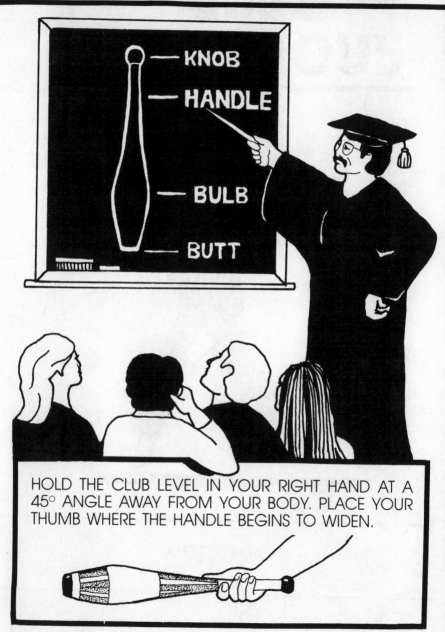

KNOB

HANDLE

BULB

BUTT

HOLD THE CLUB LEVEL IN YOUR RIGHT HAND AT A 45° ANGLE AWAY FROM YOUR BODY. PLACE YOUR THUMB WHERE THE HANDLE BEGINS TO WIDEN.

THROWING ONE CLUB

CLUB JUGGLING REQUIRES A SMOOTH "SCOOP" ACTION. THE BUTT OF THE CLUB MAKES A "U" IN THE AIR.

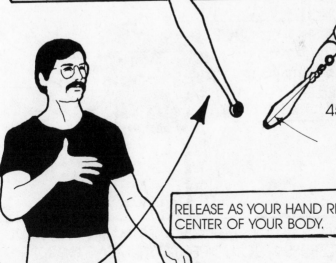

45°

RELEASE AS YOUR HAND REACHES THE CENTER OF YOUR BODY.

171

AIM HERE AT FIRST,

2 FEET

THEN AFTER A FEW
THROWS COME DOWN
SLOWLY. EVENTUALLY
THE ENTIRE PATTERN
TAKES PLACE BELOW
EYE LEVEL.

THE CLUB SHOULD MAKE
A SINGLE FLIP AND
END UP POINTING TO
THE LEFT
AT A 45° ANGLE.

NOW, REPEAT FROM LEFT TO RIGHT. WHEN YOU HAVE
A GOOD TOSS IN BOTH DIRECTIONS, MOVE ON TO THE
NEXT STEP

EXCHANGING 2 CLUBS

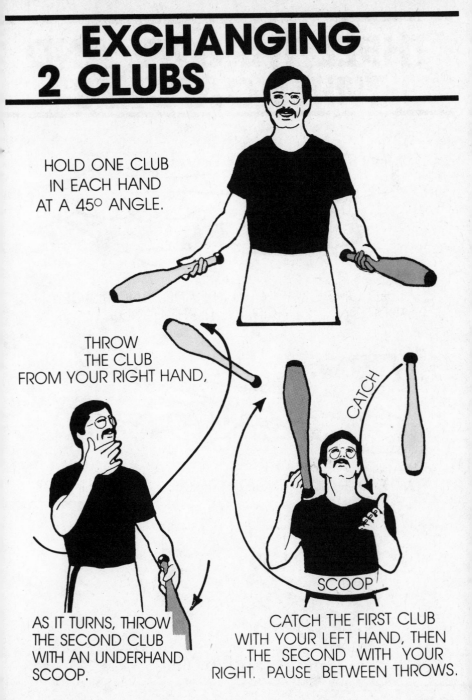

HOLD ONE CLUB IN EACH HAND AT A 45° ANGLE.

THROW THE CLUB FROM YOUR RIGHT HAND,

CATCH

SCOOP

AS IT TURNS, THROW THE SECOND CLUB WITH AN UNDERHAND SCOOP.

CATCH THE FIRST CLUB WITH YOUR LEFT HAND, THEN THE SECOND WITH YOUR RIGHT. PAUSE BETWEEN THROWS.

THREE THROWS AND THREE CATCHES

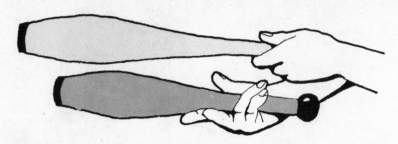

HOLD ONE CLUB IN EACH HAND, AND PLACE AN ADDITIONAL CLUB IN THE RIGHT HAND...

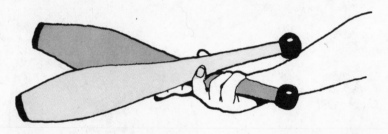

WITH YOUR INDEX FINGER EXTENDED ALONG THE NECK OF THE CLUB.

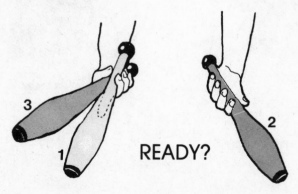

3

1

READY?

2

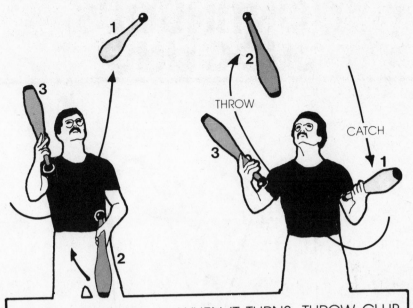

THROW CLUB NO. 1, WHEN IT TURNS, THROW CLUB NO. 2.

WHEN CLUB NO. 2 TURNS, THROW CLUB NO. 3.

TA-DAH!

CONTINUOUS JUGGLING

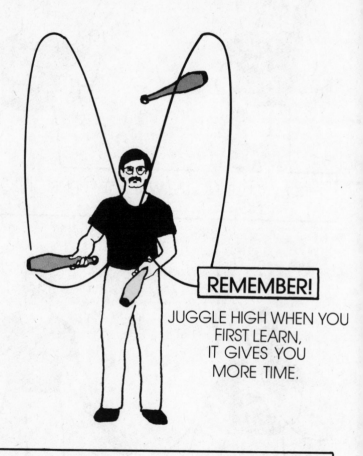

REMEMBER!

JUGGLE HIGH WHEN YOU
FIRST LEARN,
IT GIVES YOU
MORE TIME.

NOW EVERY TIME ONE CLUB SPINS, THROW ANOTHER. KEEP ALTERNATING: RIGHT-LEFT, RIGHT-LEFT.

EVENTUALLY, YOU SHOULD LOOK OVER THE TOP OF YOUR PATTERN.

AS YOU INCREASE YOUR SKILLS, BRING YOUR PATTERN DOWN SO THE CLUBS GO NO HIGHER THAN THE TOP OF YOUR HEAD.

HERE'S SOME TIPS FOR CONSISTENT CLUB JUGGLING

Get good scoops. Try to throw the clubs about a foot over the shoulder on each side, no higher. You should eventually be able to bring the pattern down and to bring your eyes down to the point where you can look directly ahead. This will be important when you start passing clubs. You want to look straight ahead, at your partner's eyes, not up in the air. Now learn to catch half spins and one and a half spins, regaining your pattern from the erratic throws. Relax your arms and shoulders. Keep your hands down, with your forearms parallel to the floor. As time goes by, use less shoulder and upper arm to throw the clubs, and use more wrist and forearm. Experiment with the use of your thumb to push down on the handle, giving the club faster spin and reducing your effort even further.

HAVING SOME PROBLEMS?

Q. WHY DO MY CLUBS COLLIDE?
A. 1. YOUR PATTERN IS NOT WIDE ENOUGH. EXTEND YOUR "SCOOP", OR . . .
   2. YOUR TIMING IS OFF—BE SURE ONE CLUB HAS PEAKED WHEN THE NEXT CLUB IS THROWN.

Q. I'VE MOVED ON TO 3 CLUBS, AND NOW I CAN'T CATCH ANYTHING.
A. TOO MUCH SPIN OR NOT ENOUGH SPIN — GO BACK TO ONE CLUB AND BUILD UP YOUR PRECISION

Q. MY CLUBS ARE "RUNNING AWAY" FROM ME.
A. REMEMBER JUGGLING TAKES PLACE IN A PLANE IN FRONT OF YOU. IMPROVE YOUR SCOOPS AND THROWS FROM SIDE TO SIDE.

Q. MY CLUBS ARE ATTACKING ME. I KEEP GETTING HIT IN THE CHEST.
A. STAND YOUR GROUND AND THROW SIDE TO SIDE — DON'T BACK UP.

FOR EXTRA CREDIT

UNDER THE LEG

*IN ORDER TO THROW A CLUB UNDER THE LEG, START WITH A SINGLE CLUB.

LEARN TO THROW THAT ONE CLUB UNDER THE RIGHT AND LEFT LEG FROM THE RIGHT AND LEFT HAND.

YOU CAN THROW UNDER THE SAME, OR . . . OPPOSITE LEG.

NOW TRY THE MOVE WHILE JUGGLING. START BY THROWING EVERY THIRD CLUB UNDER. IT MAY HELP TO TOSS THE PREVIOUS ONE A BIT HIGHER THAN USUAL TO GIVE SOME EXTRA TIME. TRY EVERY SECOND CLUB, THEN CONTINUOUS THROWS WITH ONE HAND.

FLOATERS

THE CLUB DOESN'T FLIP AT ALL. HOLD THE CLUB HIGH ON THE NECK AND SPIN IT A BIT FOR STABILITY.

REVERSE SPIN

THE HANDLE
GOES UP
AND AWAY FROM YOU.

PUSH THE KNOB END OF THE CLUB UP AND AWAY FROM YOU. THIS REQUIRES A GOOD DEAL OF FORCE, AND SEEMS AWKWARD AT FIRST, BUT EVENTUALLY CAN BE AS EASY AS NORMAL SINGLE SPINS.

BALANCING

BALANCE ONE CLUB ON YOUR CHIN OR NOSE, PAUSE AND DROP IT BACK INTO THE JUGGLE.

BEHIND THE BACK

NOTE

DOUBLE FLIPS WORK TOO!

OVER THE HEAD

THROW WITH A HIGH WIDE ARC . . . . EITHER DOUBLE OR SINGLE FLIP.

HOW TO GET HOT

★ SEVERAL HOURS PRACTICE A DAY ARE RECOMMENDED.

★ KEEP A RECORD OF PRACTICE SESSIONS.

★ STRIVE TO DO MORE EACH TIME YOU PICK UP THE EQUIPMENT.

★ YOUR MOTIVATION MUST COME FROM WITHIN.

KICK UPS

IN ORDER TO PICK UP A CLUB WITH A "KICK-UP", PRACTICE BY SETTING THE CLUB ON YOUR FOOT. THE HANDLE SHOULD POINT INWARD AND REST ON THE AREA BETWEEN YOUR FOOT AND SHIN. FLEX YOUR FOOT AS YOU KICK UP AND BACK. THE KNOB OF THE CLUB SHOULD CATCH YOUR SHIN AND THE CLUB SHOULD DO A SINGLE FLIP TO YOUR HAND.

REMEMBER

IN ORDER TO KEEP YOUR CLUBS IN GOOD SHAPE, THE BEST AREAS TO JUGGLE ARE:
A PADDED FLOOR, CARPETED AREA, GYM MATS OR A CLEAN, DRY LAWN.

STYLE

Shoulders up, throwing with entire arm

Shoulders down and relaxed, using wrist to throw.

QUESTION

Which looks better? You be the judge.

COLUMNS

Variation 1

1 While juggling, throw a left hand club straight up with a double, it will return to the left hand.

2 As it descends toss the next club from the left hand across to the right with a single spin (this is called a "vamp").

3 Catch the left hand double, then toss a double straight up with the right hand, and catch the single with the right hand.

4 Vamp the right hand across to the left, and catch the right hand double.

NOTE: In this variation, one club goes from hand to hand with singles, and two clubs go straight up and down with doubles.

Variation 2

Throw a right hand club straight up with a double. As it peaks, throw both the remaining clubs straight up with doubles.

Catch the solo club, and as the two clubs peak, throw the solo club up again from the right hand. Catch the two clubs and repeat.

NOTES—

• The single club can go straight up on either side, up the middle, or over the top.
• Keep the rhythm — catch and throw one, catch and throw two, catch and throw one, etc.
• Try this same move with singles and triples.
• It looks great if you get wide separation between the path of the solo club and the duo.

PIROUETTES

TOSS THE SOLO CLUB UP THE MIDDLE WITH A DOUBLE

Throw one club up. Just before it peaks, spot the club and spin rapidly, holding the other two.

When you get around, toss one club up under the descending club, catch the solo club and renew the cascade.

FLASH

To throw a flash, toss all 3 clubs in a cascade in rapid succession. Throw right, throw left, throw right. Then as soon as you catch, throw again. Catch and throw left, catch and throw right, catch and throw left. Now you should have time to clap when all 3 clubs are in the air. Toss-toss-toss-clap-toss-toss-toss-clap.

HEAD FLIP

Start with the club balanced on its knob on your nose.

Drop your head forward rapidly. The club will roll from knob to butt, do a complete flip, and come down in front of you.

3 CLUB START

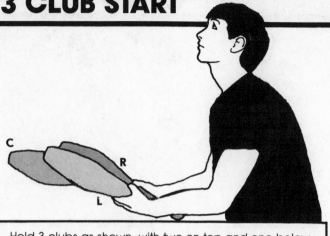

Hold 3 clubs as shown, with two on top and one below.

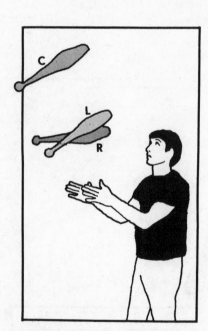

Throw all 3. The center club does a high triple. The outside clubs do doubles.

Catch the two clubs simultaneously. When the solo club comes down, start juggling.

UNDER ARMS

Clubs 1 and 2 are juggled in a cascade with singles. Club number 3 is thrown by the left hand with a double up under the right arm.

It is caught in the right hand, carried across, and thrown with a double up under the left arm.

NOTE: CLUB #3 is always carried under the other clubs, and thrown straight up. Clubs #1 and #2 are simply juggled in a cascade. The cadence is: right-left-right under the arm with a double-left-right-left under the arm with a double-right-left-right under the arm with a double.

For style points — lean far forward at the waist and exaggerate side-to-side movement.

CHOPS

The chop is a method for carrying a club quickly through the pattern, throwing it straight up on the opposite side. The right hand throws on the left side, the left hand throws on the right side.

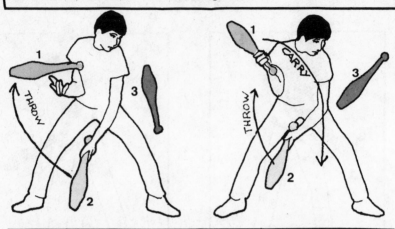

As you catch club #1 with the right hand . . .

Bring it smartly down across your chest over the ascending left-hand club #2 . . .

And toss it straight up the left side with a single or a double.

NOTE: Widen your stance, keep your elbows in at your sides, and look from side to side.

Now carry the club you just caught in your left hand down in a chop toward the right,

and toss it straight up under the left hand with a single or a double.

HEAD SPIN

Instead of throwing a right-hand club, place it on your head and spin it as shown.

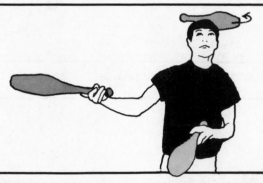

Reach out with the right hand and catch the preceding club as the one on your head turns.

The club on your head falls toward the left and you continue to juggle by tossing the left–hand club, reaching up and removing the spinning club from your head.

BETWEEN THE LEGS

BACK TO FRONT

This move is like an under-the-leg throw, except that both feet stay flat on the floor and you reach way down between your legs to throw. Use your wrist to throw.

FRONT TO BACK

Every club is carried between the legs and thown up over the opposite shoulder.

HINT: Use knobs to throw and switch your head from side to side.

BACK CROSSES

Give yourself 2-3 hours per day for a week to get this one. It is hard, but worth it.

Learning Steps:

1. Start with 1 club and toss it back and forth over your shoulder.
2. While juggling 3 clubs, toss an occasional right hand throw over your shoulder. Work your way up to every other right hand throw.
3. Now do the same with the left hand.
4. Shift back to the right hand and work your way up to every throw going over the left shoulder.
5. Now try two throws in a row while juggling, one over each shoulder.
6. Work your way up to successive over the shoulder throws. Count your throws. Keep a record.

Alternate throws behind your back. Use singles. Bring your hands up high to throw, shift your head from side to side and focus on that moment when the club comes over your shoulder. Try doubles and then triples. Go for 100 throws straight.

> **HINT:** Practice turning your head from side to side without any clubs. Then practice the same move with the appropriate arm movements, but still don't throw. Raise your arms high to throw. Remember, you only get to see that incoming club for a micro-second as it comes over the shoulder — not when you catch it.

TURNING ON STAGE

To turn slowly throw a shower from the right hand and slowly turn to the right, one small step with each throw.

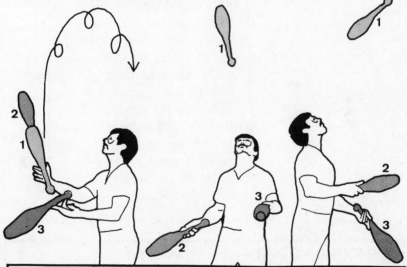

To turn quickly, throw a high right triple over your head, turn to the left, look up, throw from the left hand as the incoming club descends, and keep juggling. Remember—the descending club is turning away from you.

COMBINED MOVES

You can combine between-the-leg throws from back to front and from front to back for a **super** effect. One full set of these throws would be:

Right front to
back—
Left self throw—
Right back to
front—
Left self throw—
Right self throw—
Left front to back—
Right self throw—
Left back to front—
Right self throw—
Left self throw—
Repeat

DROP INSURANCE—

Dropping is embarrassing, so take out drop insurance. How? Easy, practice repetitions, and **COUNT!** Let's say you are working on double back crosses. You get going and after a while you fall apart. Just count the successful catches. Now try again, but add at least one more successful catch. What to count then becomes a problem. Why not count every time a club lands in your left hand? Set a goal, for instance 50 successful throws and catches. When you succeed reward yourself with a glass of ice water.

Prof Confidence

FOR EXTRA POINTS —Add under-arm throws and back crosses to this combination for an unbelievable set of moves. You will have to take small steps in place to keep going, and keep turning your head from side to side. Give it a try!

FANCY FINISH

Toss one club high, with a double. While it is in the air, transfer the club from your left hand to your right.

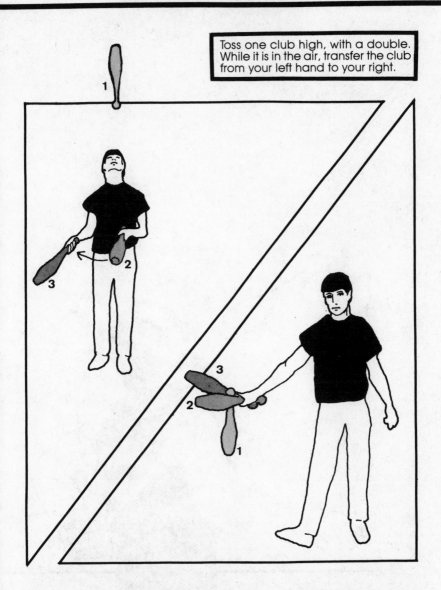

Make a "V" between the two clubs in your right hand and catch the third club between these two, trapping the knob.

ALBERT PETROWSKI

Juggling 4 & 5 Clubs

Certification Requirements

1. With 4 clubs demonstrate simultaneous and alternating throws with double spins in either outside circles or columns.
2. Demonstrate single spins in columns with 4
3. Demonstrate s split for at least 8 throws with 4
4. Demonstrate "triple/singles" for 5 right hand throws with 4
5. Successfully kick up to four clubs from three
6. Complete 40 throws with 5 clubs and finish cleanly
7. Demonstrate one additional move with 5 clubs such as
   a. One club under a leg,
   b. At least one successful throw behind the back.

4 CLUBS

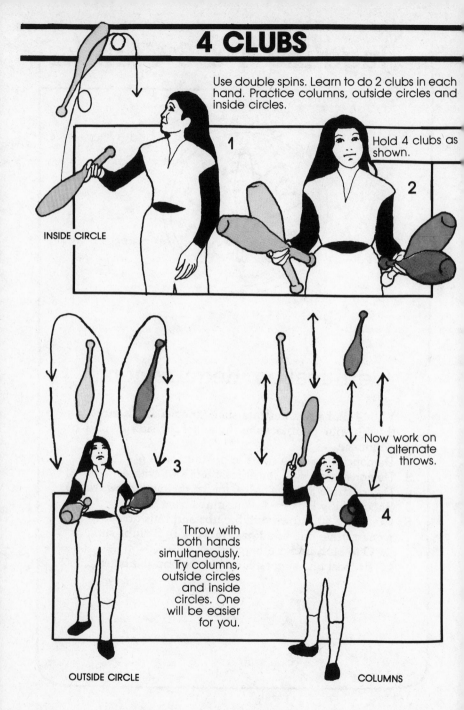

Use double spins. Learn to do 2 clubs in each hand. Practice columns, outside circles and inside circles.

1

Hold 4 clubs as shown.

2

INSIDE CIRCLE

3

Now work on alternate throws.

4

Throw with both hands simultaneously. Try columns, outside circles and inside circles. One will be easier for you.

OUTSIDE CIRCLE

COLUMNS

SINGLE SPINS

Every club goes straight up and down in its own column.

The easiest single spin pattern with four clubs is to alternate your hands and throw columns.

SPLITS

Throw two clubs up on the right. When they peak, throw two up on the left. Shift quickly back to catch the first two.

Now shift quickly from side to side, catching and throwing as rapidly as possible, but keeping control.

TRIPLE/SINGLES

FRONT
VIEW

SIDE
VIEW

Throw singles with the left hand and triples with the right.

The rhythm is the same as for 3-club juggling, except the right hand throws much higher and harder.

The same move, behind the back.

Once you can throw the triple in front, practice throwing it as a back cross. The rhythm is the same.

KICK UP TO 4

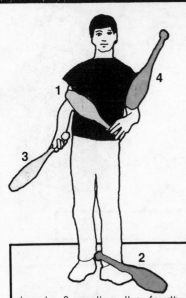

Juggle 3, resting the fourth club on the top of your foot, knob hooked under the shin of your left foot.

As you toss a left hand vamp, kick up. Now you shift from a cascade pattern to two in each hand, with an alternating or simultaneous rhythm.

BALANCE TO 4

Start with a chin balance while juggling three.

Throw a left hand vamp, drop your head forward and shift from cascade to two in each hand.

5 CLUBS

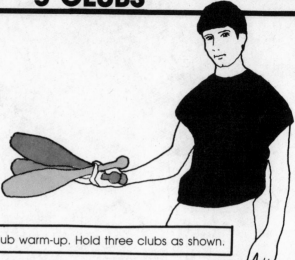

Start with a three club warm-up. Hold three clubs as shown.

Throw doubles. Toss all three quickly from right to left. This is a five club pattern with two empty spaces.

Without pausing, catch and throw them back from left to right.

Keep alternating hands. Three throws in a row from right, three throws in a row from left. Learn to catch three in either hand when you finish a run.

GO FOR IT!

Five clubs are hard to start. Bend your knees a bit to give the clubs more momentum.

This is John a split second later. He has thrown #s 1, 2, 3 and 4.

He is just about to catch #1 and throw #5.

Now throw high and hard, but keep your rhythm. No time to think. High, wide, accurate and rhythmic throws are the key.

5 CLUB TRICKS

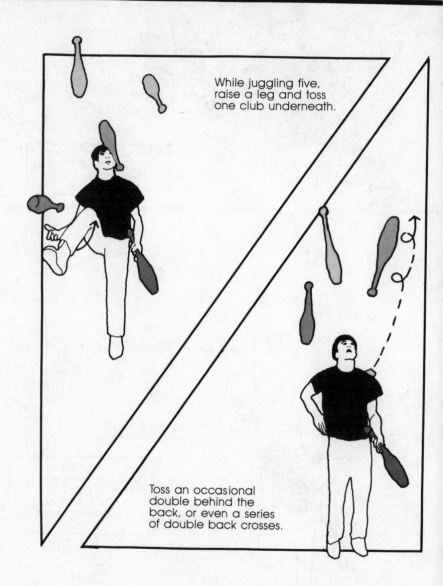

While juggling five, raise a leg and toss one club underneath.

Toss an occasional double behind the back, or even a series of double back crosses.

COLLECTING 5

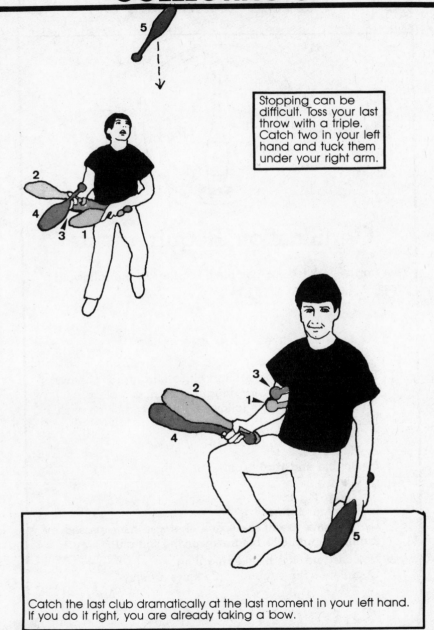

Stopping can be difficult. Toss your last throw with a triple. Catch two in your left hand and tuck them under your right arm.

Catch the last club dramatically at the last moment in your left hand. If you do it right, you are already taking a bow.

Club Mastery

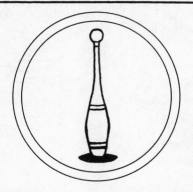

Certification Requirements

This pin is awarded for complete mastery in the following areas:

I Three Club Interaction

1. Demonstrate the run-around with a partner (3 take aways each) and side by side juggling sharing 3 clubs
2. Run 3 clubs using the following (throw and catch each at least once)
   a. Floater
   b. Helicopter
   c. Double and triple spin
   d. Chop
   e. Under leg throw
   f. Shoulder throw
3. Demonstrate use of the space after you have passed by turning a pirouette before receiving the clubs
4. Demonstrate side by side juggling
5. Complete a run-around three times around

II Passing Six Clubs

1. Complete a 3-3-10 with six clubs
2. While throwing every other club (4 count) throw and catch the following:
   a. Floater
   b. Helicopter
   c. Double and triple spin
   d. Chop
   e. Under the leg throw
   f. Shoulder throw
3. Pick up to six clubs while showering (2 count)—
4. Demonstrate at least one diagonal passing pattern both as passer and receiver (for example, left hand double to your partner's left)—
5. Pass six clubs around a "volunteer" for at least 10 throws—
6. Complete one of following:
   a. Back to back passes, or
   b. Kick up a dropped club while passing, or
   c. Pass between legs and over shoulder
7. Pass seven clubs for at least 20 throws and finish by collecting all seven clubs

III Club Passing Configurations

1. Serve as the post in a continuous feed of 40 or more throws with two or more additional jugglers—
2. While in the feed demonstrate your ability to:
   a. Throw under the leg, floaters and at least two other fancy passes;
   b. Recover from a drop and continue the feed—
3. Pass doubles and triples in a feed—
4. Pass around and across in a triangle—
5. Demonstrate your ability to successfully take every position in a line of 3 or more jugglers—
6. a. Successfully pass for 10 throws as either the top or the bottom man in a two-high feed, or
   b. Successfully participate in a carousel
7. a. Complete a 3-3-10 in a box with 4 jugglers, or
   b. Complete a pivot with 4 jugglers
8. Complete one of the following:
   a. A four person line
   b. A "Y" with four jugglers
   c. A five person star
   d. A double feed with two feeders and three feedees

CLUB PASSING

RUNNING 3

Running 3 clubs between two jugglers is the first step in club passing.

Juggler No. 1   Juggler No. 2

Start with 1 club. Throw it from your left to your right hand with a single flip. Then drop your right hand down so the club hangs parallel to your leg. Bring your arm up and release the club at chest height as shown above. The club does 1½ turns and ends up in your partner's upraised left hand, knob down. Now he throws from his left to right and back across to you. This is a single flip.

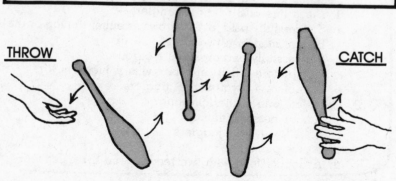

THROW   CATCH

Now that you can run one club from person to person, you can see the pattern. From above it looks like this:

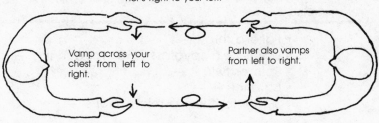

Pass comes in from your partner's right to your left.

Vamp across your
chest from left to
right.

Partner also vamps
from left to right.

Pass from your right   To your partner's left.

Remember: Drop your arm to throw, raise your hand to catch.

Now move on to three clubs. Pass one at a time, following this path. All left hand throws go across your chest to your right hand. All right hand throws go to your partner's left.

Remember: Thrower—alternate your hands, pass club 1 from the right, vamp to yourself with your left, pass 2 with the right, space where the left should be, pass 3 from the right. Catcher—after receiving club 1 in your left hand, wait until you see club 2 on its way to you, then throw your left club to your right. Now you have one in each hand. As club 3 comes in, start the cascade with a lefthand throw.

213

KEEP A CLUB

Instead of throwing all three clubs to your partner, you can throw two, and keep the third one. Now you have an extra two beats to clown around with that one club. You could:

- Fake a throw —
- Use it as a spyglass or a wooden leg —
- Spin or twirl it —
- Balance it —
- Sing into it like a microphone —

Then the retained club becomes number one in the next round of incoming clubs.

MORE HELPFUL HINTS FOR RUNNING 3

1. Learn to catch, and recover from, just about any sort of throw—a lob, a helicopter, a 1½ or a double throw, a kicked or bounced club, or one skittering along the floor.
2. Remember, in running 3 clubs the objective is to keep going **no matter what**; so stay with the rhythm of the pattern and keep extending yourself. This dedication to continuation will help a lot when passing 6 or 7 or more clubs.
3. Be patient with your partner. Build up your throwing and catching skills slowly, working first with one club, then with two, and finally with three.

HINT: Practice with one club first, then move on to three.

CLEANING UP YOUR ACT

1. After you get all three clubs, juggle them for a while, breathing normally. When you have stabilized, throw them back to your partner slowly, one at a time.
2. Take your time. The beauty of this exercise is that you have time to pause between throws. Gradually increase your tempo, and eliminate any pauses.
3. Throw across with your palm up, fingers pointed toward the midline. Catch with palm out, fingers toward the outside.

ADDING SPICE

Running 3 clubs can be exciting for the jugglers and for the audience. When you don't have anything to juggle, you have time to do something else. For instance, you could:

- Clap
- Turn a pirouette
- Do a front roll
- Take off a piece of clothing
- Turn and blow a kiss
- Take a bite or a sip

Turning back to your partner just in time to catch the first incoming club.

TRICKY TOSSES

You can return clubs to your partner in any of a number of difficult ways.

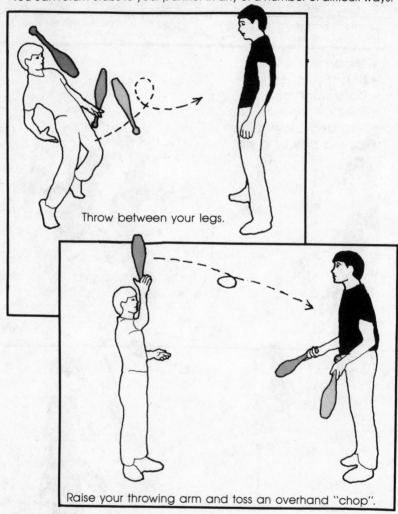

Throw between your legs.

Raise your throwing arm and toss an overhand "chop".

Throw over your own shoulder. "Shoulder throws".

Or with reverse spin.

Or a helicopter.
This can turn
inward or
outward.

CATCHING A CLUB

Your partner makes the hard throws look easy, why not make those easy catches look hard?

A
For most catches your elbow is down—and the knob of the club is down. Catch up and around your bicep.

B
When your partner throws with a bit too much or too little spin, the knob may point up. Just catch and recover by tossing a 1½ to your other hand. This is also a convenient way to catch a chop.

C
If the chop is thrown to waist height, allow ¼ more turn and catch as shown.

D
When your partner tosses a helicopter spin, catch it with your fingers pointed up or down depending on the direction of spin.

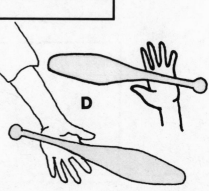

AMAZING CATCHES

One mildly spectacular catch requires you to reach around your back with your right hand.

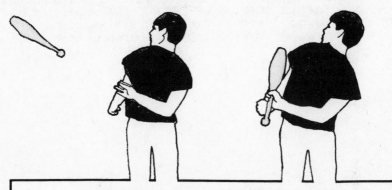

Turn 90 degrees and reach as far as you can.

Quickly turn back to catch the next incoming club in the normal manner.

BREAKING THE RULES

By now you know enough about juggling to know that there is only one rule — "KEEP GOING NO MATTER WHAT!" This rule has a corollary — "TURN ALL DROPS INTO OPPORTUNITIES." With this in mind, invent your own novel methods to deliver a club to your partner, and exciting ways to catch. You could bounce a club across.

NOTE: Toss without a spin so the knob and bulb hit the ground simultaneously.

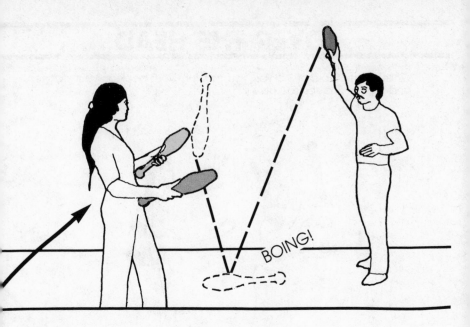

BOING!

or slide it
or even run over, hand it to your partner, and run back to
your own position.

You can hand the last club across instead of throwing it. But jump
back in position with your left hand up to get that first catch.

OVER THE HEAD

While on the topic of 3 clubs, you can turn your back on your partner and toss all 3 clubs rapidly---

back over your head

SIDE BY SIDE

Right
hand
person
uses
only
right
hand

Left
hand
person
uses
only
left
hand

Stand beside one another and share 3 clubs.

RUN AROUND

Come in from your partner's left and take the left hand club as it comes in by reaching up and substituting your left hand for his.

Now reach rudely across and take the next club with your right hand in place of your partner's.

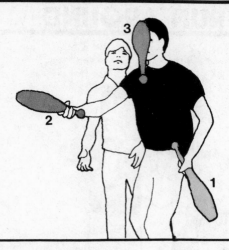

The last club comes up under your outstretched right arm, and you step in, taking over the three clubs.

PLAYING WITH THE RUNAROUND

- Remember to keep your arms separated after you get clubs one and two so your partner can toss number 3 up between your arms.
- As soon as you have reached for that first club, you are committed and must move aggressively to Numbers 2 and 3.
- Once you gain accuracy and speed, you and your partner can run around one another continually sharing three clubs. You can eventually go so fast that the first object you catch is the last one you threw.
- Now you can add objects, such as a hat. Grab the hat, put it on your head, then take the clubs. Add a towel and a cigar. Take the hat, take the towel, put it on your shoulder, take the cigar, put it in your mouth, then take the three clubs.
- Who said juggling wasn't exercise?

PASSING 6

This is it folks, the big time!

Learn to run 3 clubs, then
learn to pass 6!

Start with your clubs raised, two in the right hand, one in the left. Bring your hands down, and start juggling together. Counting "One, and, two, and, throw, one, and, two, and, throw," etc.

Toss every third club from the right hand across to your partner. Then try every second from the right. Finally, try every righthand club. This is called "solids" or "shower passing."

NOTES —

- Your stance in passing is important. The right leg is slightly back, and your weight evenly distributed on both feet.
- Just before you throw, pull your right hand down so that the club to be passed is parallel to your right leg.
- Throw with your full arm, but also use your thumb to push down on the handle of the club just below the knob. Try to make the same throw each time. **CONSISTENCY IS KEY!**
- Throw straight across in a plane with knob and butt turning in this plane, not tilted inward or outward.
- Minimize extraneous body movement. Look at the whole pattern, but focus on your throws and catches.

UNDER THE LEG

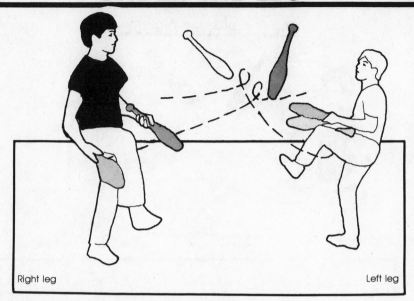

Right leg

Left leg

Raise your leg and throw underneath. You can toss under your right leg by pointing your right toe out and opening your stance, or under your left leg, by bringing it across your body and pointing your toe to the right. Either way, raise your leg high!

VARIETY

To add spice to your passing, you can both toss the same way at the same time, or alternate fancy passes with one another. We covered a few of these throws in the section on running 3. Try:

- **Chops**
- **Shoulder throws**
- **Helicopters**
- **Reverse Spin**

HINTS

— Be patient with each other.
— Invent different throws.
— It is easier to pass every other throw than every one.
—One person learns it. The other person learns it. You do it simultaneously. You do it alternately.

KICK UP TO 6

Start passing in a shower pattern with 5 clubs. While passing with 5, rest the 6th club on your left foot as shown, knob under your shin. Establish a space where club 6 should go. Every time that space comes to your left hand, raise your hand to show the space.

Just before the space gets to your left hand, kick up, toss your left hand club, the next one in your left hand is the kicked-up club. Keep tossing.

WOW

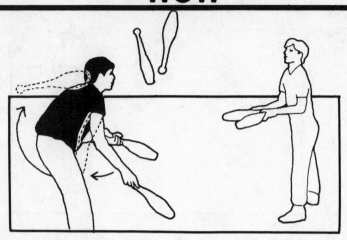

One particularly tricky and impressive throw is a shoulder throw from between the legs.

- Reach deeply between your legs —
- Hold the knob to throw —
- Bend forward so the club skims past your near shoulder —

BACK TO BACK

HINTS:

- Throw every 3rd —
- Use double spins —
- Focus on the incoming club —
- Count out loud at first —

ULTIMATE THRILLS

Aside from exchanging lit dynamite sticks and live skunks, one of the greatest thrills in passing is to try everything backwards. That means you vamp across your chest from right to left and toss across to your partner with your left hand. Both of you toss with the left and catch with your right. It is a very humbling experience, as clubs crash around you.

Another exercise in patience and agility is to pass with both hands. Now nothing crosses the chest. All throws are to your partner. To avoid collisions, toss under the incoming club. See "one count" in ball passing section.

THE "THUNDER SHOWER"

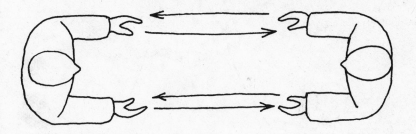

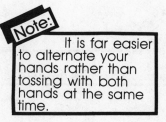

Note: It is far easier to alternate your hands rather than tossing with both hands at the same time.

DOUBLE AND TRIPLE SPINS

Hint: Juggle slower and look up. Throw higher—not harder. The extra height means more spin.

Start with every third right toss as a double then try every second. Finally every right hand throw is a double.

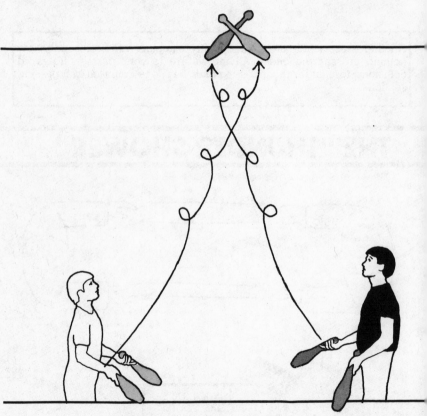

You can both throw doubles or triples at the same time.

SINGLE, DOUBLE, TRIPLE

NOW ... start showering 6 clubs! Now we get tricky! A double takes one extra beat, a triple takes two beats. So, you can toss a single with your right hand; on the next beat you can throw a double diagonally across with your left hand. The double arrives in your partner's left just at the moment that the next single should have gotten there. And just to make it a bit harder the next throw can be a right hand triple, caught at the moment that the NEXT single should have arrived. So the receiving juggler doesn't change the pace, but the sending juggler throws right (single—straight across), left (double—diagonally from left to left), right (triple—straight across).

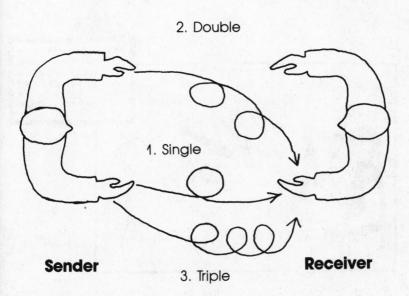

2. Double

1. Single

Sender

Receiver

3. Triple

7 CLUBS

HINT: Learn to do 6 "solids" with double spins first.

The person with 4 clubs starts with a high double.

The person with 3 clubs waits.

NOTE: The rhythm for each person is the same as for 6 clubs, but you are throwing with your right hand at the same time that your partner throws with his left.

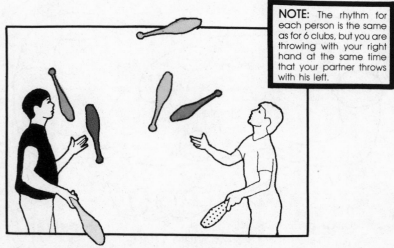

As soon as that first club peaks, the second person throws across. Now you just keep going, but notice that you do **NOT** throw simultaneously with your partner.

Try some tricks with 7 clubs, such as —

- Passing under the leg —
- Leaving a space and picking up or kicking up the 7th club.
- Going from doubles down to singles and back up.
- One person collecting all the clubs at the end (a really fast and difficult feat, but a great finale!)

TA DA!

NOTE: 7 clubs is slower than you think. Remember to alternate your hands. Don't rush the pattern or throw with right and left hands at the same time.

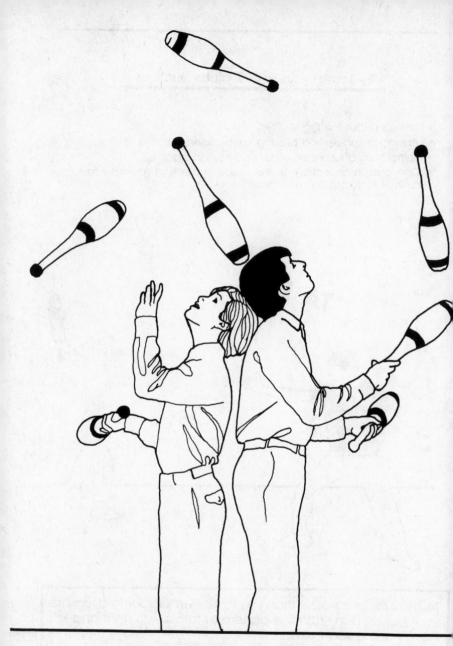

THE GENTLEMAN JUGGLERS
JOHN WEBSTER AND ROBERT STUVERUD

8 CLUBS

Remember, the pattern is the same as for 6, right, left, right, left. Only the tempo is stepped up a little bit.

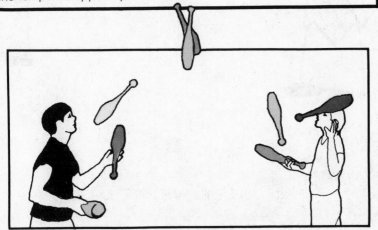

Pass at the same time, with simultaneous high doubles. This is fast, but you and your partner are throwing at the same time again.

AMY

JOYCE

THE PHILIPPINE PRIDE JUGGLERS

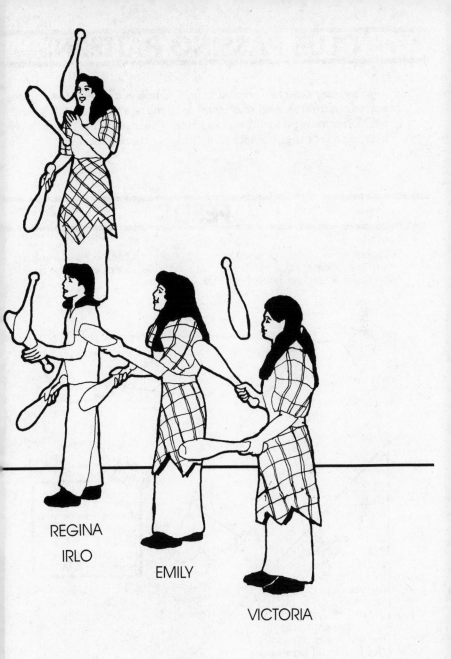

REGINA
IRLO

EMILY

VICTORIA

CLUB PASSING PATTERNS

Juggling starts out as a solo endeavor. Once you have three objects under control the next challenge is to share and pass with a partner. Eventually you will want to bring others into the act, and play with nine or more objects and three or more jugglers.

FEEDS

The feeder, or "post," passes to each person in turn. The "feedees," therefore, alternate passes with the feeder. The feeder passes twice as often as the feedees when there are two feedees.

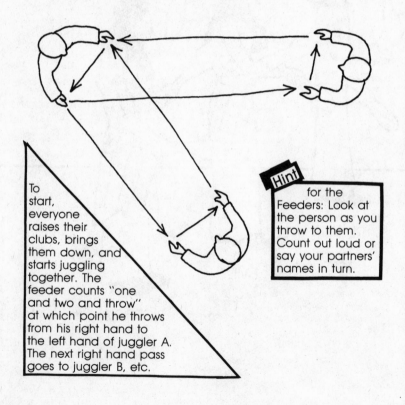

To start, everyone raises their clubs, brings them down, and starts juggling together. The feeder counts "one and two and throw" at which point he throws from his right hand to the left hand of juggler A. The next right hand pass goes to juggler B, etc.

Hint for the Feeders: Look at the person as you throw to them. Count out loud or say your partners' names in turn.

OPTIONS

Once you have the general idea you can begin to experiment with:

TEMPO—The post passes every other right hand throw across, giving partners more time between their passes (4 counts to be exact).

SPINS—Instead of tossing single spin passes, everyone can pass doubles or triples. As long as everyone does it, the beat is easy to keep.

TRICKS—After you can pass without dropping, try some fancy tosses. Under the leg and floaters are the easiest, but who said we wanted to do easy tricks? Of course you can do a fancy self throw while the post tosses to your partner, or turn a pirouette and face the post just in time to throw across.

How complex can we get?

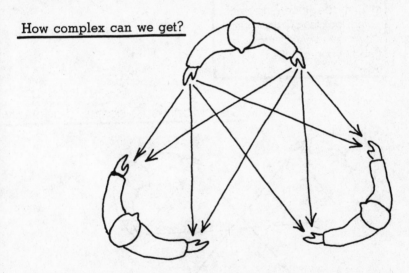

If we look at the options which are possible just from the view of the post, there are four places he can pass with the right hand and four places he can pass with the left hand. Add tempo, spin and trick options and you can come up with some pretty wild and complex feeds.

TRIANGLE

Three people can pass around in a triangle.

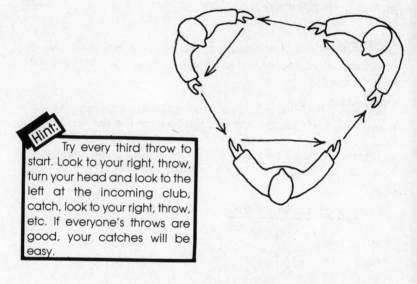

Hint: Try every third throw to start. Look to your right, throw, turn your head and look to the left at the incoming club, catch, look to your right, throw, etc. If everyone's throws are good, your catches will be easy.

Or you can pass across, diagonally.

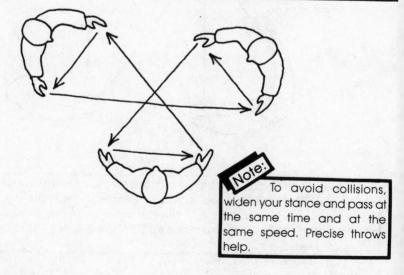

Note: To avoid collisions, widen your stance and pass at the same time and at the same speed. Precise throws help.

LINE

To avoid C's pass hitting B's shoulder, throw high and a bit to the outside. Also, B could offset ½ step to the left.

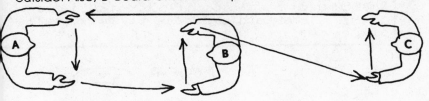

A passes short throws to **B**, single or double.
B passes a "drop back" double to **C**.
C passes long throws to **A**.

Hint: C should throw a bit to the outside to keep from hitting B's elbow.

JUGGLING PEOPLE

Now that there are three of you passing 9 clubs, and you can do a feed, a triangle and a line you can begin to experiment with movement. Here are a few ideas:

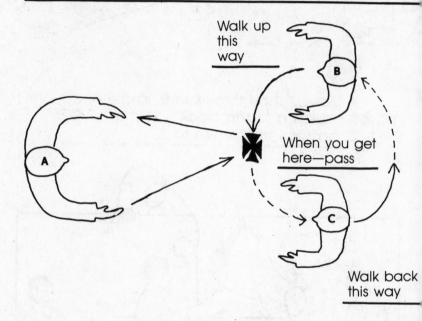

Walk up this way

When you get here—pass

Walk back this way

A passes every third right hand throw across and feeds either B or C.

B and C walk rapidly around in a circle facing A and juggling. Each throws on every sixth count. Try to throw when you reach point X.

NOTE: Now the question becomes, how to get to X when it's your turn? Can you go between your partner's legs or vault over? You'll have to hold your clubs for a few counts rather than juggling, but it can be done.

While passing in a triangle, the entire triangle walks slowly around in a circle. Here it helps to decide on a specific number of steps between throws.

In a line the center person can do a half turn and face the other end. That means a rhythm like "one and two and throw and half turn and two and throw." On "half-turn" you throw a right hand double over the shoulder, turn and catch it yourself in the left hand, still juggling. The next right hand throw goes over the shoulder to the former head of the line who is now the tail of the line.

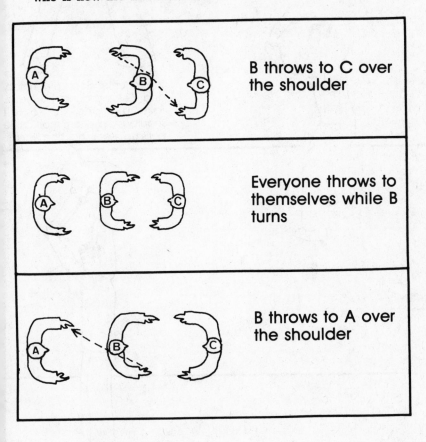

B throws to C over the shoulder

Everyone throws to themselves while B turns

B throws to A over the shoulder

TWO-HIGH FEED

THE MOUNT —

Bottom man squat and hold your hands up crossed left over right. Top mounter step with your right foot high up on his thigh.

Top mounter step on right foot and pivot around his back. Take big step up to left shoulder of bottom man as he pulls up. Keep holding hands.

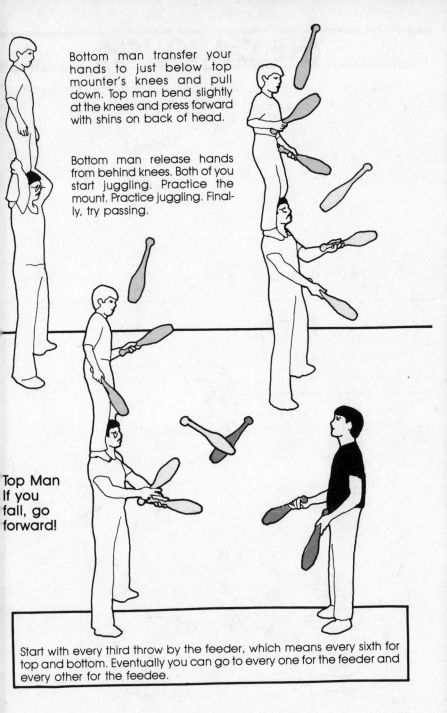

Bottom man transfer your hands to just below top mounter's knees and pull down. Top man bend slightly at the knees and press forward with shins on back of head.

Bottom man release hands from behind knees. Both of you start juggling. Practice the mount. Practice juggling. Finally, try passing.

Top Man
If you
fall, go
forward!

Start with every third throw by the feeder, which means every sixth for top and bottom. Eventually you can go to every one for the feeder and every other for the feedee.

THE CAROUSEL

Three people can juggle six clubs in a fast-paced and relatively simple pattern called a carousel.

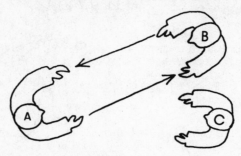

A and B are passing. C comes in to the left of B and raises his left hand.

Now A passes to C and receives from B, until B has no more clubs. At which point...

B runs over to the left of A, raises his left hand and catches C's next pass.

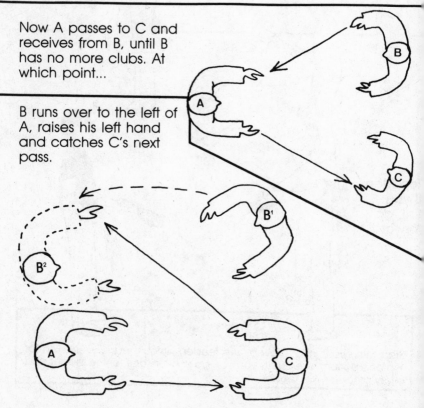

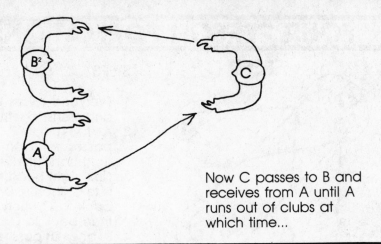

Now C passes to B and receives from A until A runs out of clubs at which time...

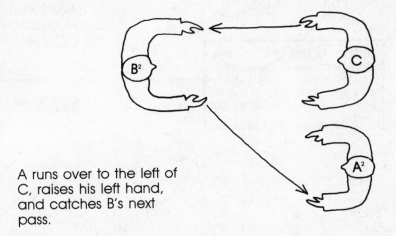

A runs over to the left of C, raises his left hand, and catches B's next pass.

To keep the carousel going:
- As soon as you are out of clubs, run, turn and catch—
- If anyone drops a club, the next person to run can pick it up on the way to their new position—
- By taking a side step just after the person moves you can occupy their exact position and stay lined up on stage.

FOUR PERSON FORMATIONS

FEED

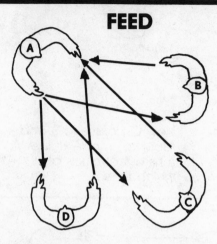

STEPS

1. Everyone raises club and starts together.
2. A looks at B and passes to B on third right hand throw.
3. Next right hand throw is to C, then to D, then back to C, then to B then back to C.
4. B and D pass every third throw, C passes every other throw.
5. A looks at and names each juggler in turn.

Drops: If B or D drop there is plenty of time to get a club and get back in. If A drops he can fail to pass to B or D and let them retrieve the dropped club.

WEAVE

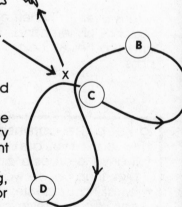

STEPS

1. A passes every third right hand throw to point X.
2. B, C and D rotate along the path as shown, throwing every ninth right hand toss from point X.
3. Immediately after catching, step back to clear the way for the next feedee in order.

Note: Your people pattern is actually a cascade juggling pattern.

BOX

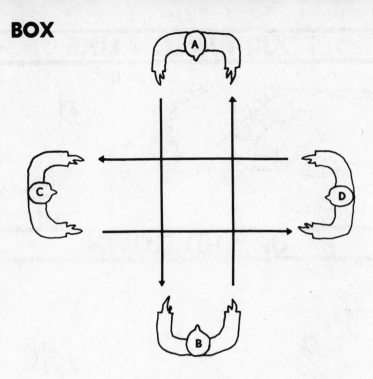

STEPS

1. All raise hands simultaneously.
2. A and B bring hands down and start together.
3. C and D wait one count, bring their hands down and start together.
4. A and B toss the third right hand throw across.
5. C and D toss the third right hand throw across.
6. Now A and B toss every others, alternating with C and D.
7. Once you can get the rhythm for this pattern it doesn't matter if one pair drops, you can get back in with a "live start" when it is your turn.
8. Eventually try a "3-3-10" in this formation. Throwing "solids" is tough, but possible if you get your timing right.

FOUR PERSON LINE

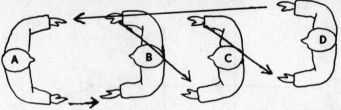

Now B turns around and you can go—

Get it? (If not, see Three Person Line and figure it out!)

UP AND DOWN

A and C pass every third. They then squat while B and D stand up and pass.

Alternate—throw,
squat, stand,
throw, squat,
stand, etc.

250

As long as you are facing this way why not try—

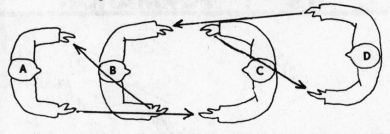

Or use double spins and try—

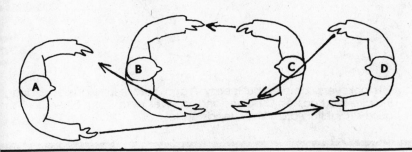

Also, facing this way—A and B circle and pass every third at point X. C and D circle and pass every third at point Y.

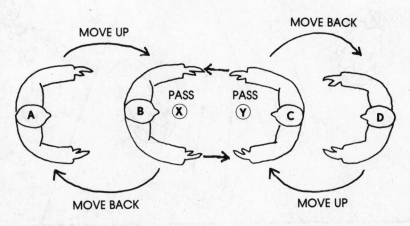

MOVE UP

MOVE BACK

PASS (X) PASS (Y)

MOVE BACK

MOVE UP

THE "Y" FORMATION

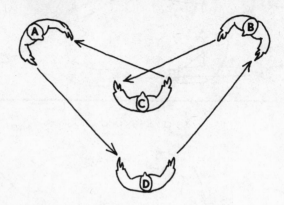

This looks very complex, but is easy. A and D make long passes. C and B make short passes. C passes and receives across, but otherwise it's quite straightforward. Which leads up to:

THE PIVOT

As long as C is in the middle he can pivot around throwing first to A (while B and D exchange) then to B (while A and D exchange) then to D (while B and A exchange).

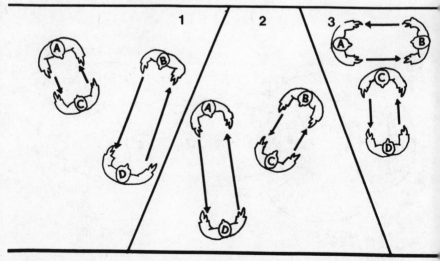

FIVE FOLKS

The Star

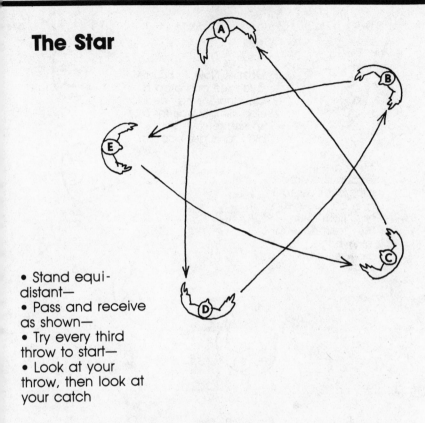

- Stand equi-
distant—
- Pass and receive
as shown—
- Try every third
throw to start—
- Look at your
throw, then look at
your catch

> **Note:** Most collisions are caused by juggling at different tempos.
> Pass at the same time with the same force.

The star looks great as is, but you can also:
- Turn the entire formation while passing;
- Alternate singles, doubles and triples;
- Pass floaters on a specific count
- Put a sixth member in the middle, also juggling.

Drops: Now if you are a feedee and drop a club there is no need to stop. Simply wait for a space, retrieve your club, and get back in.

If you are the feeder and drop, skip your pass to B or E, but receive a pass from them. They then have to retrieve the dropped club.

Note:
This is just like a feed with three but the feedees have so much time they can do tricks while waiting. Why not:

- Turn a pirouette—
- Throw a back flip—
- Do a quick solo series of tricks—

THE DOUBLE FEED

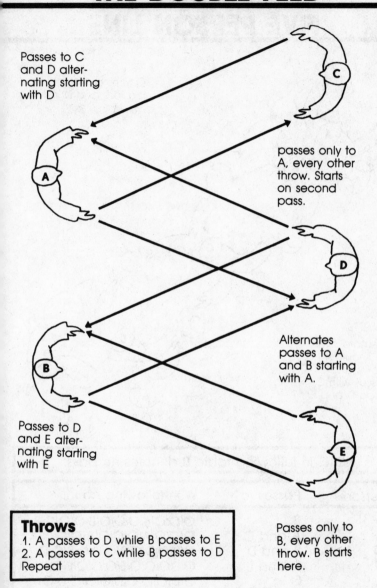

Passes to C and D alternating starting with D

passes only to A, every other throw. Starts on second pass.

Alternates passes to A and B starting with A.

Passes to D and E alternating starting with E

Throws
1. A passes to D while B passes to E
2. A passes to C while B passes to D
Repeat

Passes only to B, every other throw. B starts here.

VARIATIONS ON FIVE PERSON LINE

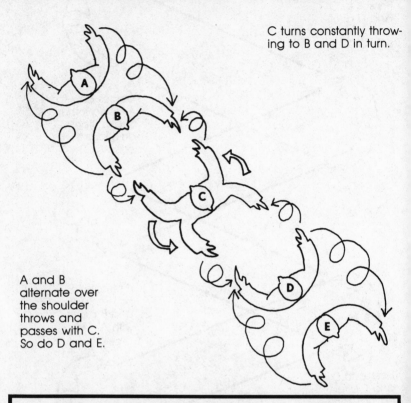

C turns constantly throwing to B and D in turn.

A and B alternate over the shoulder throws and passes with C. So do D and E.

NOTE: In following table 0 denotes no pass.		

Person	Passes to	With following count
A	B	O/O/O/B/O/O/O/B/O/O/O/B
B	A and C	O/C/O/A/O/C/O/A/O/C/O/A
C	B and D	O/B/O/D/O/B/O/D/O/B/O/D
D	C and E	O/E/O/C/O/E/O/C/O/E/O
E	C	O/D/O/O/O/D/O/O/O/D/O

DOUBLE FEED WITH SEVEN

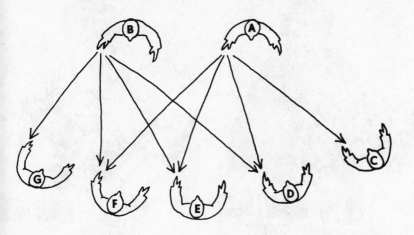

A and B start with C and D, sweep down to F and G and back again.
For all the feedees the trick is to get the count. Use the table below to
get your count.

Person	Passes to	Starts with	This person's count
A	C, D, E and F	C	C/D/E/F/E/D/C/etc.
B	D, E, F and G	D	D/E/F/G/F/E/D/etc.
C	A	A	A/O/O/O/O/O/A/O/O/etc.
D	A and B	B	B/A/O/O/O/A/B/A/O/O/etc.
E	A and B	O	O/B/A/O/A/B/O/B/A/etc.
F	A and B	O	O/O/B/A/B/O/O/O/B/A/B/etc.
G	B	O	O/O/B/O/O/O/O/O/B/O/O/etc.

BILL GALVIN AND STEVE MOCK

Cigar Boxes

Certification Requirements

1. Half turns and full turns on both ends
2. Take outs on both sides moving down through and up over
3. Spin the center box 3 ways
4. Under the leg and out again on both sides
5. Behind the back with all three boxes and out again
6. Any three vertical moves
7. a. Release all 3 boxes, clap twice and regrasp
   b. Release all 3 boxes, cross your arms and regrasp
   c. From crossed arm position, uncross
8. Hand a box across
9. Demonstrate a fancy start
10. Demonstrate a balance move
11. One of the following
    a. A four cigar box move
    b. A pirouette move
    c. A stack of eight boxes

LEARNING TO DEFY GRAVITY—WITH AMY

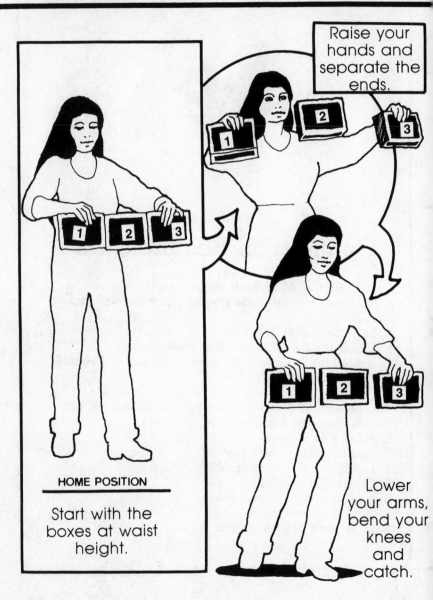

HOME POSITION

Start with the boxes at waist height.

Raise your hands and separate the ends.

Lower your arms, bend your knees and catch.

TURNING ONE END BOX

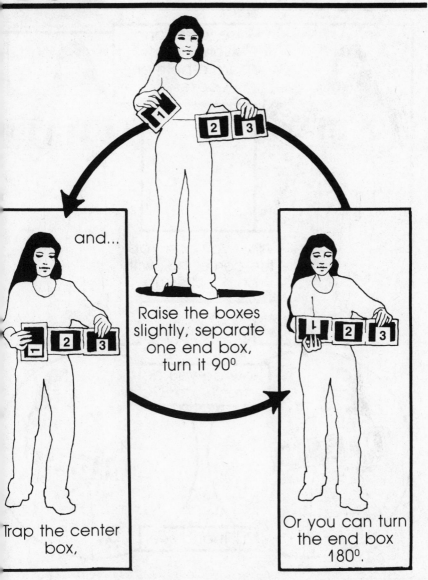

and...

Raise the boxes slightly, separate one end box, turn it 90º

Trap the center box,

Or you can turn the end box 180º.

TURNING BOTH END BOXES

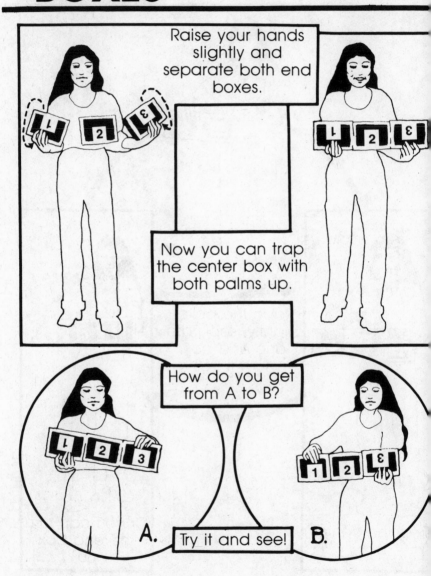

Raise your hands slightly and separate both end boxes.

Now you can trap the center box with both palms up.

How do you get from A to B?

A.

Try it and see!

B.

TAKE OUTS

NOTE: Just for fun Amy will show you this move left-handed. Learn all moves both ways.

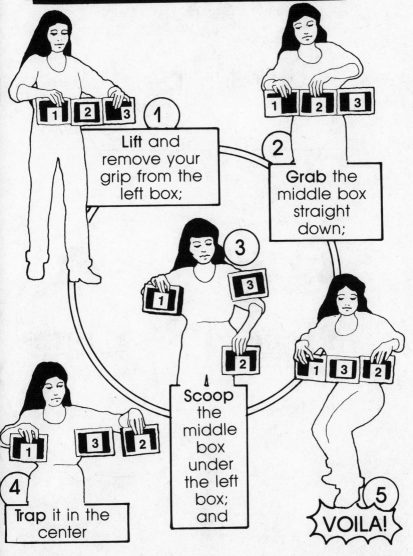

1 Lift and remove your grip from the left box;

2 Grab the middle box straight down;

3 Scoop the middle box under the left box; and

4 Trap it in the center

5 VOILA!

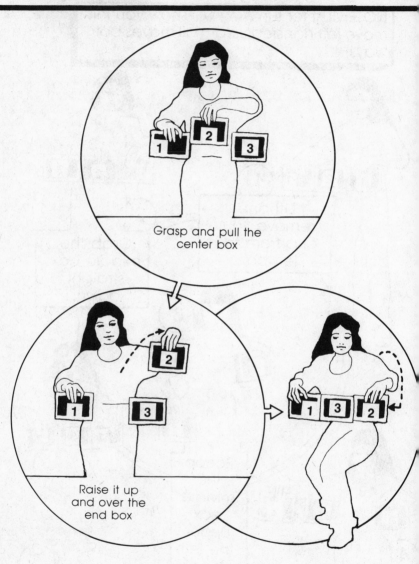

Grasp and pull the
center box

Raise it up
and over the
end box

SPINS

When you release the center box spin it slightly so it turns 90°, 180° or 360° and trap it again.

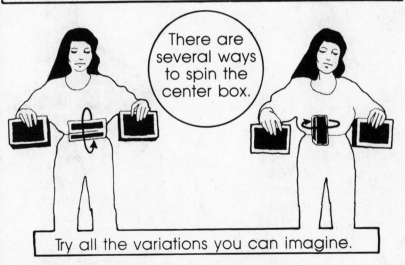

There are several ways to spin the center box.

Try all the variations you can imagine.

BODY MOVES

Swing the boxes to one side

Separate them on one side

Your leg goes through the gap

Trap them again, under your leg

or trap your knee for a laugh

Move your whole
body through
the gap.

Trap your waist

Trap your head

VERTICAL TRICKS

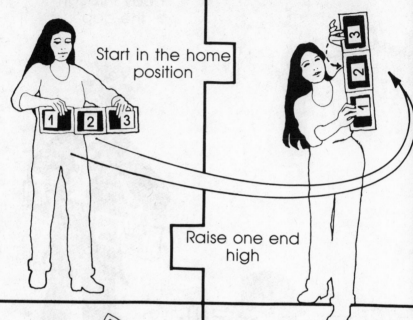

Start in the home position

Raise one end high

Bring your top hand off and through the center, tumbling the top box

Trap the tumbling box in the center

A VERTICAL SEQUENCE

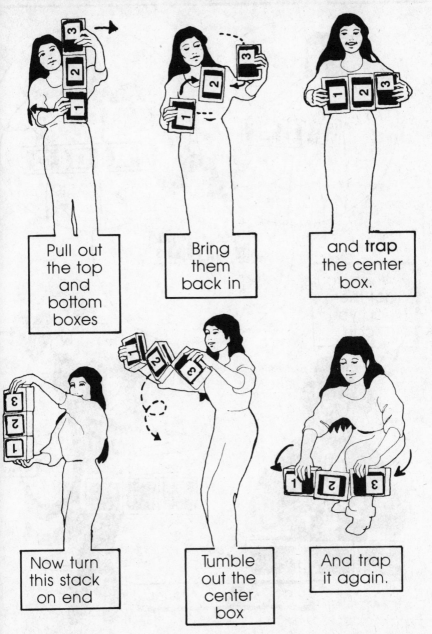

Pull out the top and bottom boxes

Bring them back in

and **trap** the center box.

Now turn this stack on end

Tumble out the center box

And trap it again.

Now its time to learn to **release** and **regrasp** all the boxes.

When you let them go you can:

clap **or...** pirouette

or...

Now that you have all that time on your hands, why not do something with those floating boxes?

You can tumble them toward you.

or catch them with your arms crossed.

slap cheeks

and...

catch

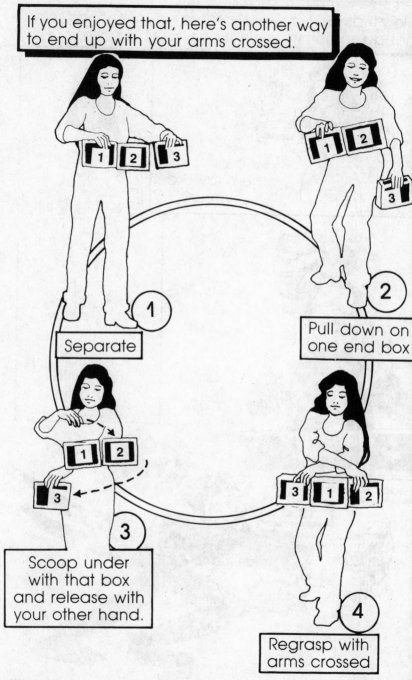

If you enjoyed that, here's another way to end up with your arms crossed.

1 Separate

2 Pull down on one end box

3 Scoop under with that box and release with your other hand.

4 Regrasp with arms crossed

273

CLAP TRAP

Here is a **FAST** move

① Raise

② Separate, lift and pass the box across

③ To the other hand

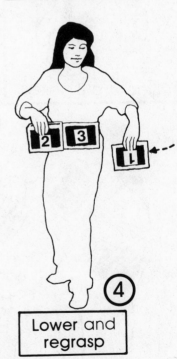

④ Lower and regrasp

A FANCY START

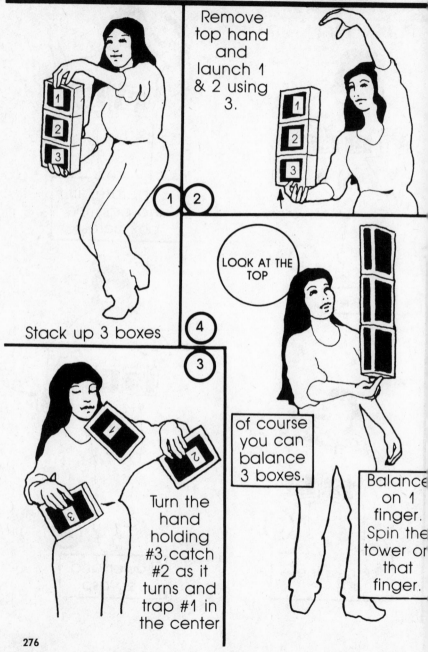

Remove top hand and launch 1 & 2 using 3.

① ②

Stack up 3 boxes

④

③

LOOK AT THE TOP

of course you can balance 3 boxes.

Turn the hand holding #3, catch #2 as it turns and trap #1 in the center

Balance on 1 finger. Spin the tower on that finger.

THE GRAND FINALE

1 FOR A GRAND FINALE, YOU WILL NEED 8 BOXES. STACK THEM LIKE THIS, PULLING THE CENTER BOX OUT APPROXIMATELY 2 INCHES...

PICK THE STACK UP FROM THE SIDES AND SLOWLY & CAREFULLY INTEGRATE THE BOXES LIKE THIS!

2

3 PLACE THE LAST BOX AS SHOWN HERE

4 TURN THE WHOLE STACK 90°...

5 MOVE THIS BOX TO THIS POSITION

6

BALANCE THE PILE ON YOUR CHIN

THE FLOWER STICK

Devil Sticks

Certification Requirements

1. Demonstrate double sticking
2. Demonstrate single sticking
   a. Complete a half flip
   b. Complete a full flip
3. Pick up from the ground
4. Helicopter spin
   a. With two sticks
   b. With one stick
5. Airplane propeller
6. One additional one stick trick
7. One crossed arm move
8. Under both legs
9. Behind the back on one side
10. Either
    a. A balance move or
    b. A partner move

THE DEVIL STICK

By Todd Strong

A Few Preliminaries

Work in short blocks of time, 5 to 10 minutes are fine when you are just starting and don't yet have the "bug."

- If you get frustrated, take a break or try a different challenge.
- Never be satisfied. Keep trying new tricks and polishing those you know.
- Keep your mouth closed and your tongue inside, common problems when you first begin.
- Breathe normally while practicing. Holding your breath hinders progress.

Two points from Aikido:

"Stay with the experience"

It's important to concentrate on what you are doing if you want the sticks to dance. Should your mind wander to paying the rent or what is for dessert, you may find it is gravity and not you in control of the choreography. You have to focus and concentrate in order to play with the sticks, but the more you practice the better your focus and concentration.

Beginners make large circles, masters make small circles.

Most devil stick moves are fairly subtle. As beginners we guess at the proper pattern, drop frequently and make mistakes. These errors provide the feedback that helps us tighten our patterns. This tightening is called "education." Beginners in anything make large jerky patterns; masters make smaller, more precise patterns.

VOCABULARY

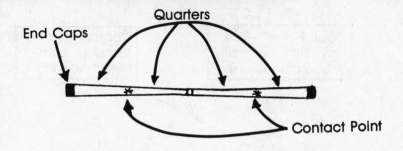

End Caps

Quarters

Contact Point

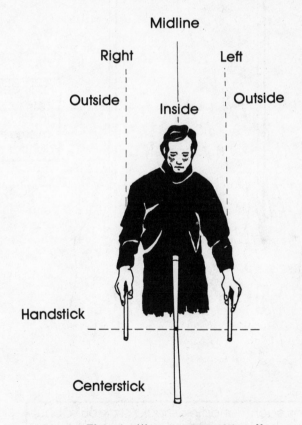

Midline

Right

Left

Outside

Inside

Outside

Handstick

Centerstick

This is "home position"
— Forearms are parallel to the ground —

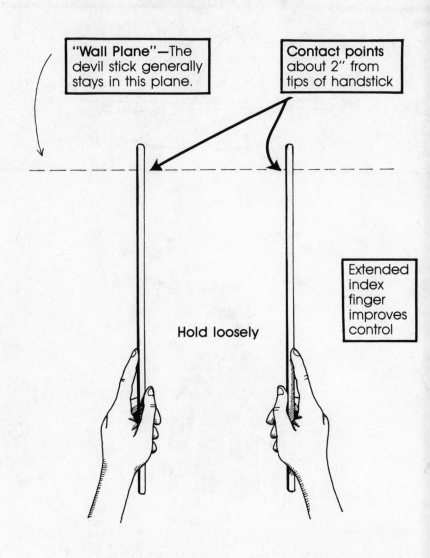

"Wall Plane"—The devil stick generally stays in this plane.

Contact points about 2″ from tips of handstick

Extended index finger improves control

Hold loosely

Butt of each handstick should stick out about 2″. This improves grip and reduces fatigue.

GETTING STARTED

GROUND SCHOOL

- Kneel with the stick standing upright
- Toss it back and forth with your hand
  (The bottom end of the stick
    never leaves the floor).

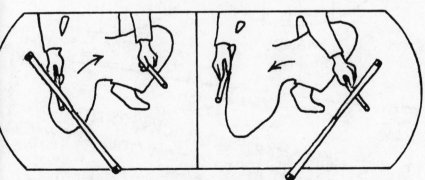

- Now use the handstick in place of your hands

REMEMBER

CATCH AND THROW DON'T HIT

FLIGHT TRAINING

- Now stand up and try it in the air
- Repeat the previous steps with the bottom of the devil stick off the floor
- Remember, a drop is a sign of progress

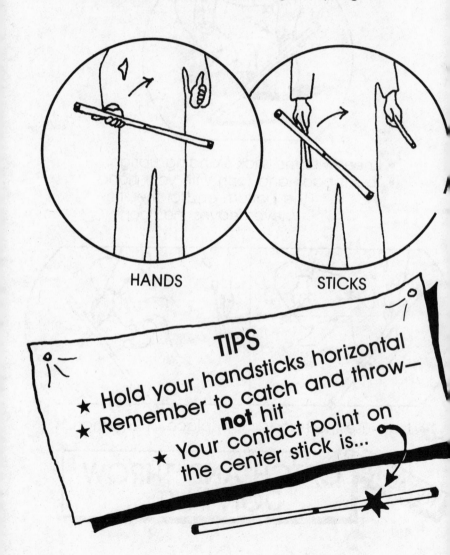

HANDS

STICKS

TIPS

★ Hold your handsticks horizontal
★ Remember to catch and throw— **not** hit
★ Your contact point on the center stick is...

HAVING SOME PROBLEMS?

Q. Why does my centerstick roll over the top of my handstick?

A. You are catching it too close to the center tape—remember your contact point.

Q. I'm losing control of my centerstick. It seems to be going too fast.

A. You may be hitting too close to the top—lower your contact point a bit.

Q. Why is my centerstick running away from me?

A. Your handsticks are "V"ed out—keep them parallel to one another and horizontal.

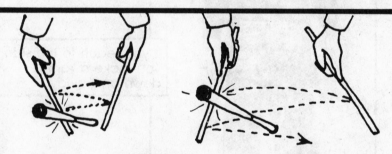

"V" IN—stick goes toward hands   "V" OUT—stick runs away

• REMEMBER THE BASICS •

★ Toss and catch: don't hit
★ Aim for the contact point
★ Keep your handsticks parallel to each other and horizontal
★ No practice = no progress

STILL DROPPING?

Keep your forearms and the handsticks parallel to the ground by using your elbow, shoulder, waist and knee joints, as well as your wrists. The more you move—up and down and side to side—the more fluid your control.

If you reach down, you make a ramp down. Don't just reach down—go down!

If you reach to the side, you make a ramp down and away.

Don't just reach to the side—move to the side.

DOUBLE STICKING
(TRAPPING)

Double sticking is the term for hitting the centerstick with both hands simultaneously, one above and the other below the center tape.

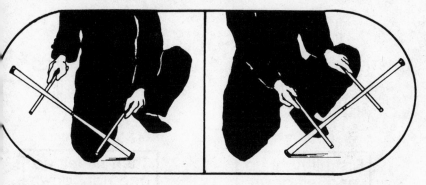

Begin with one end of the centerstick on the floor.

CONTACT POINTS

NOW!

Gain your rhythm and try it in the air.

POINTERS

- Lift the centerstick 1 or 2 inches with each tap.
- Slow and soft is the key.
- Use your shoulders and elbows to raise and lower the handsticks, not your wrists.
- Alternate your hands up and down, like 2 reciprocating pistons.

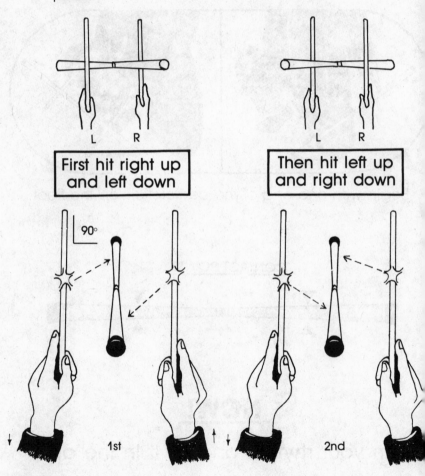

First hit right up and left down

Then hit left up and right down

1st

2nd

GAINING CONTROL

- Balance the centerstick on the handstick.
- Bounce the centerstick up and down a few inches.
- While the centerstick is in the air, cross your hands and catch.
- Toss again and uncross.
- Try right over left and left over right.

TOSS AND CROSS

HALF FLIPS AND FULL FLIPS

- Balance the centerstick on the handsticks.
- Toss the centerstick up so it does a half turn and catch it on **both** handsticks again.
- Now try a full turn.
- Learn half and full flips in both directions. Then try 1½ and double flips.

And catch on the handsticks.

Remember:
- Finesse is more important than strength.
- Toss only as high as is necessary to complete the move.

NOW LET'S GET FANCY
AND DO THAT SAME MOVE WHILE DEVIL STICKING

HALF FLIPS

Get a good "tic toc" rhythm with your handsticks, tapping the centerstick back and forth.

With your right wrist, flick up a little higher and impart more force so the devil stick spins 180 degrees before you catch it on the other handstick.

FULL FLIPS

Same as a half flip, but flick the centerstick higher and with more spin to allow for a 360 degree flip.

FLIP TIPS

Pull your receiving stick out of the pattern of the spinning centerstick — then re-insert the handstick for the catch.
- First try one isolated flip with either hand.
- When you gain more control — progress to flipping in a steady rhythm. For example one...two...three...flip, one...two...three...flip.
- Finally you can flip continuously from either hand alternating half flips, full flips, one and one halfs and doubles.

If you have progressed this far, you know all of the most important basic moves. Here is where your real learning will begin, so let's start with a few hints.

POINTERS

★ If you aren't dropping, you aren't learning.
★ Work on perfecting each move (depth) and learning new moves (breadth).
★ Several short sessions are more productive than an overly long session. You may find you do better after a break.
★ Practice to music if you can. It cuts out the rest of the world and gives you a rhythm to follow. If you put on a 45-minute tape, you know when you have practiced for 45 minutes.

PICK-UPS

NOTE: By now you are an expert at one move, for sure—the drop. Here are two methods for getting started again. If done properly your audience will think it's part of the act.

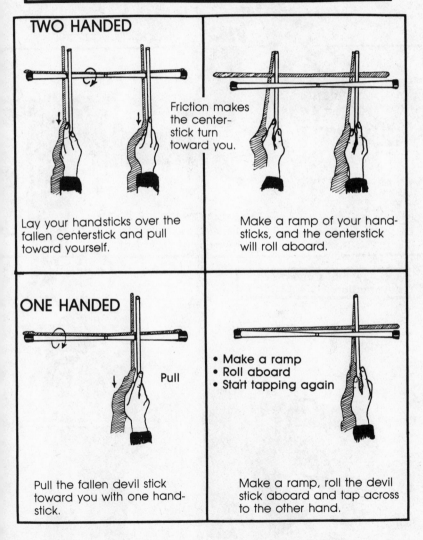

TWO HANDED

Friction makes the center-stick turn toward you.

Lay your handsticks over the fallen centerstick and pull toward yourself.

Make a ramp of your hand-sticks, and the centerstick will roll aboard.

ONE HANDED

Pull

- Make a ramp
- Roll aboard
- Start tapping again

Pull the fallen devil stick toward you with one hand-stick.

Make a ramp, roll the devil stick aboard and tap across to the other hand.

AND KICK-UPS

NOTE: Even fancier and guaranteed to gain applause is a kick-up back into the pattern. The key is practice, practice, practice.

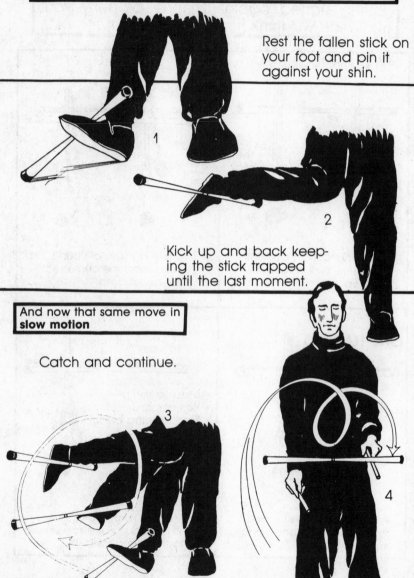

Rest the fallen stick on your foot and pin it against your shin.

Kick up and back keeping the stick trapped until the last moment.

And now that same move in **slow motion**

Catch and continue.

ALTERNATE KICK UP

Maneuver your foot under the exact center of the devil stick.

KICK
STRAIGHT
UP IN
FRONT—
CATCH
AND
CONTINUE

HELICOPTER SPINS

NOTE: Pulling hand is palm up. Pushing hand is palm down.

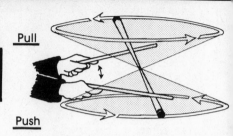

Pull

Push

- While you are double sticking, push slightly with one hand as you pull with the other.
- Stay close to center tape for more control.
- Use tips of handsticks for better clearance.

★ Keep your helicopter spin with one hand stick.
★ Remove the pulling stick, keep pushing with the other stick.
★ Contact point is right on the center tape.
★ Every time the devil stick makes a half turn, tap upward.

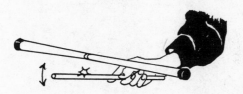

ULTRA-SNAZZY MOVE—
• Learn the helicopter with each hand.
• Start a helicopter spin, and switch hands. If done with flair, a real crowd pleaser!!!

AIRPLANE PROPELLER

(FRONT VIEW — PERFORMER'S PERSPECTIVE)

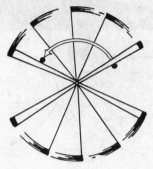

To begin the propeller, maintain contact with the centerstick a bit longer than usual.

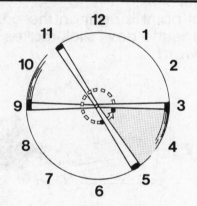

Circle the centerstick with the handstick, then push up in one move from 5 to 3 o'clock.

For this pattern, move your handstick closer to the center tape for your contact point.

ONE STICK TRICKS

Tap across with your right handstick and pull your right handstick out.

Move your right arm across, insert and tap back using the same handstick.

TIPS—
- A half flip or full flip may be easier than no flip at all, since you gain time while the devil stick is turning.
- Pull out, move across and insert quickly. Tap back slowly and gently.

Using one handstick, balance the devil stick horizontally with tiny taps on both sides in succession.

CROSS ARM VARIATIONS

All sorts of possibilities open up when you learn to work the devil stick with your arms crossed.

Start on the ground and hit back and forth using the tops of the handsticks. Stand up, bringing the devil stick up with you, and experiment with crossing and uncrossing your arms with a half flip.

UNDER THE LEG

Reach under your leg with one handstick, tap, and pull out. Then try your other leg. Eventually you may be able to jog in place hitting under the leg with alternating right and left handsticks.

BEHIND THE BACK

After hitting the centerstick, drop your hand and handstick behind your back to reappear by your waist on the other side of your body. Instead of home position, you now work with one hand around your back. It is easiest to use trapping in this position.

TIPS

- Move quickly.
- Point handstick straight down while moving.
- Toss a half-flip to gain time as you move into and out of this position.

THE BUZZ-SAW

- Hold the handsticks horizontally.
- Move your hands as if they were pedaling a bicycle.
- Trap the devil stick between the handsticks.
- Lift with the near handstick.

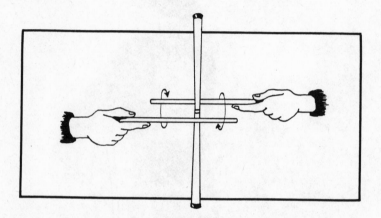

- Once you can pull up and under, toward your chin, learn to pedal your hands the other way, lifting with the far handstick.

CAUTION: Watch out for your chin, your ego, and other breakables!!!

CHOP STICKS

We are grateful to the Chinese for both the devil sticks and chopsticks. Now let's combine the two!!

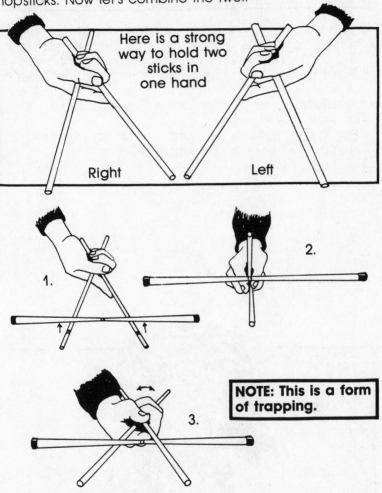

Here is a strong way to hold two sticks in one hand

Right   Left

1.

2.

3.

NOTE: This is a form of trapping.

1. Balance a devil stick on two handsticks and toss it straight up.
2. Pull your hand back and reinsert the handsticks.
3. Gently rock the devil stick back and forth by rotating your wrist.
4. Handsticks stay almost horizontal.

Now with your free hand you can try another set of chopsticks. A kick up is a good way to start your second devil stick. Here are a few multiple devil stick variations:

- Try a flip with one hand, then a flip with the other, alternating hands. The key is to focus on the devil stick in the air and just keep rocking with the other hand.
- Toss flips with both hands simultaneously; the devil sticks cross in mid-air and change hands. The trick is to establish a near plane and a far plane and to toss one devil stick in each.
- For the "pièce de résistance" kick up devil stick number three, and start juggling.

DUAL DEVIL STICKS

Start as shown above.
- Establish two separate wall planes, one near tips, one near hands.
- Hit both devil sticks simultaneously.
- Hit perfectly straight across, so they don't collide.
- Lift higher on the near plane devil stick.
- Separate your hands, hit close to the tape, and go slowly.

DUAL PROPELLERS

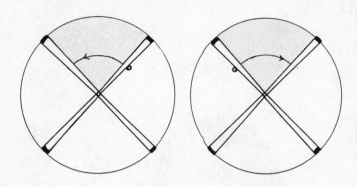

- Start by holding a handstick and a centerstick in each hand, tossing the centersticks in the air simultaneously, and turning outward.
- One advantage is that you can use just one wall plane and avoid collisions by keeping your hands wide apart.

NOTE: If you can accomplish all of the feats described so far you know that this chapter is only a rough outline of possible devil stick moves. Use your imagination to invent your own variations.

BALANCE

The Principle of Balance: Keep your eye on the top and your body adjusts automatically.

You can balance it on your foot, on your chin, or on a handstick. You can also toss from one balance point to another.

Variations of Balance...

which may not work

PARTNERS WORK

Two partners, sharing one devil stick set.

ALSO: If you face one another and stand one arm's length apart sharing a devil stick in a single plane you can both use your right hand.

Two partners with two sets of handsticks and one centerstick:

PLAY CATCH WITH THE CENTERSTICK

HINTS:
- Pass high.
- Give it at least one full spin.
- Use trapping method to catch.

For extra points try helicopter passes also.

Drop Back

Back to Back

TAKE AWAYS

The "thief" can come in from behind and "steal" from the "victim."

Victim   Thief

HINT: The thief comes in quickly, substituting his hand-stick for the victim's. The victim quickly removes both handsticks from the scene of the crime.

THE DIABOLO

Diabolo

Certification Requirements

1. Start your diabolo and show how to keep it from running away or turning
2. Throw and catch at least 3 times in succession
3. Demonstrate whipping
4. Catch on both handsticks
5. Climb the string
6. Hop the diabolo over your leg 3 times in succession
7. Either of the following
   a. Throw, jump the string, and catch, or
   b. Throw, do an acrobatic stunt, and catch
8. Demonstrate a move ending up with crossed arms, then uncross your arms
9. One of the following
   a. Send a diabolo up a fixed string to an 18 foot ceiling
   b. Toss a diabolo back and forth with a partner
   c. Demonstrate a one-wheeled diabolo

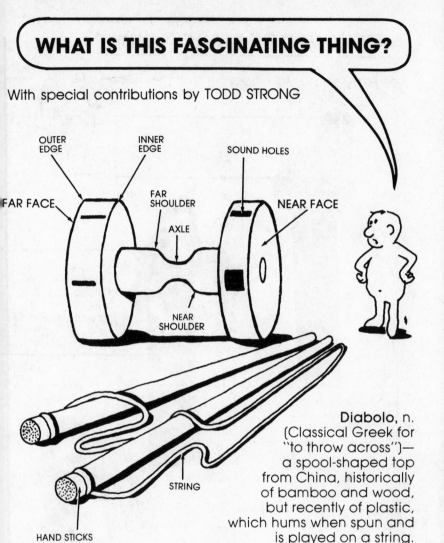

WHAT IS THIS FASCINATING THING?

With special contributions by TODD STRONG

OUTER EDGE

INNER EDGE

SOUND HOLES

FAR FACE

FAR SHOULDER

AXLE

NEAR FACE

NEAR SHOULDER

STRING

HAND STICKS

Diabolo, n. (Classical Greek for "to throw across")— a spool-shaped top from China, historically of bamboo and wood, but recently of plastic, which hums when spun and is played on a string.

NOTE: A yo-yo is just a captive diabolo! Think of all the things you have seen done with a yo-yo. Now imagine that the yo-yo could leave its string, fly high, and return. That is a diabolo!

319

AND HOW DO I MAKE IT SING?

Let Amy show you how.

Start with the right hand-stick pointed down, and the left handstick at waist height.

Diabolo on the ground about 1 foot to the right of your right foot.

Pull up with the right handstick so the diabolo rolls up along the string. Increase speed as the diabolo gets higher up the string.

REMEMBER—
The diabolo is like a pulley.

PULL

PULL

As the right hand goes up, the left hand goes down slightly, to absorb the pull.

Now lower the right hand, and raise the left slightly.

The right keeps going down. The left comes up until the right is a few inches below the left.

Then it "whips" up again, as the left "drums" down.

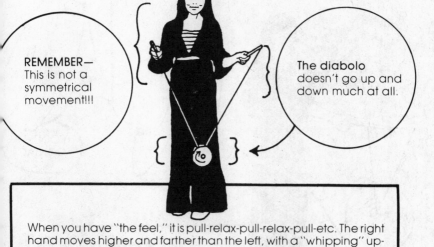

REMEMBER— This is not a symmetrical movement!!!

The diabolo doesn't go up and down much at all.

When you have "the feel," it is pull-relax-pull-relax-pull-etc. The right hand moves higher and farther than the left, with a "whipping" upward motion and a relaxed down stroke. The left hand goes down like a drum beat.

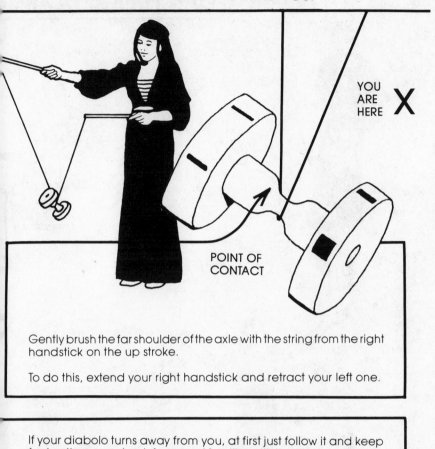

YOU
ARE
HERE **X**

POINT OF
CONTACT

Gently brush the far shoulder of the axle with the string from the right handstick on the up stroke.

To do this, extend your right handstick and retract your left one.

If your diabolo turns away from you, at first just follow it and keep facing the near wheel. As you get familiar with the diabolo you can stop this "wandering" by gently touching the inner or outer edge of the near or far wheel with your right handstick.

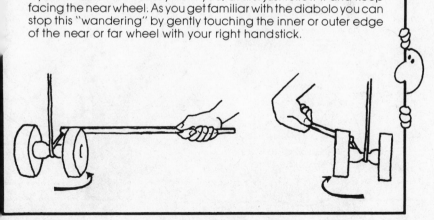

1 Start your diabolo spinning until it sings.

2 Raise and spread your arms, tightening the string.

3 Sight along your a and handstick.

As it comes down, point your right handstick at the center of the axle.

AVE THE STRING?

WARNING! Practice over a mat or thick carpet. When you throw your diabolo, avoid breakable items such as vases and your front teeth!

6 Now you should be back where you started.

5 And immediately drop your right hand. Absorb the impact on the string by raising your left hand.

4 Catch near the right handstick.

WHIP YOUR DIABOLO TO GIVE IT MOR ZING!

The diabolo flies from side to side as your right hand whips back and forth across your body.

1 Use your right arm and shoulder. Raise your left elbow.

2 The right hand stick crosses under your left elbow. Snap your wrist after you have extended your arm across your chest.

3 On the recovery stroke you are still accellerating the diabolo as it comes back across your chest.

Toss your diabolo up. Point your handsticks in...

and catch it on a handstick.

While it is still spinning, you can toss it from one handstick...

to the other.

Bounce your diabolo up and down,

In the center of the string.

When it is in the air...

cross your handsticks...

and catch it in the "V"

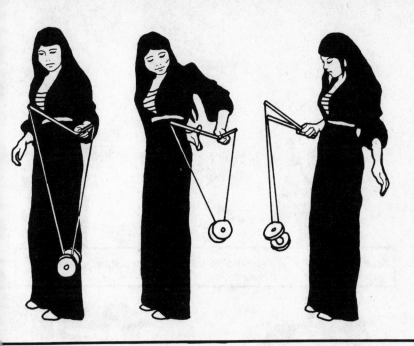

Pass the handsticks behind your back.

Loop the right handstick over the inner wheel, pull down, and the diabolo will climb the string.

Next time you throw, quickly reposition the handsticks and catch with the string behind your back.

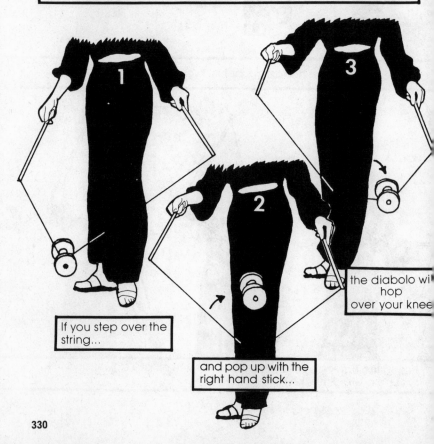

1

2

3

If you step over the string...

and pop up with the right hand stick...

the diabolo wi[ll] hop over your knee

AROUND THE WORLD

NOTE: These tricks are dangerous!

Build up your rpms.

1

...nd end up ...ith crossed ...rings. ...everse the ...rocess to ...ncross.)

4

2

Swing the diabolo in a big arc.

3

It will circle over your head.

331

AROUND THE WORLD THE DANGEROUS WAY!
(WATCH OUT FOR YOUR CHIN PLEASE!)

Face the diabolo as shown.

Swing it out and away in a big circle.

The diabolo comes over the top.

And down the center, back to the starting position.

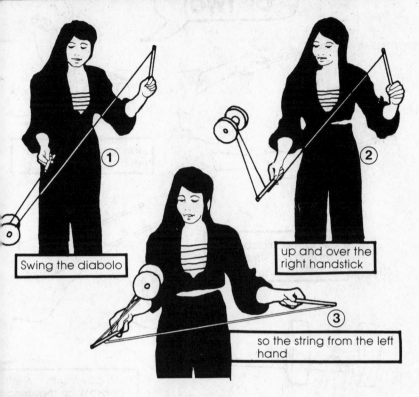

Swing the diabolo

up and over the right handstick

so the string from the left hand

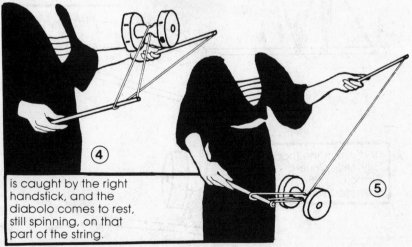

is caught by the right handstick, and the diabolo comes to rest, still spinning, on that part of the string.

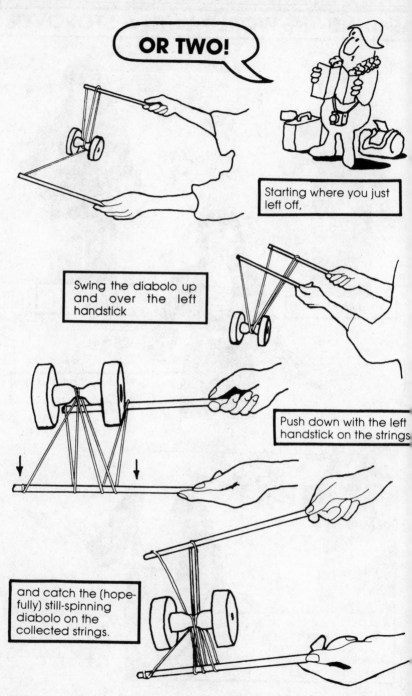

OR TWO!

Starting where you just left off,

Swing the diabolo up and over the left handstick

Push down with the left handstick on the strings

and catch the (hopefully) still-spinning diabolo on the collected strings.

Just imagine all the things you can do while your diabolo is in the air.

You can jump over the string.

But beware of the falling diabolo!

You could even do a fancy pirouette while the diabolo is in the air.

PRETTY FANCY, EH?

Now let's make those easy tricks a little more complicated.

Instead of hopping the diabolo over your foot or knee, try catching it behind the back, and

over

hopping it

your tummy

pull up on the left hand-stick.

1 If you loop your right handstick

2 over the far wheel

3 and pull down

4 **5** The diabolo will climb up...and over the left handstick.

Once the diabolo is spinning rapidly,

2 Lower the right handstick,

3 quickly circle all the way around the spinning diabolo,

4 and pull up, recapturing the diabolo on the string.

5 You end up with crossed hands.

HERE IS A SHOW STOPPER.

Attach a string to the ceiling.

Whip your diabolo to get it moving.

Get a friend to help you loop it with the string...

and pull down sending the diabolo to the ceiling.

THERE ARE TWO WAYS TO HOLD TWO STICKS IN ONE HAND.

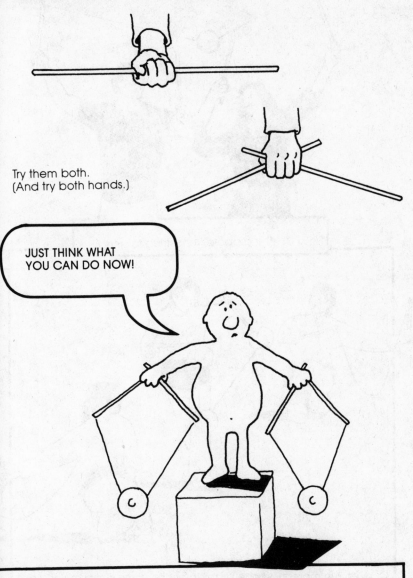

Try them both.
(And try both hands.)

JUST THINK WHAT YOU CAN DO NOW!

Now you should be able to do two diabolos simultaneously. (Have a friend start the second one and hand it to you.)

WITH TWO OR MORE PLAYERS YOU CAN:

Pass the diabolo from string to string.

Or even run more than one diabolo on the same string, by having your partners toss them to you.

SIDE BY SIDE

FRONT TO BACK

FRONT TO FRONT

BACK TO BACK

THERE ARE SOME "ONE-WHEELED" VARIATIONS OF THE DIABOLO.

There are two ways to start these diabolos.

①

Start with the diabolo on the ground. Wrap the string around the spindle 3 times.	Lift and pull gently on the right handstick. As the string slowly unwinds the diabolo starts turning.

Starting method #2

A

Twist the string four or five times while holding handsticks in one hand.

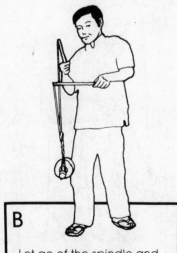

B

Let go of the spindle and begin raising and lowering handsticks as the string slowly unwinds.

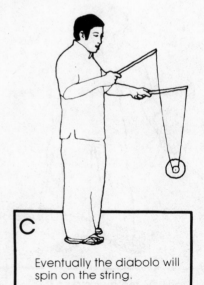

C

Eventually the diabolo will spin on the string.

HERE ARE SOME TRICKS FOR ONE-WHEELED DIABOLOS

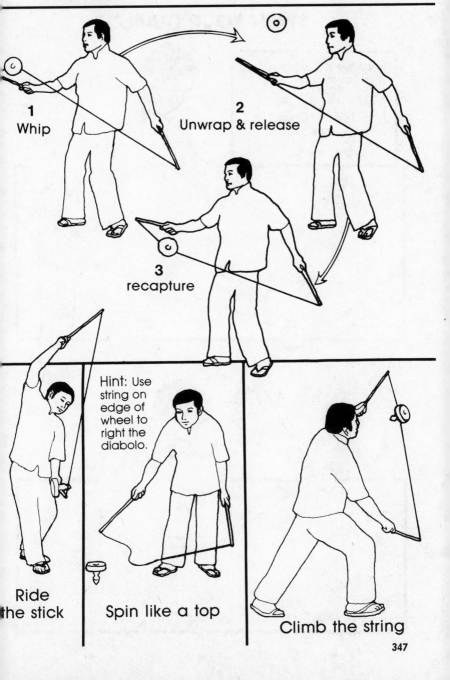

1 Whip

2 Unwrap & release

3 recapture

Ride the stick

Hint: Use string on edge of wheel to right the diabolo.

Spin like a top

Climb the string

A MORE PROFESSIONAL WAY TO START YOUR DIABLO

Loop the string around the spool as shown.

Right hand pulls up. Left hand pushes.

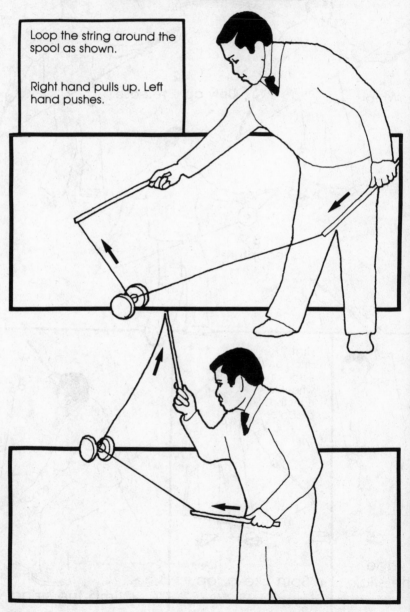

With string wrapped around the spool, diablo can be made to jump up and down several times in a row without unwrapping.

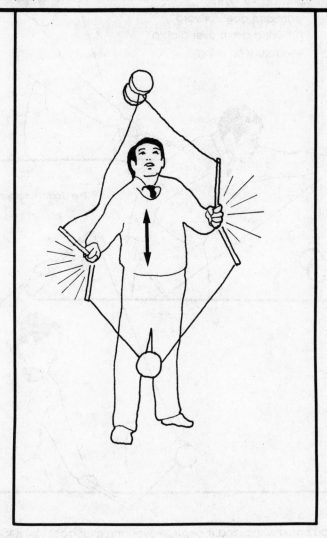

Unwrap and recapture

Left arm goes forward.
Unwrap with left.
Right arm goes forward.
Pull string down over diablo.
Recapture on string.

The diablo is suspended in ai

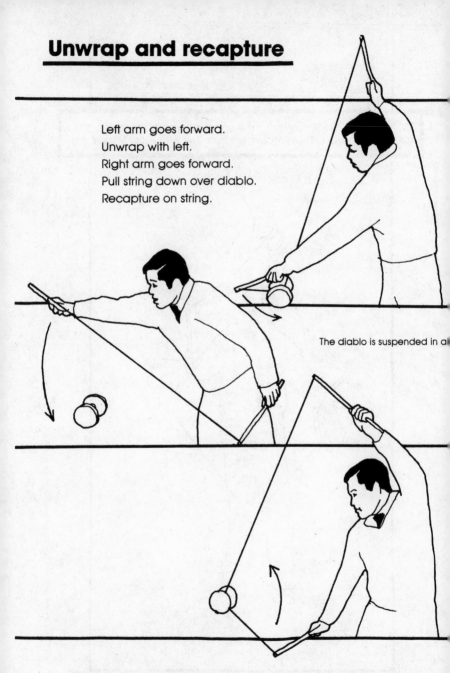

You can unwrap and recapture over and over again in quick succession.

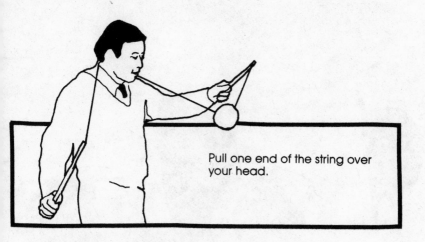

Pull one end of the string over your head.

Toss the diablo and hold both sticks in front as shown with the string around your neck.

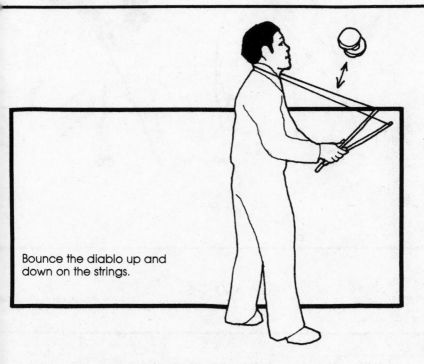

Bounce the diablo up and down on the strings.

BELLA AND KRIS KREMO

Hat Manipulation

Certification Requirements

1. Roll your hat down your arm and replace it on your head on both sides
2. Roll your hat from your outstretched hand to your head on one side
3. Turn your hat off, and back
4. Show 3 ways to flip, flop, or tumble a hat
5. Toss your hat up to your head with a single and a double flip
6. Toss your hat to your foot and kick it back up to your head
7. Balance your hat in a tricky fashion
8. Roll your hat down your arms, across your back, to a catch
9. Either
   a. Juggle three hats using two hands and your head, or
   b. Roll your hat backwards to a catch, and back up your back to your head
10. Throw a hat onto a partner's arm or head
11. Show a combined move with your hat and at least one other object

Hat Manipulation

Hat manipulation can be a show-stopper with plenty of comic moments and surprises for your audience.

Any topper or derby will do, but try to get an all felt hat. Real beaver hats or those with cardboard stiffening get broken and beat up in very short order. A heavy hat is better than a light one.

ENOUGH OF THIS SERIOUS RECREATIONAL JUGGLING. LET'S HAVE SOME FUN. I'LL CHANGE INTO MY PERFORMING TOGS AND SHOW YOU SOME HAT TRICKS DEVELOPED DURING THE VAUDEVILLE ERA.

ROLLING THE HAT DOWN YOUR ARM

To take your hat off, tap it upward with a finger at the back, and aim it down your outstretched arm, palm up.

The front of the brim should touch your shoulder (1), the leading edge of the crown should touch your elbow at the top of the joint (2), the trailing edge of the crown will hit just above the wrist (3) and you should catch the hat in your hand by the brim (4).

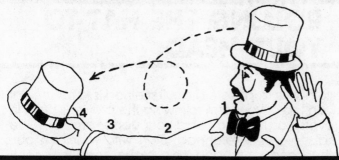

REPLACING THE HAT BACK ON YOUR HEAD

From the final position in the last move, to get the hat back on your head flip the crown back past your wrist.

Bend your arm at the shoulder and elbow and place the hat on your head. Let go of the brim after the hat is securely on your head.

ROLLING THE HAT TO YOUR HEAD

An alternative and more difficult method is to roll the hat back on top of your arm following the previous steps in the reverse order, and using your upper arm to guide the hat onto your forehead. Start with your arm outstretched and your hand held higher than your forehead. Let gravity assist you.

TURNING YOUR HAT OFF AND BACK

Put both hands up with your thumbs up, elbows out and forward, fingers beneath the brim. Rotate your wrists forward. Once the crown is down you can roll the hat once or twice more by turning the brim over your fingers like a baton. To return the hat to your head, just reverse the process.

FLIPPING YOUR LID FROM SIDE TO SIDE

Hold the hat on the right side with the right hand. Flip it by pulling up to the right, so the brim rotates around the crown. Catch it with the left hand on the left side.

Once you can flip singles, try doubles.

Practice reaching out to catch, as if the hat were escaping.

FLOPPING YOUR LID
ACROSS YOUR THUMB

Hold the hat by the front of the brim with your right hand as shown, with the crown to the left.

Flop it over your thumb. Remove and replace your hand in the original position, so the hat is suspended in air for just a second.

TUMBLING YOUR HAT

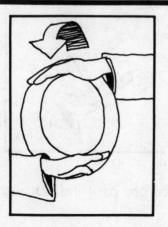

The hat can be tumbled with the crown toward you, or away. Place one hand on the top brim and one on the bottom. Your hands rotate over and over one another, and the hat tumbles, rolling around each wrist in turn.

TOSSING AND CATCHING YOUR HAT

Practice throwing the hat with a single flip. Hold it thusly and flip it toward you. Catch with the same hand or the other hand. Teach both hands to flip and catch. Once you can do a single, learn a double flip.

Once you can flip it to your hand, practice the same flip, but duck your head under the hat. Gradually work on accuracy of the flip so you can toss it to your head without ducking. once you learn singles, learn doubles.

Use this same flip to your extended arm held high over your head. Look out at the audience and catch "blind."

ROLLING DOWN THE BACK
(AND UP AGAIN)

Roll your hat down your back by tipping your head back.

Catch it "blind" at waist level.

Bend forward at a 45 degree angle, and roll it up your back.

The hat teeters on your neck and plops onto your head.

ROLLING YOUR HAT
ON THE BRIM

Hold the hat with the crown toward the audience.

Toss it up and spin it like a ring or Frisbee.

Let it roll down your arm, across your back, and out to your other hand.

Reverse that hand and catch the hat. (Got it? Now practice the other direction.)

TOSSING UNDER THE ARM

Toss your hat under your opposite arm, turn slightly, and let it plop onto your head.

Note: Look up until the very last second, then duck under the hat.

THROW TO A "HATRACK"

Hold your hat as shown.

Throw hard. The hat turns once.

Toss directly at an outstretched arm, a hatrack, or your partner's head.

Practice playing "catch" with your partner to develop this skill.

Remember that you can place or toss a hat to your elbow or your knee.

For a super effect, toss your hat with a single flip. Or tip it off your head with a flip. Catch it on your foot. Readjust the hat so it is balanced on your toe. Then flip it back to your head with a high kick.

ONE POINT OF CONTACT

SPINNING YOUR HAT ON YOUR FINGERS

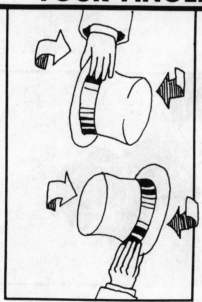

Hold the hat with your thumb under the brim, and the hat hanging vertically. Lift and spin the hat around your extended fingers and as it finishes its full spin reinsert your thumb and grasp it again. Lift, spin and let go, extend your arm and regrasp.

This same move can be done with the hat held vertically over your head, spinning it around your extended fingers. Push it up, spin, regrasp.

JUGGLING THREE HATS

METHOD 1—ONE SIDE AT A TIME

The easiest way to learn to manipulate 3 hats simultaneously is to work with one hand and two hats at a time. Put one hat on your head and another in your hand ready to toss onto your head with a single flip. Throw the hat from your hand and with the same motion reach up and remove the hat from your head. Catch the thrown hat on your head.

Now try it on the other side with the other hand. Once you can do this on both sides simply alternate, right hand throw—remove—catch on head, left hand throw—remove—catch on head.

METHOD 2—FLAT THROWS Hold one hat in

each hand by the brim, with the third hat on your head. The left hand throws its hat across toward the right and in the same motion removes the hat from the head, thumb up and toward the front. The right hand places its hat on the head and catches the hat thrown from the left. At this point you can pause, readjust the hats and prepare to throw again.

The movement with both arms is simultaneous and rythmic.

LEFT: THROW, TAKE...

RIGHT: PLACE, CATCH.

(PLACE)

(CATCH)

METHOD 3—FLIP TO THE HEAD You get

more time with this move. However, instead of placing
the hat on your head, you flip it to your cranium. Hold
one hat in your left hand, and another in your right hand.
Put the third hat on your head. Toss the left hat across
your body with a high flip. As it peaks toss the right hat
with a single flip and simultaneously remove hat from
your head with your left hand, thumb above the brim.
The right hat lands on your head.

LEFT: FLIP, TAKE... (TAKE)

(FLIP)

RIGHT: FLIP, CATCH.

(FLIP)

(CATCH)

BALANCING YOUR HAT

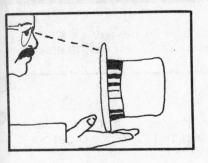

You can balance your hat anywhere on your body as long as you can see the uppermost part of the brim. For instance, you can balance it on your hand, your foot, or your nose.

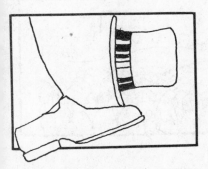

Place the front edge of the brim on the bridge of your nose, tilt your head back and look up.

Focus on the center of the sweat band. Keep the hat balanced by moving underneath the hat. To put it on your head just tilt your head forward.

AND FINALLY, PASSING YOUR HAT

This is the most dangerous part of the act. If done incorrectly, you can become a magician and the entire audience will disappear.

Steps in hat passing include:

1. THE WARNING Just before your spectacular finale, tell the assembled throng that they should get out their wallets; you will soon be passing the hat.

2. THE REQUEST Immediately after your finale crescendo, take off your hat with a flourish, pull out a dollar bill and let the audience know that..."This is the **average** donation, although some generous fans do give more".

3. THE PASS Keep talking. "That's it folks, don't be bashful. It's just like church. Give today so you won't feel guilty tomorrow. I've done my part, the rest is up to you." Look each donor in the eye, smile and thank them profusely.

Now that you and your hat have become working partners its time to use your imagination and invent some moves of your own. Just remember that the two of you will have to spend many hours in practice together. Here are a few ideas to explore:

1. Interactive hat manipulation between two or more jugglers;
2. "Blind", behind the back catches with the hand or on the foot;
3. Rolling the hat on its brim across the chest or over the back;
4. Flipping the hat from foot to foot;
5. Catching objects on the brim or crown of your hat;
6. Leaving the hat on the stage and getting into it with a front roll or a back bend;
7. Combining hat manipulation with toss juggling.

Have fun, and treat your hat with love and respect.

PLATE SPINNING

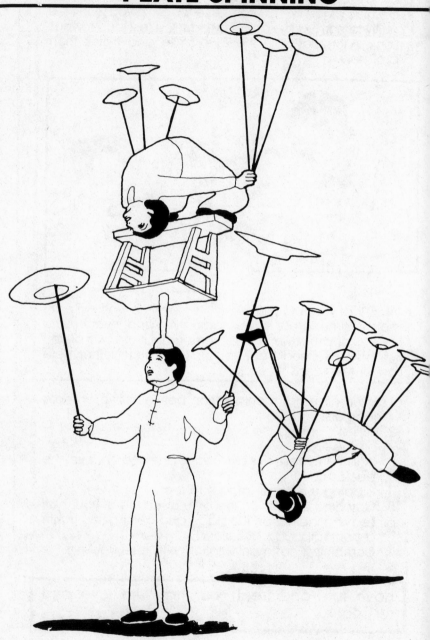

Plate Spinning

Certification Requirements

1. Demonstrate starting and accelerating a plate with each hand
2. Toss a spinning plate and catch it again on the stick
3. Pass a spinning plate behind your back and under the leg (using a stick)
4. Curl a spinning plate under each arm (using a stick)
5. Demonstrate one move on your finger
6. Demonstrate one balance move and either juggle or swing clubs while the plate is balanced
7. Either
   a. Demonstrate an acrobatic move while spinning one or more plates, or
   b. Spin three or more plates in one hand, or
   c. Spin three or more plates on anchored sticks, or
   d. Demonstrate plate spinning skills using a frisbee, a weighted cloth or a rectangular object (tray, board, book)

GETTING STARTED

Instant success guaranteed!
- Put the point of the stick in the center of the plate.
- Hold the stick straight up and down in your right hand.
- Hold the rim of the plate between your left thumb and finger tips as shown.
- Spin the plate toward yourself.

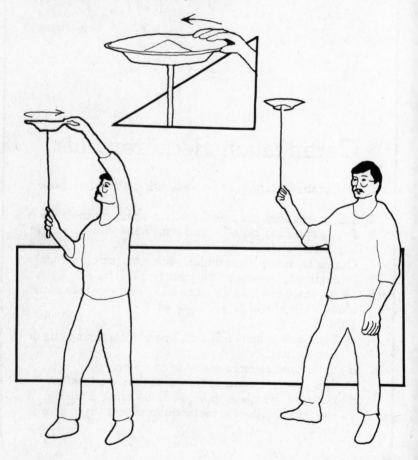

ACCELERATING

STEP 1—Spin an invisible plate.

Make small
circles with
the tip
(apx. 6″ diameter)

Keep stick
straight
up and down

Point
index finger
up along
stick

Turn your
wrist

STEP 2—Accelerating a real plate.

Start spinning as shown on
previous page.

As the plate spins, start turning
your wrist, and catch the point
of the stick in the ridge on the
bottom of the plate.

Suddenly freeze your wrist and
the plate will jump to the
center, spinning faster than
before.

373

STARTING THE HARD WAY

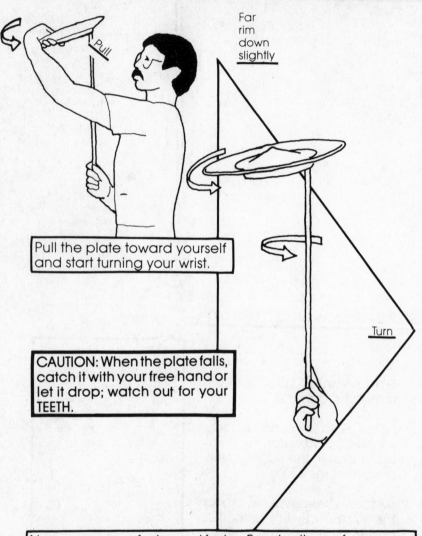

Pull

Far
rim
down
slightly

Turn

Pull the plate toward yourself and start turning your wrist.

CAUTION: When the plate falls, catch it with your free hand or let it drop; watch out for your TEETH.

Now you can go faster and faster. Eventually you freeze your wrist and the plate jumps to center.

THROWS

Start spinning	Toss the plate up from the stick	Catch it again on the point

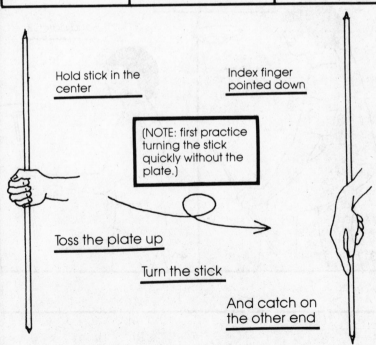

Hold stick in the center

Index finger pointed down

(NOTE: first practice turning the stick quickly without the plate.)

Toss the plate up

Turn the stick

And catch on the other end

PASS UNDER YOUR LEG

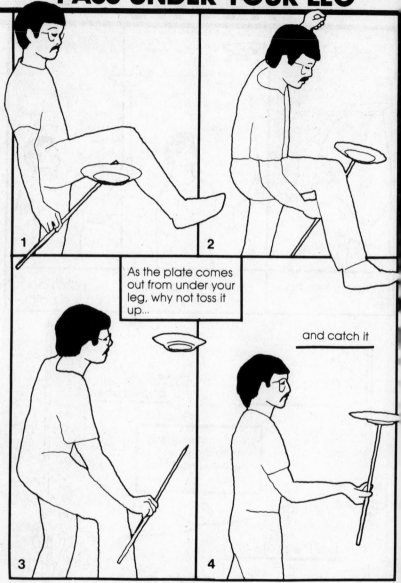

As the plate comes out from under your leg, why not toss it up...

and catch it

CURLS

(NOTE: with most moves you can practice first with a stick and no plate, later add the plate.)

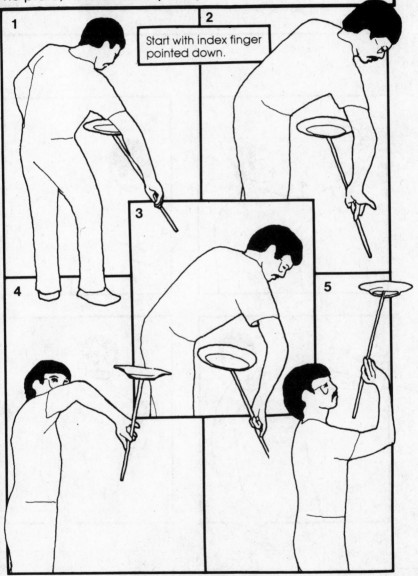

1

2

Start with index finger pointed down.

3

4

5

SPIN ON FINGER

You can start the plate on your fingertip and then: curl under your arm—

PASS BEHIND YOUR BACK

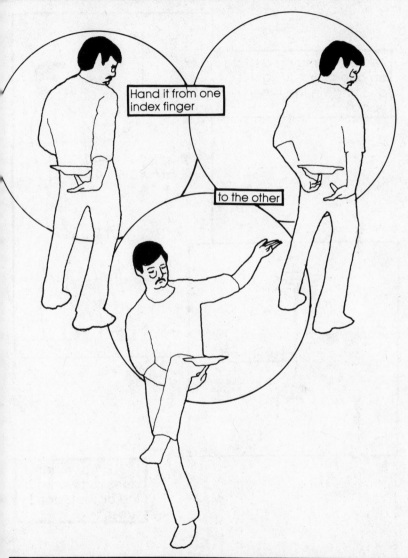

Hand it from one index finger

to the other

NOTE: practicing with a spinning plate can help you to learn to spin, balance and curl a spinning ball.

BALANCES

While balancing a plate on one palm, juggle 2 or 3 rings in the other hand.

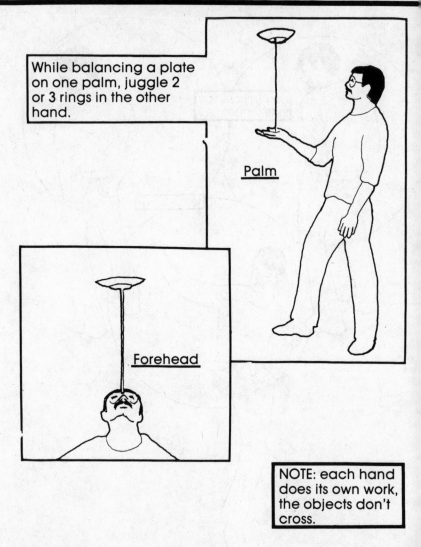

Palm

Forehead

NOTE: each hand does its own work, the objects don't cross.

While balancing a plate on your forehead, juggle an even number of rings or plates.

MULTIPLE PLATES

You need a friend to help you get your plates started. They hand you spinning plates one at a time.

Hold them as shown, and keep your wrist turning.

SPINNING ON AN ANCHORED STICK

Get a slender stick about 5 feet long and anchor it firmly at the base.

WHAT'S NEXT?

Now that you can spin a plate you can transfer the skill to other objects, even rectangular ones like notebooks and trays. You can also start working on ball spinning skills, or on spinning a large cloth, cut round, with weights sewn in the hem. The same principles apply.

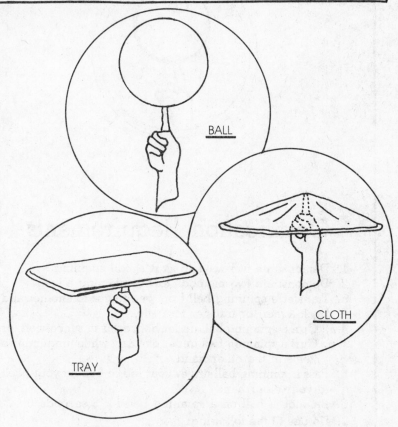

BALL

CLOTH

TRAY

Ball Spinning

Certification Requirements

1. Demonstrate two ways to start a ball spinning
2. Demonstrate two methods for maintaining a spin
3. Transfer a spinning ball from one finger to another and back again, or transfer to a stick
4. a. Curl a spinning ball under both arms in succession, or
   b. Curl a spinning ball under one arm while juggling two items in the other hand
5. Pass a spinning ball under your leg or behind your back to your other hand
6. Balance a ball on a spinning ball for 5 seconds
7. Do one of the following:
   a. Roll a ball from your forehead to one temple and back again, or
   b. "Head" two balls (3 times each) or
   c. Catch a ball on a mouth stick (3 times in a row) or
   d. Either a chest roll or a back roll

SPINNING
ONE HANDED START

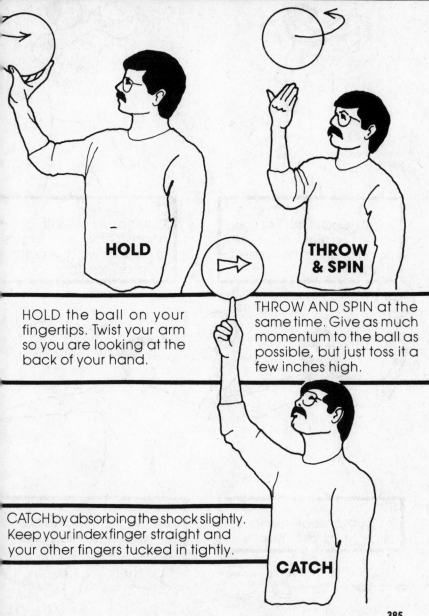

HOLD

THROW & SPIN

HOLD the ball on your fingertips. Twist your arm so you are looking at the back of your hand.

THROW AND SPIN at the same time. Give as much momentum to the ball as possible, but just toss it a few inches high.

CATCH by absorbing the shock slightly. Keep your index finger straight and your other fingers tucked in tightly.

CATCH

TWO HANDED START

GET MORE INITIAL RPMS!

HOLD
Right hand in front of your face, palm out—left hand on the other side of the ball, palm in.

SPIN
Pull sharply out with both hands. Leave your fingers in contact with the ball as long as possible.

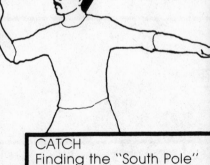

THROW
About a foot high, as straight as possible.

CATCH
Finding the "South Pole" on your spinning ball comes with practice.

HOLD THAT SPIN

Q. Where on my fingertip do I balance the ball?

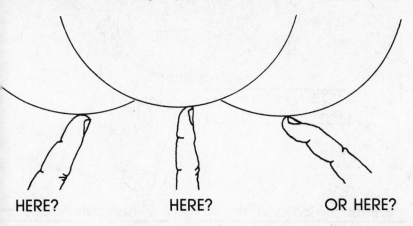

HERE?   HERE?   OR HERE?

A. Try all 3. Choose one and stick with it. They all work.

Q. How can I balance the ball once it is spinning?

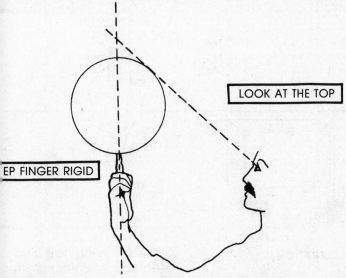

LOOK AT THE TOP

EP FINGER RIGID

A. Imagine a rod running through your finger and the ball. Keep this rod straight up and down.

Q. How can I keep the ball spinning longer?

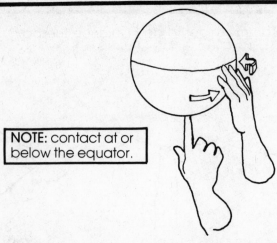

NOTE: contact at or below the equator.

A. Brush the ball toward you lightly with your free hand.

A. Use the tip of your middle finger to give a delicate push to the ball.

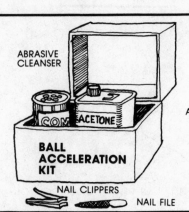

ABRASIVE CLEANSER

ACETONE

BALL ACCELERATION KIT

NAIL CLIPPERS

NAIL FILE

A. Clean your ball and keep your nails clipped.

TRANSFER TO A STICK

- Hold the stick steady in your hand or your mouth.
- Hit the exact center when you transfer.
- Resist the impulse to move the stick.

SPINNING 2 BALLS

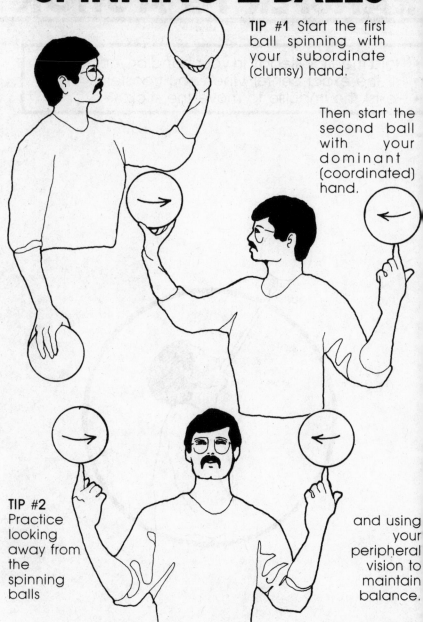

TIP #1 Start the first ball spinning with your subordinate (clumsy) hand.

Then start the second ball with your dominant (coordinated) hand.

TIP #2 Practice looking away from the spinning balls

and using your peripheral vision to maintain balance.

Q. Why spin the ball inward? Don't most basketball players spin outward?

A. That brings up the topic of....

A spinning ball naturally migrates in the direction of spin. If you spin a ball with your right hand toward the outside (or clockwise when seen from the top), and then try to "curl" it under your arm, you fight the natural inclination of the spinning ball.

OOPS!

HOWEVER...

If the ball is spinning toward you when you curl it under your arm it is moving naturally in the appropriate direction.

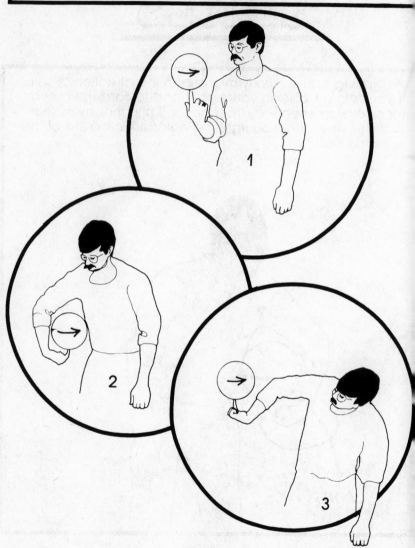

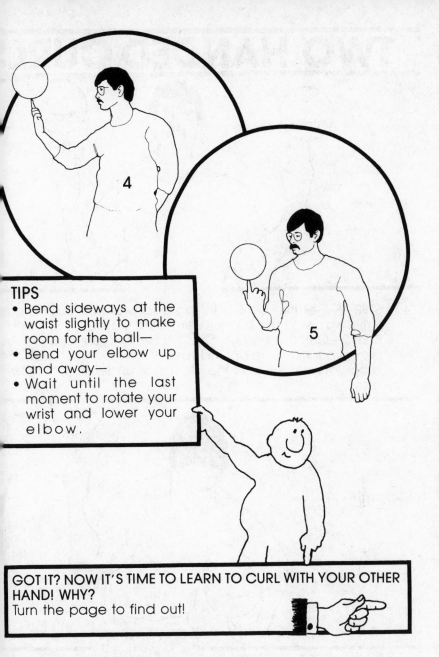

TIPS
- Bend sideways at the waist slightly to make room for the ball—
- Bend your elbow up and away—
- Wait until the last moment to rotate your wrist and lower your elbow.

GOT IT? NOW IT'S TIME TO LEARN TO CURL WITH YOUR OTHER HAND! WHY?
Turn the page to find out!

TWO HANDED CURL.

STEP 1—Get two balls spinning and practice curling one while spinning the other. Learn both sides.

STEP 2—Curl the ball which is harder for you, and as you bring your hand up behind your back, twist your wrist and drop your elbow, start the other ball under your opposite arm.

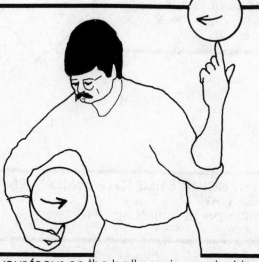

STEP 3—Keep your focus on the ball coming up behind your back each time, and continue. Each time your wrist "breaks" start the other side under.

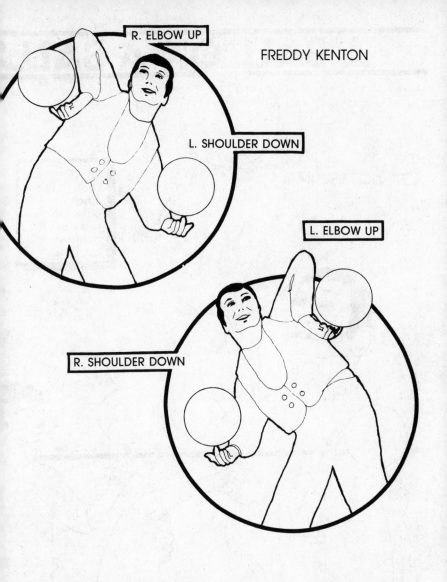

FREDDY KENTON

R. ELBOW UP

L. SHOULDER DOWN

L. ELBOW UP

R. SHOULDER DOWN

A GOAL Eventually you want to be able to stand in one place, face the audience, bend your body as little as possible, and curl spinning balls continuously with both hands.

A BALL ON A BALL

FRANCIS BRUNN

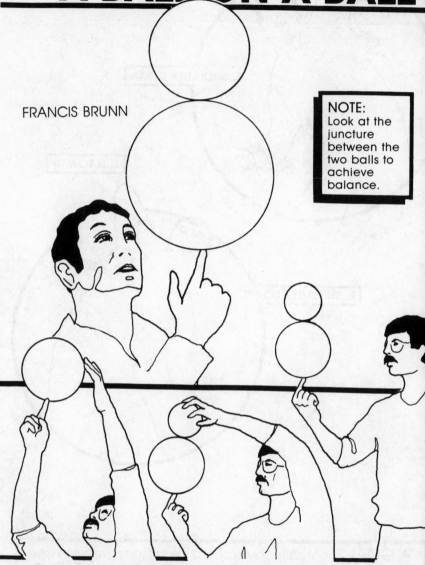

NOTE:
Look at the juncture between the two balls to achieve balance.

To balance a ball on a ball spin the first ball on your fingertip. Place the second ball on top of the first, right in the center. Don't give it any spin. After a careful release it will roll around on the first ball.

NOW FOR SOME STYLE

HIGH THROWS The high throw is a fancy way to start a spin. Toss the ball several feet in the air and absorb the shock when it comes down. It may help to use a two-handed start to get extra torque.

FOR EXTRA CREDIT Pop the spinning ball up from your finger and catch it again...still spinning.

REMEMBER—
- STAY ERECT.
- EXTEND YOUR ARMS AND LEGS.
- MOVE PRECISELY.
- DANCE WITH THE BALL.
- MAKE THE HARD TRICKS LOOK EASY.
- HOLD STRIKING POSES LONG ENOUGH TO ACCEPT APPLAUSE.
- COMBINE SPINNING WITH OTHER SKILLS.
- TO BECOME A GREAT JUGGLER LOOK AT OTHER ART FORMS, NOT JUGGLING.
- PRACTICE, PRACTICE, PRACTICE.

COMBINATION MOV

Work step by step to build up a combination move.

STEP 1—Juggle 2 in one hand while spinning with the other.
STEP 2—Juggle 3 in one hand.
STEP 3—Juggle 3 in one hand while spinning with the other.
STEP 4—Add a forehead balance.
STEP 5—Add the mouth balance.
STEP 6—Add a ring on the upper portion of balance arm.
STEP 7—Get an agent

BEHIND THE BACK

Execute this move after transfer of spinning ball from hand to hand has been perfected.

UNDER THE LEG

Once you can transfer a spinning ball from hand to hand these tricks are quite easy.

CHEST ROLL

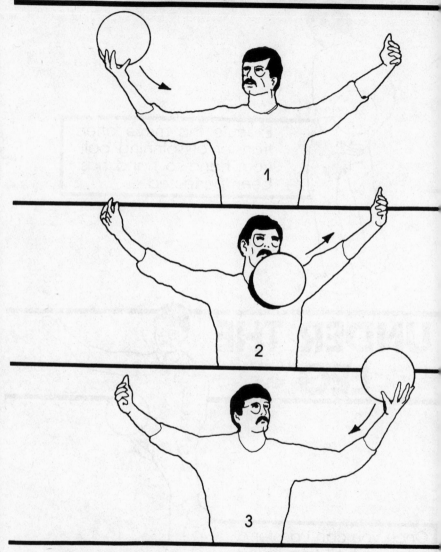

Here again practice pays off. A fingertip flip starts the ball off, keep your chin clear. Then flip it back.

BACK ROLL

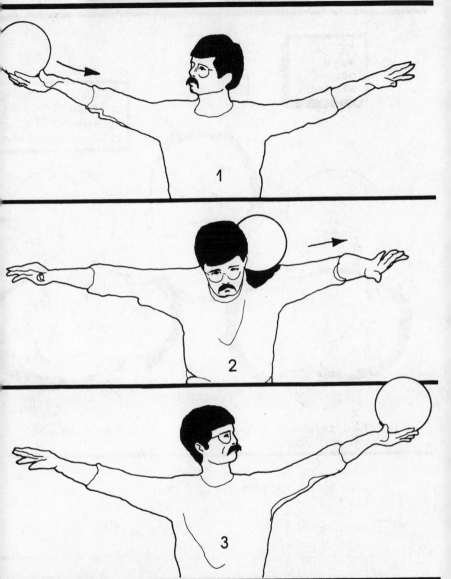

Try to create a ramp across your shoulders for this move.

HEAD ROLLS

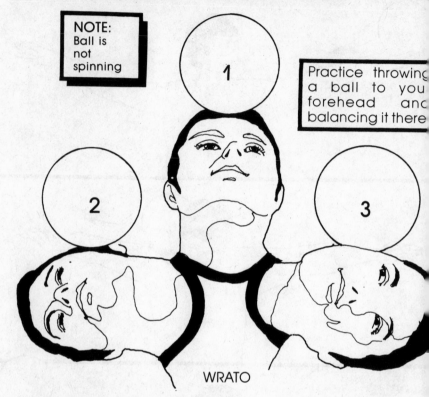

NOTE:
Ball is
not
spinning

Practice throwing
a ball to you
forehead and
balancing it there

1

2

3

WRATO

Practice balancing the
ball on one side.

And the other side.

Now practice moving in this order:
STEP 1 to STEP 2
STEP 1 to STEP 3
STEP 2 to STEP 1
STEP 3 to STEP 1
STEP 2 to STEP 3
STEP 3 to STEP 2
The ultimate move is:
STEP 2 to STEP 3 around the back, circumnavigating the
cranium.

HEADING THE BALL

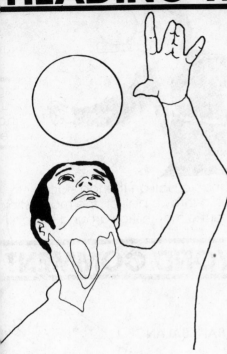

Straight up and
down is the key.

FRANCIS BRUNN

HINT
Bounce 1 ball
straight up and
down, and prac-
tice with an imag-
inary second ball.
The body move-
ment and the ball
work can be prac-
ticed separately.

THE MOUTH STICK

STEP 1—Learn to balance a ball on the top edge.
STEP 2—Learn to catch a thrown ball on the mouthstick.
STEP 3—Learn to rotate the mouthstick around the ball.

MOVES BEYOND COMMENT

THREE BALL BALANCE

MICHAEL CHIRRICK

THE FRONT ROLL

ENRICO RASTE

STILL NEED INSPIRATION?

RUDY CARDENAS

PAOLO BEDINI (Rastelli's nephew

GREGOR POPOVITCH

Balance And Auxiliary Equipment

Certification Requirements

1. Go from standing to lying and back to standing with a linear object balanced on forehead, nose or chin
2. Balance a linear object of no more than 12 inches length for a period of 10 seconds or longer
3. Balance 3 linear objects simultaneously for 10 seconds or longer
4. a. Without spinning, balance a ball on a ball, or
   b. Balance a club on a club as part of a juggling sequence, or
   c. Balance a club on your chin or forehead as part of a juggling sequence and return to juggling
5. Juggle 4 or more rings, balls or clubs while balancing a linear object on the nose, chin or forehead (20 throws)
6. Juggle 3 clubs for 20 throws while:
   a. Riding a unicycle, or
   b. Balancing on a rolling globe, or
   c. Balancing on a rola-bola, or
   d. Riding or balancing on any similar piece of equipment (stilts, unsupported ladder, etc.)

BALANCE AND AUXILIARY EQUIPMENT

Jugglers like to combine their unique abilities with a number of related skills such as balance, unicycling, tightwire, the rola bola and stilt walking. Books are available on most of these topics. We will merely provide some hints and pointers for those who wish to combine juggling with other activities.

BALANCE

Balancing a long object is easier than balancing a short one. Simply get a long skinny object, put it on your palm, and look at the top. Peacock feathers are ideal. As long as you keep your eye on the eye on the top of the feather, it will stay upright. Your hand adjusts automatically underneath.

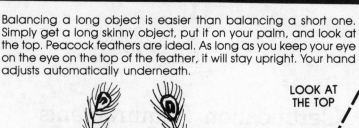

LOOK AT THE TOP

Now that you can balance the feather on your hand why not try.

YOUR ELBOW

YOUR KNEE

YOUR FOOT

YOUR SHOULDER

OR YOUR PROBOSCIS?

Once you can balance a feather you can:

This makes a GREAT relay race, by the way!

Let it fall forward and follow it wherever it goes, pushing slightly with your nose. Or you can...

GO DOWN ON ONE KNEE

SIT DOWN

OR EVEN LIE DOWN

BALANCING SHORTER OBJECTS

Some skilled jugglers can balance teaspoons or ballpoint pens on their noses. They weren't born with this skill. Here's how **you** can learn it.

Start with a dowel about 36 inches long. Balance it on your nose.

When you can balance it easily, cut about 3 inches off at a time. (Off the dowel, not your nose.)

Finally you should be able to cut the dowel down to about 6 inches. Then try other objects. Eventually you should be able to pick a pen out of someone else's pocket and balance it at will.

SIMULTANEOUS BALANCES

REMEMBER: You have to be able to see the object to adjust to it.

Again, longer is easier. Start with feathers. Do both hands. Then try one hand and your nose. Now switch to something that is relatively stable, like a pool cue, or a spinning plate on a stick.

BALANCE AND JUGGLING

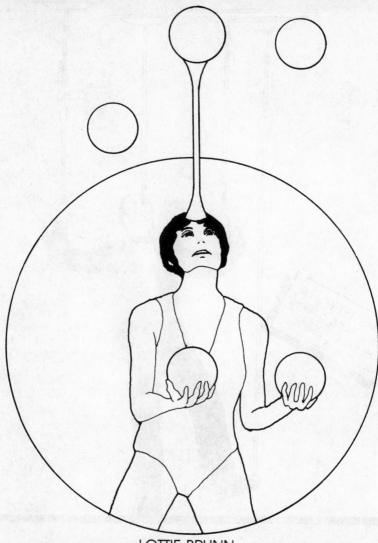

LOTTIE BRUNN

You can juggle while balancing as long as you can see the peaks of your juggling pattern. That means juggling even numbers of objects since they go up each side of the balanced object. Rings are easiest.

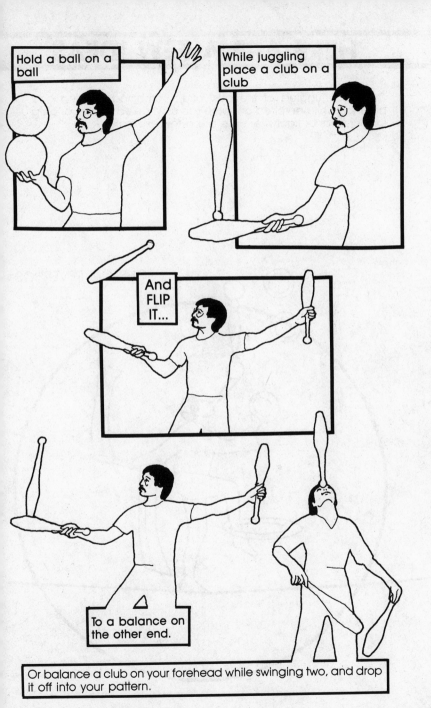

Hold a ball on a ball

While juggling place a club on a club

And FLIP IT...

To a balance on the other end.

Or balance a club on your forehead while swinging two, and drop it off into your pattern.

HERE ARE A FEW IDEAS

The great jugglers of the past often combined juggling and balance while perched on some sort of wheeled device or on a ladder, stilts or tightwire. Here are a few examples—

GUSTAVE REVERHOS

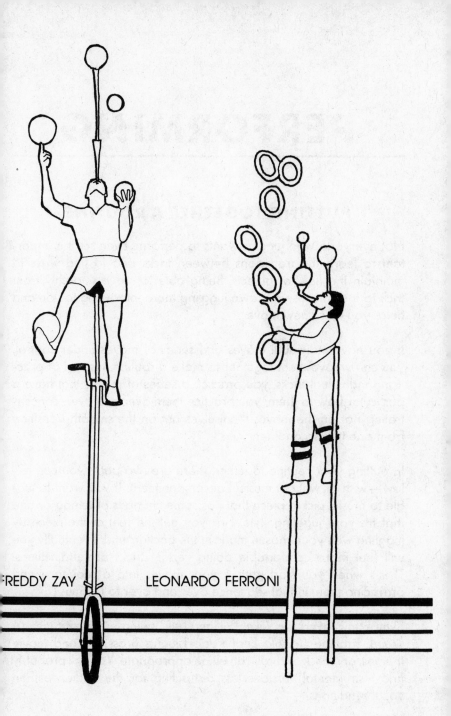

FREDDY ZAY   LEONARDO FERRONI

PERFORMING

PUTTING TOGETHER A ROUTINE

Not everyone who juggles wants to perform. Even so, it is impor-tant to learn the transitions between tricks and to find ways to maintain the flow of objects. Being able to move smoothly from trick to trick makes your own juggling more interesting to you and helps you learn new moves.

If you have individual moves and series of moves under control, you can weave them together to make a routine. Instead of prac-ticing individual tricks, you practice a series of moves that have a particular flow to them; you practice them over and over, concen-trating not on the moves themselves but on the smooth transition from one trick to another.

In putting your routine together, there are two paths you can fol-low—with or without musical accompaniment. If you want to jug-gle to music, pick a piece that has some changes of tempo or one that fits your juggling style. First you get the feel of the piece by juggling with your chosen music in the background. Eventually you will feel more comfortable doing certain tricks at certain times. That's when you start putting your moves into a sequence and practicing them in that sequence over and over to the music.

Symphonic overtures (like *William Tell*), swing-era jazz tunes (*A Train*), ragtime (*Maple Leaf Rag*), Tijuana Brass, TV and movie themes, and rock and roll can all be appropriate. You will probably find instrumental versions less distracting for the audience than vocal renditions.

To fit your juggling to the music, remember that you not only have a list of tricks from which to choose, but that these tricks can be done higher, wider and more slowly or tighter, smaller and more quickly, and that you can use the height and breadth of your stage as well. You can use minimal arm movements or big swinging motions. You can incorporate movement from side to side, turns and spins, leaps and acrobatics into your routine. You can sit, kneel or stand. Rastelli lay down to juggle, and Bobby May stood on his head. You can surprise the audience with a high throw out of a low pattern, a bounced ball that goes away and comes back again, movement of your head from side to side, an abrupt kick, a bounce off the forehead or bicep or even a sudden stop, balancing a ball on your forehead or a club on your foot. If your music is full of surprises, your juggling should be also. If your music is lyrical or driving or silly, so should your juggling be.

Use a friend, a mirror or, best of all, a video camera to look at your routine. Remember that a routine has highs and lows. Your first trick should be impressive, and your last should be a crowd-pleaser, but in between you want some applause points to give the audience a chance to show their appreciation.

When you decide to put together a routine *without* musical accompaniment, you can perform in silence or you can join the ranks of talking jugglers. Comedic patter may appear easy, but it requires the same discipline as a tightly scripted musical routine and the same attention to tempo. Now, however, we call it "timing."

Often a juggling trick reminds you of something else—a yo-yo, a tennis match, a volcano. So use a few of the easy ones that already have names. Generally speaking, you name the trick at the moment audience recognition takes place. In other words, you say "The juggler's Yo-Yo" just as you begin to do it. If you start doing it first, people will titter and giggle, and this noise may drown out your pronouncement. If you announce the trick too soon, the element of surprise is reduced. The verbal and visual images should register on the brain of the audience members simultaneously.

Also, the order in which you present "silly stuff" is important. For instance, you announce "Juggler's Tennis" and use as much of the stage as you can, running from side to side doing that trick. Each time you throw a long one you say, "Smash" or, "It's a long one." Suddenly you throw one to center stage and do the same move tightly, look up and say, "Fast volley at the net," toss one high and say "Lob," throw it off stage and say "Lost ball." If you drop, it's "Love—15."

In comedy juggling, keep your words to a minimum. You generally do the setup verbally, then the objects you are juggling deliver your punch line. Don't forget that you can accentuate your comedy juggling with funny faces or postures that reinforce the moves.

Silent juggling can be both musical and comic, since the audience will hear the music of your hands slapping the equipment, and you can use facial expressions and the element of surprise to elicit laughter. With a devil stick, or three clubs with sleigh bells taped on them, or cigar boxes, diabolos or torches you can use the noise made by the equipment to create a beat.

GUIDELINES FROM THE GREATS

Now let's look at a few of the guidelines the great jugglers of the past have given us. The combined wisdom of Francis and Lottie Brunn, Nick Gatto, Bobby May, Homer Stack and Enrico Rastelli provides some rules an aspiring performer ignores at great risk.

1. Practice every day for 20 minutes (Stack), one hour (Gatto), two hours (May) or as much as you can (Brunn, Brunn and Rastelli).

2. Count your repetitions of difficult moves and always do more than you did in the previous practice session.

3. Practice your routine over and over again from start to finish, until you can perform without any drops.

4. Don't copy other jugglers; instead, look at other art forms for your inspiration, such as dance, acrobatics, theater, comedy or music.

5. Use your entire body and plenty of variety in your juggling to cover the entire stage, just as a painter covers an entire canvas.

6. Use costuming, makeup, lighting, stage props and assistants to give your act a well-prepared, clean, polished look.

7. Develop a stage character and juggle in character.

8. Project vitality and enthusiasm with your body and your face. Smile and have fun. If you do, the audience will enjoy themselves too.

PRESENTATION

As a performer, you want to have as much control as possible over the environment in which you perform. Sometimes you will have to work under severely restricted conditions. The ceiling of the cruise ship may be so low that you have to omit your flashy start. The corner of the room in the comedy club may be lit by a single blinding spotlight. The circus may have three rings full of jugglers and be playing the other guy's music. The only half-decent street corner in town may be next to a major bus stop. But when you can find a good spot or a good stage, you can make it a great experience for your audience.

If it is your show from the opening curtain to the final act, start by making sure that the audience is comfortable and everybody can see and hear you. As they come in, if it is in character to do so, you might greet them and start to make friends before the show starts.

If possible, music should play in the background as your audience assembles. Show tunes, movie or TV themes or circus music will each set a different mood. Try them all and see which one suits you.

If there is a curtain, have it closed and direct every light you have on it. Someone introduces you, the house lights dim, the curtain opens, and all your butterflies flutter away as you meet your audience.

Here you have a decision to make. You can start out already standing on stage, or you can come on in character. Are you a comic juggler? Perhaps you want to walk on slowly. Are you a speedy Las Vegas—style performer? You may run in juggling to fast music. No matter how you come onto the stage and no matter how primitive that stage may be, take the time to stop, look slowly around the room (the street corner, the field, the beach), smile and make eye contact. A bow, a wave, or "Hi, everybody" may be appropriate. Acknowledge the audience.

Once that first contact has been made, you can proceed with the show, but give the audience frequent opportunities to release their tension through laughter, applause or both, and acknowledge their appreciation. Nod your head, say thanks, look directly at them and speak in a natural voice. As someone once said, "Pretend you are playing to that one little buckaroo."

I like to think of a performance as a string of jewels. The performer's task is to polish and perfect each jewel and string them in an order that is esthetically pleasing. Old vaudevillians used to say, "Don't try to follow a banjo act with a banjo act," and in our necklace analogy it makes sense to balance your gems, not lump all of the same type together.

Whether you present an eight-minute circus-style show or an hour or more of material, you need to vary the presentation to keep interest high. You can use different kinds of equipment. You can bring on your partner, and he or she can do a solo number or the two of you can juggle together. You can alternate comedy and musical numbers. Bring a volunteer or two on stage or go out into the audience yourself. A number under black lights with fluorescent equipment, torch swinging or juggling, the use of apparently dangerous equipment, madcap antics, a lyrical number with scarves to ballet music, a balance routine or a chase scene can all be strung together in a logical order. With some forethought you may even be able to weave a story line through the whole show. If not, there should be some consistent threads of style, characterization and/or running gags that help tie all your baubles together.

NOVELTY ROUTINES IN THE PUBLIC DOMAIN

When you are first starting out, you need some material. Fortunately, there are many routines in the public domain. Some are classic moves, like changing the color of juggling rings or eating an apple while juggling, and these are included in their respective chapters. Others are bits of lore from vaudeville days. A partial list includes:

Apple and a Fork

Balance a fork on the back of your hand with the handle running up your forearm. Hold an apple in your hand, fingers pointed down around the apple. Bring your hand up quickly, tossing the apple and look up simultaneously. Quickly withdraw your hand, catch the handle of the fork and spear the apple as it comes down.

Apple and Fork (Audience Participation Version)

Build up the handle of a fork with wood and wrap it with foam tape to make it soft. Toss an apple (or a turnip) into the audience. Tell them that it is an old vaudeville tradition to toss fruit at performers. Have them throw with a high lob, and catch the fruit on the fork, which you hold in your teeth.

Ball on a String

Attach a piece of thread or nylon fishing line that blends in with your costume to one ball. Tie the other end of the string to your belt buckle. Juggle three balls and drop that one. It swings between your legs and back up into the pattern.

Musical Juggling

Tambourines can be juggled like rings and slapped on your hip or knee while juggling. Sleigh bells can be tied together in clusters and juggled like balls, or taped to clubs for a special Christmas effect. Of course you can juggle balls off of a drumhead, or use heavy drumsticks which can be juggled in various patterns while you play the drums. Several vaudeville-era jugglers could keep three or more banjos going and play a tune on them at the same time.

Tennis Theme

There are a number of tennis variations. One is to juggle a ball, the can the balls came in and a racket. For a finale, catch the can, catch the racket, hit the ball with the racket, and catch the ball in the can. Many jugglers use tennis rackets the way others use clubs. Buy the most inexpensive rackets you can find. You might as well go all the way and use a tennis outfit for this routine. You can balance a tennis racket on your chin while juggling three tennis balls. Or you can hit a tennis racket back and forth with two hand sticks, just like a devil stick.

Parasol Work

Get a Chinese or Japanese parasol made of coated paper and experiment with the following: balancing the parasol on its handle or on the rim; juggling the parasol and two other objects; spinning the handle of the opened parasol in one hand while a large ball or a rubber quoit circles around on the top. (Hint—Hold the top of the parasol at eye level, tilt it away slightly and gently roll the ball against the direction of the turn.) You can "gimmick" the ball by attaching it by a string to the top of the parasol, but you may as well put in the time to learn the move.

Ball on the Nose

Coat a Ping-Pong ball with rubber cement. Put rubber cement on the end of your nose. After a suitable buildup and a drum roll, toss the Ping-Pong ball high in the air, tilt your head back and let it hit your nose. It will stick there. For a few seconds you seem to be balancing the Ping-Pong ball on your nose. The audience bursts into spontaneous applause. Then tilt your head forward so they can see that the ball is stuck to your nose.

Juggling Blindfolded

It is possible to juggle blindfolded, and practicing this skill will help you to be a more precise juggler. It will also help you to stay in control when blinded by spotlights. However, there are blindfolds that can be bought in magic stores, through which you can see perfectly. For a comedy routine, you tie on a blindfold and juggle with your right side to the audience. After they are suitably impressed, you turn toward them and they see that there is a hole cut in the blindfold for your left eye.

Giving Yourself Awards

When you do a particularly good trick you can get out your diploma and display it on your prop case. When you miss, go over to the case and turn the diploma face down. Pin a medal just inside the handkerchief pocket of your jacket. When you execute a good trick, pull out the medal so it hangs in front of the pocket. Later, when you miss, tuck it back into the pocket. When you do a really good trick, open your jacket to reveal a large number of medals pinned on the inside.

Balancing a Paper Cone

Roll a sheet of newspaper into a cone shape. Soak the lower five or six inches of the cone in heavily salted water. Then let it dry. In your act, light the upper end and balance the burning cone on your nose, forehead or chin. The rising heat will help you to balance the cone until it burns all the way down to the salted portion. (Warning—Perform this trick only where there is a high ceiling and no wind. Kids perform under adult supervision only, please.)

Hat and Stick Tricks

If you have a soft, floppy round hat made of felt or canvas, you can keep it spinning vertically in front of you by hitting upward on the outside edge of the brim with a stick about two feet long. The "hit" gives the hat enough momentum to keep spinning and enough lift to keep it aloft. Combine this with ideas from the plate-spinning and hat-manipulation chapters to put together a unique act.

Coin Tricks

Start by juggling three 50-cent pieces or silver dollars. Toss one flat so it lands on your forehead. (Charles Carrer could slide a coin from this position onto his eye, where it became a "monocle." Ginquevalli is said to have been able to kick a coin directly from the tip of his toe to be caught on his eye as a monocle.) Line the three coins up on the back of your hand and wrist. Toss the coins into the air and catch them in three quick clawing motions with the

424

same hand. Put a long line of coins on the back of your forearm; toss them all up and catch them in one forward swoop with that hand.

Palm Rolling

Start with two bumper pool balls. Turn them around one another in the palm of one hand, then learn with the other hand. Next, learn to send three balls around in a circle in each hand. In general, your thumb does most of the work pushing the balls around. If you tilt your hands forward, gravity will help. Now learn to "weave" three, five and seven balls by allowing them to roll from hand to hand in an infinity sign pattern. This can also be done with eight balls, which turn like interlocking gears, or with nine balls, which weave from hand to hand.

Magic and Juggling

There was a time when magic and juggling were much closer, but with the increase in recreational juggling, the two art forms have diverged. In magic stores you can find devices and books that describe methods for producing your juggling props "from thin air." Your juggling scarves, for instance, can come out of an apparently empty coin purse. Your juggling balls can appear in a production tube and disappear in a collapsing box. Look in the Yellow Pages under "Magicians' Supplies" to find your nearest magic store.

Croquet Ball off the Head

Show the audience three balls which are apparently the same. Drop one or two on the floor with a thud. Explain that these are "rock-hard croquet balls" and that you will toss one high into the air and bounce it off your head. After a few false starts, toss one high up and let it bounce off your head with a resounding "crack." Actually, the ball that bounces off your head is a hollow rubber ball. They are all wrapped in plastic tape to look similar. The noise is caused by hitting the actual croquet balls together as the rubber ball bounces off your forehead.

Hoop Juggling

Plastic "Hula Hoops" can be used for a number of tricks. While juggling them, toss one across the floor with reverse spin. It will return, and you can resume juggling just as it gets to you. Or roll all three away from you with reverse spin, one at a time, and juggle them on the floor in this manner, using both hands. Experiment with rolling the hoops across your back, or rolling one away with reverse spin, pointing your toe in the path of its return, and allowing it to roll up your leg and back into the juggling pattern.

Hat, Cane and Cigar

One common trick in vaudeville days was to balance a hat and cigar on the foot, as shown. The cigar was actually made of wood. You kick the hat to your head and the cigar to your mouth in a single move. Some jugglers spiced up this trick by adding a whisk broom, which went into the jacket pocket (held open with a wire loop), or a cane, which ended up in the hand.

Raid the Equipment Locker

If a school show takes place in the gym, you can run into the equipment room and toss out whatever you find: a plastic baseball bat, Hula Hoops, traffic cones, bowling pins, basketballs, etc. Run through them quickly, showing how they can all be juggled, then toss them back and close the door. The entire routine can be done in three minutes.

Rubber Chickens

You can do a hilarious routine with three rubber chickens, which can be bought in any magic store. Put a dowel through the chicken from head to tail and secure it with a nail. Now think of all the fowl humor you can: "Don't be chicken." "Only a dumb cluck wants to lay an egg." "The yolk's on the audience." Of course, chickens are flying in a passing pattern while the patter flies back and forth as well. For variety add a plastic fish or a rubber dolphin to this act: "Something fishy here, folks."

Egg and Plate

This trick takes plenty of practice. You will break some eggs. A metal plate works best. During practice you may want to cover the plate with a layer of foam-backed tape. Once you have the knack, remove the tape.

The trick is simple enough. You toss an egg into the air and catch it on the plate. However, to keep it from breaking, you must absorb the shock by cushioning the fall with a scooping catch.

After you have tossed and caught the egg several times, going higher each time, you can deliberately fail to cushion the fall, and let the egg crash on the plate.

Egg Juggling

Call a volunteer up on stage. Have him choose three eggs from a carton. Explain that you will be juggling the three eggs, but at a certain point in time you will toss the third egg to your volunteer. Now run around the audience juggling the eggs. If they are seated on the floor or on the ground, so much the better. Warn them to move away when you come near. Children will shriek.

For your finale, toss the third egg high up for your volunteer. Holding your two eggs high, go back to the stage and break your eggs into a jar. Have your volunteer do the same, to prove that you were not using fake or hard-boiled eggs.

Eating an Apple

Eating an apple while juggling it is relatively easy. The trick is to do it with style. This may mean eating mixed fruit (an apple, a pear and a peach). It may mean eating fast and very sloppily so that the apple dribbles down your shirt front. It may mean eating a balanced meal of an item from the vegetable group (a cucumber), one from the grain group (a whole wheat roll) and one from the protein group (a mozzarella cheese).

To learn to eat while juggling, simply bring the item to your mouth before tossing it. If you can kiss it, you can bite it. Practice with a beanbag. Then try an apple. Learn to bite from both the right and left hands.

Taking a Bow

If you are juggling three rings, toss one high with a pancake flip, catch it around your neck and hold out your arms with one ring in each hand. Your audience will automatically applaud. If you catch a beanbag on your neck in a deep bow they will applaud also. What are they responding to? Body position.

Some performers, like Francis Brunn, continually punctuate their acts with striking poses. Others flow through without a pause and take their bow at the end, depriving the audience of a release for their tension. Poses should become second nature to you. Practice looking in a mirror. When you catch that last beanbag, stretch your arm out to its full length. While juggling four balls, casually cross one foot over the other in a pose of supreme ease. Or hold your three clubs like a bouquet of flowers at the end of your routine.

The art of taking a bow is an important one to master. It is tempting to bow once, turn and run out. But remember your character. If you just finished a funny routine, walk out funny. If you were flashy, you can run out, but wave goodby as you do, and you'll probably get a curtain call. Keep your body turned toward the audience and your smile bright and shining until you are fully off stage.

SHOWMANSHIP

Showmanship is often more important than skill, and confidence in your character is a key element in developing it. It is gained through practice and paying attention to the messages your audiences give you.

Jugglers have an enhanced opportunity to develop showmanship because of their fallibility. You can memorize the lines of a play or rehearse a song over and over until it is perfect and then present it without a fault. Even if you miss a line or forget a word or two, the audience probably won't notice. But when you drop a juggling prop, everyone sees it.

If you have developed showmanship, after the performance people will say, "Did you drop that on purpose?" or, "I really liked it when you pretended to miss and dropped that club." What they mean is, your recovery was so natural, or so funny, that they thought it was part of the show.

To accomplish this miracle, be relaxed. Don't rush your recovery. Make it part of your routine with a witty line or a "cover-up" move. Drop lines include:

- "Three tries for the hard ones!"

- "A sudden gust of gravity!"

- "Someone in the front row moved his foot!"

- "I just washed my hands, and I can't do a thing with them!"

- "The sun got in my eyes!"

- "Nobody noticed!"

- "Almost dropped one!"

- "That one's yours!" (If it goes into the audience.)

- "Don't worry, it's part of the show!"

- "That's my floor show!"

Cover-up moves include:

- Dropping to your knees and picking up the prop while still juggling.

- Having an audience member toss the prop back into the pattern.

- Throwing all three things down and doing something else for a while, then coming back to the fallen props.

- Going to your prop stand and getting something funny, like a book that says How to Juggle in big letters, a gigantic pair of eyeglasses or a gun to shoot the fallen item.

- Starting to do another trick. For instance, if you drop one club, start swinging the other two.

- Kicking the prop back up into your pattern.

Soon you will find you are inventing your own lines and your own cover-ups to fit your character.

A NOTE ON PLAGIARISM

Juggling has been around for so long that it is hard to prove that anyone "invented" anything. This is particularly true when you use relatively standard props and follow someone else's formula. This book is not intended to produce thousands of "copy-cat" jugglers who all do the same generic juggling show. They key ingredients in creating something of your own are imagination and experimentation.

Certain routines are so strongly identified with one person or group that if anyone else were to do them there would be an immediate outcry from other jugglers. Certainly there is nothing wrong with using the same kind of equipment as a fellow juggler, or performing in a particular style, or assuming a vaguely similar character or appearance. However, when these characteristics all add up to an overt copy of the other person's lines or costume or manner of speaking, you have crossed the boundary.

For example, the Flying Karamazov Brothers (FKB) perform a number of unique routines. If any other juggling troop urges their audience to bring difficult items from home "larger than an ounce and smaller than a breadbox" and has their "champ" attempt to juggle them or suffer a pie in the face as a penalty, that troop should at the very least publicly attribute the invention of that particular routine to the FKB.

If a solo performer juggles a bowling ball, an apple and an egg, eats the apple while juggling, and ends up smashing the egg into his face, he is directly copying Michael Davis and should get his permission or refrain from doing the trick. If a juggler were to affect the voice and mannerisms of W. C. Fields, dress in a top hat and imitate Fields' routines, he would be in jeopardy of a suit by the heirs who hold the copyright to the routines of W. C. Fields.

As you develop as a performer, don't hesitate to learn as much technical juggling as you can. Technical skill is in the public domain. But create your own style and your own imaginative routines.

SCHOOL ASSEMBLIES

Because school assemblies are the "bread and butter" of so many jugglers, I include the guidelines developed by the Juggling Institute to help you in planning a school-assembly program.

1. Get to the school at least an hour before the show and let them know you have arrived.

2. Give the principal an introduction to read and help him or her rehearse it.

3. Make the space in which you will be performing look as much like a theater as possible. This may mean using some sort of backdrop, sweeping the stage or the gym floor, and using curtains, lights and a good sound system, if available. If you are in a secondary school with bleachers on both sides of the gym, use one side only.

4. Play upbeat non-rock music as the students come into the room. Movie or TV themes or show tunes work to set the mood well.

5. Greet the students at the door. Shake hands, make eye contact, chat with them.

6. If you have your choice between seating the students on the floor or in chairs, always opt for the floor. It will make the audience more compact, quieter and easier to control.

7. Don't practice or warm up in front of your audience.

8. You may, however, do some "business" as the students file in. Play with the younger kids or with a broom or with your hat. This gets everyone excited and makes friends for you.

9. Again, after you are in front of the group, make solid eye contact with as many students as you can.

10. Have the principal or a student leader give you a solid introduction. We use: "They've toured the world—they've

been on many TV shows—now here they are at _____ School, *alive* and *in person,* Professor Confidence and Amy from the Juggling Institute."

11. Run in enthusiastically and acknowledge the applause.

12. Once the show begins, ask questions of the entire group at appropriate times in the show: "How many of you have tried to learn to juggle?" "How many have succeeded?"

13. Sometimes you may want one person to answer. Simply say, "Let's see a hand. Who knows _____?"

14. If you need a volunteer but the audience is getting noisy, say, "We have a special way of choosing volunteers. We pick the person who sits quietly and makes the funniest face," or, "We pick the person who wiggles his or her nose the best."

15. Touch the volunteer on the hands, back or shoulders in a reassuring manner as he or she joins you.

16. If you bring a member of the audience on stage, make sure he or she leaves as a hero.

17. Play to the teachers as well as the students.

18. Don't patronize or use a "special voice" for children. Play to the upper grades so the lower ones will have to stretch to keep up, but don't play so far over their heads that they get bored.

19. Keep up the pace of the show. There should never be a dull moment.

20. At every opportunity, make teaching points about topics such as:

   a. Diet and nutrition
   b. Making friends
   c. Exercise and learning new skills
   d. Helping each other to learn

e. Sticking to tasks until finished
f. Accepting challenges
g. Being different is OK
h. Anti-smoking or alcohol
i. Math, spelling, English, foreign languages

21. Drama training helps. Here are a few simple rules:

   a. Face the audience and, when turning your body, keep looking toward them.
   b. When your partner is alone on stage or making a presentation, stay out of sight. Avoid upstaging each other.
   c. Warm up backstage with easy tricks. There should be no audible drops coming from backstage.
   d. When lighting is limited, focus it on one spot and play in that spot.
   e. Wear costumes that set you apart from the rest of the world and make a statement such as "This is an athlete" (tennis outfit or muscle shirt), "This is a person with dignity" (three-piece suit for men, evening dress for women), "This is a star" (sequins, strong basic colors such as black, red or white, gold and silver), "This is a clown" (silly shoes or hat, old-fashioned clothes).
   f. Develop a character and stay in that character.
   g. Most of all, teach them to be a good audience.

Audience Training

Because you will be called upon to perform for school groups, you should learn these two methods of audience control which work well, with young people or any group in a theatrical setting.

Making Rain

Say to the audience, "Do as I do." Then show them your two index fingers, and tap the fingers together lightly. Hold up your index and middle fingers and tap them together. Hold up your first three fingers and tap them. Display your four fingers and tap them. Finally, hold up your hands and hit them together in a full burst of applause. Now work your way back down to four, three, two and one finger and finally to none. At that point you should have full attention and absolute silence. Then shout "Cloudburst!" hold up both hands and start clapping furiously. Then one finger again and silence. Now whenever the audience gets a bit noisy, simply say "Cloudburst!" and start clapping. Then go to one finger and silence. It works every time.

Hi! Hi! Hi!

Come on stage in silence. Wave to the audience and mime "Hi!" Someone will say "Hi!" to you. Mime "Hi!" back to them and encourage them to say it back to you by a thumbs up signal and/or by cupping your hands behind your ears. Now alternate with them. You mime "Hi!" and they say "Hi!" back. Now split the audience in half by indicating one side of the room. Signal that side to be quiet. Say "Hi!" to the other side. Hold your hand up palm down and wiggle it from side to side to show that that's OK but not great. Now signal to that half of the room to be quiet and get the other half to shout "Hi!" Show your pleasure at this. Now alternate back and forth from side to side, by raising one arm, then the other. Finally raise both arms together for everyone to shout "Hi!" You can start doing jumping jacks, and everyone will laugh together. Put your palms down and signal for silence. Later in the show, when you want silence, use that signal again. The principle at work here is strange. If you want the audience to be quiet, first make them noisy.

JUGGLING
GAMES

uggling is generally a cooperative endeavor with every effort bent toward keeping a number of objects aloft for as long as possible. With imagination, however, even juggling can become competitive. Most of us have, at one time or another, tried to best a fellow juggler by getting a larger number of objects into the air or by keeping them aloft longer. It is no surprise that competition is not restricted to the IJA championships. New juggling games for individuals and teams are being developed constantly. This chapter reviews a few of the most common.

Juggling games usually involve teams or sides and trying to make the other team or person stop or drop. The winner may be the person or team that is still juggling when a drop occurs, has the least drops after a certain time has passed, crosses the finish line first or scores the most goals.

All jugglers are automatically members of the Juggling Games Inventors of America. If you develop a game, refine it through practice and teach your friends. Write up a description and send it to *Jugglers' World* magazine.

STEALING

Stealing is a game that can be played by novice jugglers. One person juggles three beanbags. The other person faces him. Each juggler tries to keep the other from stealing the three beanbags by throwing doubles, overhand, high, low or wide. Once the thief gets one beanbag, she can toss it back in at the correct moment and try again or go for a second beanbag. If she gets two beanbags, the third one is hers automatically. Now the roles change; the thief becomes the juggler and vice versa.

JOGGLING

Joggling is juggling while running. You can use beanbags, balls or clubs. Three is the usual number, although some intrepid runners use five.

Although a personal goal may be to avoid drops altogether, the penalty for a drop is to stop, pick up the object, and continue juggling from the point where the drop occurred. So drops cost time; and your objective is to run a faster race than the other jogglers, or to better a previous personal best.

Joggling is touted by jugglers and by runners as a way to exercise the upper and lower portions of your body simultaneously. If you joggle with heavyweight beanbags, both the upper and lower parts of the body will be exercised equally—a guaranteed method of conditioning.

Joggling races are held at the annual IJA convention and at local and regional juggling get-togethers. Jugglers have been known to joggle their way through fun runs and marathons, attaining some respectable times even for runners. As with all running, joggling's greatest rewards are found in the rhythmic "plop" of objects in hands and the high of each moment spent controlling the flow of complex activity.

JOLLYBALL

(Invented by Prof. Confidence)

Jollyball uses five balls about 4½ inches in diameter and 6 ounces in weight. It is played by two jugglers who face each other with an imaginary net at about eye level separating them.

One person has three balls, the other has two. They volley for serve. The person with three balls starts juggling. Within seven throws he must toss one ball over the imaginary net. The opponent can either juggle or toss one back. She has a maximum of seven throws to toss a ball back across. The first person to miss, drop or throw out of bounds loses the serve. If you throw with such a low arc that the ball would have hit the net, and your opponent misses the ball, you lose a point or the serve.

The game is played much like volleyball. You have to win the serve before you can score a point. You can throw singles, or you can throw simultaneous doubles across the net. However, if you throw doubles they must be within the arm span of your opponent. If she can demonstrate that she could not reach both balls, you lose a point or the serve.

As in volleyball, you play to a score of 15. In competitive play there is a line judge and a net judge who is the official scorekeeper. All throws across the net must initially have an upward trajectory from the throwing hand. Slam dunks and smashes are not allowed. Of course, you can play with a real net, in which case touching the net is a fault and any point made on that play does not count.

RELAY RACES

Teams of about five members each are best. If the number of players is uneven, the team with one less member sends its first runner twice. A good way to choose teams is to use the calendar.

With 20 players, say, "Everyone born in January, February, or March is in Team 1; April, May, June in Team 2; July, August, September in Team 3; October, November, December in Team 4". Or you can use the calendar to divide 60 people into 12 groups or 10 people into two groups. It's easier than counting off. Once you have your teams, there are a number of relay races you can run. The following were submitted by Mike Vondruska.

Relay Race with Three Juggling Balls per Team

Each team is in a straight line, one behind the other, with the front person holding three juggling balls (or beanbags). The lead person from each team is behind the starting line. When the starter says, "Go," the first person from each team starts juggling and running (or walking fast) to a predetermined turnaround point and then heads back toward his team. He or she crosses the starting line and hands the juggling balls to the second in line, who takes off as fast as he can along the same route. The team that finishes first wins. To make this relay more interesting, if someone drops one or more balls, he has to go back to the starting line and begin all over again. The starting and turnaround points can be lines on a gym floor, or masking tape can be used to create lines. The length of the course can be left up to the organizers.

Obstacle Course Relay Race with Three Juggling Balls per Team

This race is set up and run exactly like the above relay race, but some "twists" have been added. The starter says "Go," and the first person on each team starts juggling and takes off running or walking. At a certain point along the "raceway" (a line on the floor), the competitors have to kneel down with both knees touching the floor, get back up, turn around, and continue the race juggling and running backwards to a chair on the turnaround line.

Once at the chair they sit down, still juggling, stand up again and come back to the starting line, juggling all the way.

For an added degree of difficulty and to improve peripheral vision while juggling, you can run a slalom course using traffic cones for the racers to weave around as they run. For more advanced competitors, rings and clubs can be used in place of balls and beanbags.

Relay Race—Three Ball Passing

Teams stand in line one behind the other about three feet apart and face forward. The first person in line has the three balls or beanbags and faces the second person. When the starter says, "Go," the first person starts juggling the cascade pattern and passes the balls in a right-left-right pattern to his teammate, who catches in the same order and continues juggling, then turns and passes them to the third person. And so it goes to the last person, who passes the three balls back to the second-to-last person and so on until the first person gets the three balls back. The first team to complete this wins. If someone drops the balls, the person who was doing the passing must pick them up, start juggling, and then pass them to the next person in line. This same relay race can be done with over-the-head passes from front to back. After you pass, turn around.

TIMED COMPETITIONS

If you have a stopwatch, records can be kept on how long someone can keep a certain number of items in the air. You can keep individual records, or the teams can add up their combined times to determine the winners of the event. Another timed competition is to see how many times two people from the same team can continuously pass six balls between them in one minute (see section on passing). Score is kept by counting every pass that goes across to the other person. The team that has the largest number of throws across wins.

In all timed competitions, it is good to keep the current record posted. This gives students a standard of comparison for their own efforts.

HOT POTATO

(Invented by John Dobleman)

Players stand in a circle facing inward. Each player holds two white stage balls. One player starts juggling with one stage ball of a different color. The ball is passed from player to player. You can go in either direction or throw across the circle. The recipient must catch into a juggle. The object is to "fake out" other players and not drop the ball yourself. Have the players who miss step back until only two remain. Those two keep playing until only one remains.

"J-U-G-G-L-E-R"

(Created by the Juggling Games Workshop, 1986 IJA Convention)

As long as you are in a circle, why not try a challenging game that is played like "HORSE" in basketball. One person starts with a juggling trick, then everyone in the circle executes that move. The next person to the right then does the move and adds one of his own. Everyone does the same two moves in the same order. Play progresses around the circle with each person in turn adding a trick to the sequence. If you drop, step back, until there are only two jugglers remaining. The last person gets a letter in the word "JUGGLER." The first person to spell "JUGGLER" is the winner. You can play the game the other way around—that is, every time you miss, you can gain a letter and jump back in. Decide before you start. Also, you can make it one of your local rules that every move must be a trick and that you lose a letter if you execute a simple cascade at any time.

TEAM COMBAT

(Developed at the Winnipeg Juggling Festival)

There are two teams, an offense and a defense. The game can be played with balls or clubs, so decide in advance. Teams start at the opposite end of a field or the opposite sides of a gym or room. Team A is on the offense; Team B on defense. All players start juggling at a signal. Team A's players try to cross the field or court and the goal line while still juggling. If a member of Team A stops, drops, or goes out of bounds, he is out. Team A tries to get as many jugglers as possible over the goal line, still juggling. Team B tries to stop them, also while juggling. Then switch, putting Team A on Defense and Team B on offense. Add up your scores after an agreed-upon number of rounds to determine the overall winner.

FEATHER BALANCING GAMES

Peacock-feather balancing is so easy that even first-graders and many disabled youngsters can participate in feather games. These are the games Professor Confidence uses:

Pass the Feather

Form a circle. Start with one feather. Balance it on your hand, put your hand over the hand of your neighbor to the right, and drop the feather onto your neighbor's hand. He turns right and drops the feather onto his neighbor's hand. See how quickly you can send the feather around the circle. As soon as your students gain facility with one feather, add a second one which follows the first one. Continue adding feathers as ability increases.

A Well-Balanced Student

Tell your students that you are going to choose the most well-balanced one among them. Give each student a feather and let him practice balancing it. With students from kindergarten through third grade I suggest balancing the feather on the palm, back of the hand, elbow and shoulder. With fourth to sixth graders or above, try the knee, foot, forehead, nose and chin as well.

For the contest the younger students use the palm. The older ones can use the forehead, nose or chin. The objective is to see who can balance the feather the longest. If they touch it with their fingers or drop it, they hand it in and sit against the wall until there are only a few well-balanced students remaining.

For the final elimination, instruct these few remaining students to go down on one knee and stand up again, to sit down and stand up and finally to lie down and stand up again. Whoever survives these challenges is a definite winner.

Feather Relay Races

Divide the class into teams of 4 or 5 students. Have the teams line up at one end of the room. The first person in each team goes to the other end of the room balancing a feather, touches the wall with his or her hand or foot, turns and comes back. Each team member goes down and back in turn. The first team finished is the winner. The younger students balance on their palms, older students on forehead, nose or chin.

TWO-PERSON COMBAT

(Invented by Mike Vondruska)

This game involves two jugglers standing back to back in a small, defined area. (The circles found on basketball courts for jump balls work well.) Each person has three balls and begins to juggle. The starter then says "Go," and the object of the game is to push the opponent out of the circle by backing into him. The first person who drops a ball, stops juggling, or is pushed out of the circle loses. (For safety reasons, it is a good idea to use your whole body to push the other person out of the ring. Using elbows or feet can result in injury.)

GROUP COMBAT

This is fun as long as two important rules are followed. *First,* players may not do anything that might hurt another player, and *second,* when you are no longer juggling, pick up any dropped equipment and leave the playing area until the next round. If these rules are not followed, this game can be dangerous. The author takes no responsibility for loosened teeth, black eyes or bruised egos. May the best juggler win!

This game is played with a large group of jugglers as in "King of the Mountain." The group should decide in advance whether they are going to play with beanbags or clubs. The object is to be the last player still juggling. This is not a game of endurance; it is a game of aggressiveness and agility.

At a signal, everyone charges onto the floor juggling. Players try to make each other drop, using any strategy. You can throw your own objects high, and knock your opponents' down. You can back into other jugglers, use your legs, your hips or your voice. Shouting a club out of someone's hands is possible.

Tactics include:

- Tossing one of your own clubs away and grabbing an opponent's right out of his pattern without missing a beat.

- Stalking a victim and intimidating him into dropping out of nervousness.

- Telling jokes to make your opponent laugh and drop.

Combat is a fast-moving game. Many rounds can take place in an hour, and everyone has a chance to win or to be one of the last few jugglers. The greatest satisfaction may actually come not from winning the war but from winning a particularly hard-fought battle with a renowned competitor.

Combat will improve your reflexes, your ability to recover an erratic throw and your peripheral vision. It is fun and exhilarating; but remember, play safe.

FIELD JUGGLING

(Invented by Ken Burke)

Field Juggling is to artistic juggling as hockey is to figure skating. It is fast-paced, vigorous and exciting, requiring teamwork, tactics, juggling ability and lots of running. Clubs, leagues, tournaments and fan support may follow as this game becomes a sport.

The game is played on a football field. Each player holds two dead balls. One live ball of a contrasting color is tossed in. The object is to keep the live ball in continuous motion, juggling it toward and across the goal line. The team with the most points after two 15-minute periods is the winner. Blocking and tackling are not allowed. Passing, running and skillful juggling are the tools of offense. Interceptions, noncontact interference and aggressive "stealing" are the hallmarks of a good defense.

At this point the rules for Field Juggling are quite basic and general. We look forward to the continued development of the sport and welcome your input so the rules can be standardized. Let us know what has worked for you. In the following rules, the paragraphs marked with asterisks are essential to the game and inflexible. The other paragraphs may be changed to improve the game.

1. * The game is played on a regulation 100-yard football field, marked off in 10-yard sections. There must be an equal number of players on each side, and not less than seven.

2. * All players on one team hold a white stage ball in each hand. Players on the other team hold yellow stage balls. These balls are not exchanged between players. They are called field balls or "dead" balls because they are not "live" with reference to scoring.

3. * The score ball is an orange stage ball. It must always be juggled and can never be held longer than normal in a juggling pattern. It must always be in motion. If you juggle with two balls in one hand, one of the two must be the score ball. No player may hold two balls in one hand at any time.

4. The "throwoff" is like a kickoff. Each team lines up behind its own 20-yard line. To begin play, one team member on the throwing team picks up the score ball into a juggle, maintains the juggle for at least four throws, and throws the score ball downfield to the other team. Once the score ball is thrown, players are free to cross their 20-yard lines and go anywhere on the field they choose. On the throwoff, if the ball does not land between the end zone and 20-yard line of the receiving team, it must be thrown again. If it falls short a second time, the receiving team performs a

"pickup" in the zone between the 20- and 30-yard lines. Neither team may rush until this pickup is completed and the score ball has been juggled four times.

5. * Players without the score ball may move anywhere on the field. A player with the score ball may move, while juggling, anywhere within a 10-yard length of field. If he crosses over any field lines, his team loses possession of the ball. To move the score ball out of a zone, it must be passed over two field lines or more. It must be thrown out of a juggle and into a juggle.

6. * Once the score ball is caught in a juggling pattern in the end zone and is thrown and caught four times, that team scores one point. The score ball is then thrown off to the opposing team as in the throwoff.

7. * No intentional body contact or contact with an opponent's "dead" balls is permitted.

8. * If any member of the team with possession drops either a dead ball or the score ball, the team loses possession of the score ball, and play stops.

9. When a team loses possession of the score ball, the team gaining possession may reposition the score ball anywhere in the zone in which the ball dropped, or in the zone in which a dead ball was dropped. Opposing players must vacate the zone in which the score ball is being juggled until the fourth throw with the score ball. The player picking up the score ball may not pass it until his fifth throw of the score ball.

10. * If more than one ball drops simultaneously before play is stopped, each dropped ball from one team cancels out a dropped ball from the other team. The team with the fewest dropped balls takes possession of the score ball. If both teams drop an equal number of balls, the team with previous possession retains the score ball. When play is resumed, the team in possession starts with a pickup.

11. * The score ball may be intercepted into a juggle, provided the interceptor does not drop the score ball or either of his dead balls. The interceptor may not make contact with any opposing team members or with their dead balls, with one exception: unintentional contact is not penalized if the player successfully intercepts without dropping. If the interceptor makes contact with an opposing team member or his dead balls or the score ball and does not successfully intercept, play stops, and possession is returned to the passing team wherever the score ball landed. The passing team executes a pickup from this point.

12. * Stealing the score ball from an opponent's pattern is permitted as long as there is no contact with the body or dead balls of the opponent. Unintentional contact which causes a drop gives a pickup to the offended team. Intentional contact results in a penalty.

13. Penalties for rough play, intentional contact with an intended receiver or contact with opponents' dead balls should be decided on in advance. They may include time in a penalty box, turnover of the ball if it is in the offending team's possession or yardage penalties.

14. The game is divided into two 15-minute periods. The original receiving team is determined by a coin toss before the game. The halftime lasts 5 minutes. After the halftime, the teams change ends of the field, and the team which received the initial throwoff throws the ball into play to start the second half. Each team gets three time-outs of no more than 1 minute each. If no team wins, a 5-minute tie-breaking period is played. If there is still no winner, successive tie-breaking periods are played until one team wins.

15. On the throwoff, a member of the receiving team may catch the score ball into a juggle and immediately pass it off, as long as it crosses two field lines and no balls are dropped.

16. If the receiving team elects not to catch the score ball, they must allow it to hit the ground before they contact it in any way. After it hits the ground, the receiving team may stop the ball with any part of the body except the hands. From this point, the score ball can be picked up into a juggle by a member of either team. This is the only time the score ball can be considered "live" while it is on the ground.

17. If any player touches the live score ball with his hand, he must pick it up into a juggle and throw it four times before passing it. From the moment the live, free score ball is touched with a hand, all contact, scoring, dropping, pickup, stealing, and interception rules apply.

18. If, on the throwoff, the score ball is touched and then rolls out of bounds, the team that did not touch it takes possession with a pickup from the point where the ball went out of bounds.

19. If the receiving team elects not to catch the throwoff and the ball rolls out of bounds, the receiving team picks up from the zone where the ball first hit the ground.

20. If the score ball lands out of bounds during regular play, the team that last touched it loses possession, and the opposing team executes a pickup from the point where it went out of bounds.

21. * During regular play, the score ball may be caught and then passed immediately as long as at least one dead ball is self-juggled. Alternately, it may be retained indefinitely by the same player as long as he does not juggle across any field lines.

Inventor's Notes

· Field juggling may be played with clubs, but not with mixed balls and clubs.

· In the event of limited field space, field juggling may be played with adaptations. In this version, the rules regarding field lines are omitted and the objective can be changed. For instance, it may be possible to play on a basketball court and to count baskets as goals.

TEACHING
JUGGLING

NOTES FOR TEACHERS

This book can be used as a curriculum guide. It can be used by physical education, movement, dance or drama instructors in the formal classroom setting at all levels, by recreation specialists, camp directors or individuals who want a comprehensive written guide to help them learn faster and more efficiently.

Juggling provides a model for motor skill development. The simple stepwise patterns are a paradigm for learning complex physical activities. Each student can move at his or her own pace in a self-regulated problem-solving format, with automatic reinforcement at every level of accomplishment. Every new move or piece of equipment poses a challenge to the student, with the teacher (or this text) serving as a guide and source of feedback. Each student builds his or her own repertoire through a process leading from awareness through interest and exploration to experimentation, refinement and consolidation of skills. Eventually, through the introduction of this learning paradigm, each student can become a teacher, assisting others through this same process. The product is physically adept students who know how to learn new motor skills, who appreciate the skills of others and who can transfer this knowledge and appreciation.

Learning juggling skills should be self-paced. Environmental demands are removed. Students work without time pressure, since there is no standard for comparison except each individual's previous level of accomplishment. Juggling can serve as an eye-hand training program for players in every sport. For those with learning disabilities or with emotional/attitudinal problems, it is ideal. It can improve ability to cross the midline, work bilaterally and concentrate on a task. General objectives for juggling students include, but need not be limited to:

- Improvement in eye-hand coordination
- Development of accuracy in throwing and catching
- Improvement in reflexes, timing, rhythm and balance
- Development of concentration and focus
- Improvement in self-confidence, poise and stage presence
- Development of teamwork and teaching skills

There are numerous reasons for integrating juggling into physical education, drama, or recreation programs. It is a safe activity in which boys and girls are equally adept. It involves a maximum number of students in a minimal space. It is a noncontact sport or recreational/performance activity that can be carried out by individuals or teams. It requires almost no capital equipment expenditures and can take place in almost any space, indoors or out. It is exhilarating and fun, an avant-garde activity and a great break in routine for both teachers and students.

MOTIVATION

To help with motivation and continuation you can:

1. Hold a contest at the end of class to see who can juggle or balance a feather the longest.
2. Have students sign a wall chart as soon as they can juggle three objects for 20 throws.

3. Plan to present a juggling show at the school talent night, at a PTA meeting or as halftime entertainment at a basketball game.

4. Give individual physical education credits for personal achievement in juggling.

5. Use the International Jugglers' Association (IJA) certification program and the pins described in this book as a reward system to challenge your students to achieve.

6. Become an IJA member and make information on events, skills and equipment available to your students.

7. Form a juggling club at your school, become an IJA affiliate, attend regional and national conventions and become certified as a Juggling Institute instructor.

8. Have your students plan and host a community-wide juggling festival with competitions, classes, juggling games and a show.

9. Sponsor a lunchtime or after-school juggling club.

10. Schedule a weekend outing to a juggling show or circus.

11. Give extra credit to students who run and juggle simultaneously (joggle) during daily workouts or the annual fun run.

12. Let your better juggling students teach juggling or give shows at nearby elementary schools.

13. Hold a "juggle-a-thon" in place of your annual "walk-a-thon" to raise money for school activities or for charity. (Juggle as long as you can without stopping. Every minute counts toward pledges.)

14. Take your best jugglers to the state physical-education convention to demonstrate and teach the skill. (For a schedule, contact the American Alliance for Health, Physical Education, Recreation and Dance—AAHPERD, 1900 Association Drive, Reston, VA 22091)

15. Hold a contest in your school and send the winner to the annual IJA convention.

16. Challenge a nearby school to a game of field juggling.

17. Sell juggling equipment in the student store as a fund-raiser.

18. Play juggling games on your annual field day.

19. Start a Jollyball ladder with lunchtime contests.

20. Post school-wide juggling endurance records and joggling times on the wall in the gym.

ORGANIZING A JUGGLING CLASS

In general, juggling classes can take place indoors or out. However, if you try to teach scarf juggling outside in even a tiny wind, the equipment blows away, so stay indoors until you reach the beanbag stage. A wooden floor is best for ball juggling, and you should practice rings, clubs, and other "breakables" over grass, carpets or gym mats.

Music is important to set the rhythm of your class and to inspire continuation in your students. Use a recent aerobic dance tape, ragtime, '50s rock and roll, swing, dixieland, disco or march music to provide the beat.

If you teach large groups, have your students form a circle around you and go around the circle giving assistance. A good way to exercise control is to follow these steps:

1. Have your students sit on the floor

2. Ask them to put their equipment behind them and their hands in their laps

3. Explain and demonstrate the next move *only*

4. Put on the music and let them practice

5. Go around and make corrections without using the words "no," "wrong" or "not right"

6. Once they all have the move, turn off the music and ask them to sit down and put their equipment behind them and their hands in their laps

7. Explain and demonstrate the next move, etc.

PASSING OUT AND COLLECTING EQUIPMENT

At the beginning of class have the equipment neatly organized. Tell your students, "When class is over, I expect the equipment to be put away as neatly as it is now." For scarves this means stopping your class about three minutes before dismissal and saying: "Now stack your scarves in a flat pile in front of you, like three pancakes. As soon as yours are flattened out, join your nearest neighbor and make a stack of six, then get with your next neighbor for a stack of twelve. Keep stacking them neatly until we have one big stack up in front. Then sit down here."

For beanbags or balls, put receptacles around the room. Then stop your students and say, "As politely as you can, without throwing anything, put your equipment in the nearest bucket, come over here and sit down." By having your students sit before leaving the gym you can make sure that they aren't walking off with any equipment.

LESSON PLANS

Whether you have only one hour with each group of students or meet with them daily for a school year or longer, it is good to have a plan. Consider each chapter in this book as the basis for a lesson or series of lessons.

Primary Grades   Primary youngsters are the most eager and least adept. You can play with them using scarves and peacock feathers and help them to develop prejuggling skills.

The lessons that follow are intended for students kindergarten through third grade and last from 20 to 40 minutes each. With kindergarten and first-grade students it may be best to present only lessons 1 and 2 and the first few steps in lesson 10. For second- and third-graders try the whole series, adjusting to their skill level by moving at a slower or faster pace.

This entire sequence can be presented over a full school year by holding a juggling class once every week or so. Daily juggling classes may be appropriate in some cases, but it is probably best to offer them as a treat on a specific day of the week, or as a rainy day recess or physical education activity.

Lesson 1—Scarf Play

Equipment   One scarf per student.

Objectives   To improve throwing and catching skills; to gain confidence in using both hands; to begin to learn multiple task sequences.

Teaching steps   First demonstrate step 1, then pass out one scarf per student.

1. Throw and catch, using one hand. (Have students hold onto their belt or waist with the other hand.)

2. Throw and catch, using the other hand. (Make sure they keep the palm out to throw and "claw like a lion" to catch.)

3. Throw with one hand and catch with the other. Then throw with the other hand and repeat. (Make sure they throw every time and *never* hand across.)

4. Throw, clap, catch with the other hand.

5. Throw, clap, clap, catch with the other hand.

6. Throw, clap under right leg, and catch with the other hand.

7. Throw, clap under right leg, clap under left leg and catch with the other hand.

8. Throw, clap, clap under right leg, clap under left leg, clap and catch with the other hand.

9. Throw, turn all the way around and catch with the other hand.

By now you get the idea. Make a progression out of the skill. Turn on the music and use a microphone to tell your students what to do. Don't stop the music, except to demonstrate a new move. Keep them going. As soon as most of them have accomplished a task, introduce the next one. This is aerobic activity. Some of the tasks you can elaborate on include—

1. Throw under each leg in turn.

2. Throw behind the back from the left hand, catch with the right and vice versa.

3. Blow the scarf up in the air, sit down, stand up and catch.

4. Throw, bend over and touch the floor, stand up and catch.

5. Throw, pat your head, pat your stomach, touch your knees and catch.

Got it? Great! Use your imagination. Ask the kids to invent moves. Go around the circle and let each student do a move, which everyone then copies.

Lesson 2—Two Scarves

Equipment   Two scarves per student.

Objectives   To be able to keep two objects moving; to see and understand the cascade pattern in preparation for three scarves.

Teaching Steps   First demonstrate step 1, then pass out two scarves per student.

1. Start with two scarves in your favorite hand. Throw one scarf. When it gets to the top, throw the other. Each scarf has its own pathway. (Demonstrate by throwing one scarf straight up. When it gets up, throw the other parallel to it. Then catch and throw the first, catch and throw the second, and keep them going. The other hand is kept behind the back.)

2. Throw around in a circle. Toss the first scarf out toward the side. When it peaks, throw the second in the same arc. Keep them going in a circle.

3. Throw in a circle from the outside to the center.

4. Do each of these three moves with the other hand.

5. Hold a scarf in each hand. Throw the first across like a big letter "X." When it gets to the top, throw the second up and across the other way. Catch the first, pause, catch the second. (See page 11 for illustration.)

6. Throw the first across, throw the second across, clap, catch the first, catch the second.

Got it? These last two are identical to the steps you took in "Scarf Juggling." Now your students are on the path to juggling. You can assure their success with a few more intermediate steps that involve throwing without catching.

Lesson 3—Three Scarves

Equipment Three scarves per student.

Objectives To be able to throw and catch three scarves; to see what has to be done to keep going with three scarves.

Teaching steps First demonstrate step 1, then pass out three scarves per student.

1. Start with two scarves in the dominant hand. Number 1 is held loosely on the fingertips, number 2 in the other hand, and number 3 deep in the dominant hand. Toss number 1. When it gets up, toss number 2. When that gets up, toss

number 3, but don't catch anything. Just let the scarves fall to the ground. Repeat over and over again.

2. Now toss number 1, toss number 2, catch number 1, toss number 3 and let number 2 and number 3 fall.

3. Now toss number 1, toss number 2, catch number 1, toss number 3, catch number 2 and let number 3 fall.

4. Now toss number 1, toss number 2, catch number 1, toss number 3, catch number 2 and catch number 3.

Got it? You have taken three lessons to teach the basic prejuggling skills necessary to get your primary youngsters started. Now just follow the steps in the "Scarf Juggling" chapter and go slowly.

Lesson 4—Continuous Juggling

Equipment   Three scarves per student.

Objectives   To be able to juggle three scarves continuously; to be able to adjust erratic throws; to juggle big and slow and small and fast.

Teaching steps   Follow steps in the "Scarf Juggling" chapter up to "Reverse Cascade." (See pages 7 through 12.)

Lesson 5—Juggling Three with a Partner

Equipment   Three scarves between two people.

Objectives   To be able to juggle three scarves continuously between two people; to be able to juggle with your partner with three scarves using either hand.

461

Teaching steps

1. Follow steps in the "Scarf Juggling" chapter section, "Juggling 3 Scarves with a Partner." (See page 22.)

2. Let the partners experiment. First they use the subordinate hand to juggle. Then they toss under the leg each time.

3. Have partners stand side by side. The person on the left uses the left hand and one scarf. The person on the right uses the right hand and two scarves. The unused hand is behind the back. The person with two scarves starts and the partners alternate, just as the right and left hands alternate.

Lesson 6—Tricks

Equipment   Three scarves apiece.

Objectives   To be able to do the Reverse Cascade and Columns.

Teaching steps   Follow the "Scarf Juggling" chapter sections, "Reverse Cascade" and "Columns." (See pages 13 through 15.)

In each class you can spend the first half of the period having the students go through all the lessons up to this one to music. Run it like an aerobic exericise class. Use your microphone and don't stop the music. Your students are gaining physical skills and learning to follow instructions.

Lesson 7—More Tricks

Equipment   Three scarves per student.

Objectives   To be able to juggle under the leg and behind the back; to be able to blow or kick a scarf into the juggling pattern; to be able to do a full pirouette while juggling.

Teaching steps   Follow appropriate steps in the "Scarf Juggling" chapter. (See pages 16 though 18.)

By now your students are divided into two groups—those who are "getting it" and those who aren't. Don't hold back the more capable ones. Instead, teach to them and let them practice while you re-explain and demonstrate to the others. Break each move down into the smallest possible steps, then build it up again step by step. See if you can take our five-step move and break it into 20 distinct steps. Keep everyone moving and trying and smiling!

Lesson 8—And More Tricks

Equipment   Three scarves per student.

Objectives   To be able to juggle three scarves in a shower pattern; to split three scarves; to do three in one hand. (See pages 17, 19 and 20.)

Teaching steps   Follow appropriate steps in "Scarf Juggling" chapter.

Each of these moves is done best on one side or the other. Make sure your students try a shower in both directions, learn to use their subordinate hand also and can do a split with two on the left and one on the right, and vice versa.

Lesson 9—Juggling Six with a Partner

Equipment   Four scarves per student.

Objective   To be able to keep six scarves going between two people for 20 throws. (See page 24.)

Teaching steps

1. Review Lesson 5, steps 1 and 2.

2. Follow steps in the "Scarf Juggling" chapter for juggling six scarves with a partner.

3. Make this into a cooperative challenge activity, and see which team of two can go on the longest without stopping or dropping.

Lesson 10—Peacock Feathers

Equipment One feather per student.

Objectives To understand the basic principle of balancing an object.

Teaching steps Demonstrate step 1 before passing out feathers.

1. Balance a feather on the palm of the hand (see the "Balance" chapter, pages 408 and 409).

2. Balance the feather on the back of the hand, each finger, the foot, the elbow, the knee, each shoulder, the forehead, the nose, the chin.

3. Balance on the forehead while going down on one knee and standing back up again.

4. Balance on the forehead while going down to a sitting position and back up again.

5. Hold a contest to see who can balance the feather on his or her hand the longest.

6. Hold a contest to see who can balance the feather on his or her forehead the longest.

Lesson 11—Juggling Games

Equipment   Three scarves and one feather per student.

Objectives   To be able to play games and hold relay races with scarves and feathers.

Teaching steps

1. Go through scarf and feather games in the "Juggling Games" chapter, pages 443–444.

2. Invent your own games.

3. Write down your games and send them to us for inclusion in the next edition of this book.

PRACTICE AND PROGRESS

Whether you're teaching in a school, holding a weekly workshop in a community education setting, or working your way through this book by yourself, the progress card is a handy way to keep track of achievement.

Urge your students to practice every day for *at least* 20 minutes. Remind them that they can practice during commercials or television programs. In your classes it will help to use up-tempo music to assist concentration and give students a sense of rhythm. They might want to put on their stereo earphones at home or put their favorite record on the stereo.

At first, practice should be aimed at repeating particular tricks over and over, to learn them by rote. Eventually, you will want to keep track of special series of tricks or sequences. Few people will forget the day they learned to keep three things going or completed their first successful "3-3-10" passing pattern with a partner, or that day when they threw 20 successful behind-the-back tosses in a row. We urge you and your students to keep a progress chart so you know what tricks are in your repertoire.

CLASS CONTROL

If you have not taught large groups before, here are a few guidelines to observe to help you keep control in the classroom in a friendly, pleasant manner.

1. Never pass out equipment until after you have given instructions on its use. Show the students how to throw one scarf, then pass out the first scarf. Show them how to do two, then pass out a second scarf, etc.

2. Never talk until the room is quiet. If necessary, just stand quietly and wait. If you must speak, say, "Thank you for being quiet." They will get the hint and shush each other.

3. Always collect your equipment at least 3 or 4 minutes before class is over and have the students sit down for a few words. This will help you get all your equipment back.

4. Don't use a whistle in the gym, use a microphone. It helps to play music as everyone practices. To get attention, either say, "Here comes the next point (pause) _____" or simply stop the music.

5. Because juggling equipment is small and highly valued by students, make sure they leave their coats, purses and book bags outside the gym or classroom.

6. Pass out three beanbags to each student. When class is over, they line up and quickly turn in three bean bags. This reduces your loss.

7. In correcting mistakes, praise the good work. Saying "Your catches are good now, and it's time for one more throw" is

better than "You're stuck at three throws and three catches."

8. If you want everyone to sit on the floor, say, "Wherever you are (pause) as quickly as you can (pause) *sit down.*" They will drop like stones.

9. If they are fidgeting with their beanbags, say, "Put your beanbags on the ground, put your hands in the air, put your hands on your heads, put your hands on your shoulders, put your hands in your laps and don't touch the beanbags."

10. To get one small and talkative knot quiet, either say, "Thank you for your attention," or say to the group as a whole, "I don't think I have everyone's attention." The noisy ones will be told by their peers to be quiet.

11. If beanbags start being used as weapons, stop the class and tell them that they are to be used only for juggling or you will terminate the class altogether.

A SPECIAL NOTE FOR ADMINISTRATORS

Juggling is not restricted to the physical-education setting. It provides an opportunity to look at a topic in breadth as well as depth, involving a number of disciplines and curriculum areas. Let's imagine you are about to introduce juggling in your physical education classes. How can you maximize the benefit of this novel experience?

You might arrange for a juggling team to present an assembly to pique student interest and give direction to the project. Before jugglers arrive, you can study the history of juggling.

In science class you can discuss gravity, properties of falling objects, trajectories, the physics of balance and the physiology of throwing and catching. In drama class you can find, write or adapt a play with a circus or juggling theme.

On the day of the assembly, students can practice writing thank-you letters to the jugglers; or they can draw their impressions of the show for an art project. You can use the performance as a touchstone for exploring the history of the antic arts. Older students can write short stories about jugglers, and you can read aloud books like *The Juggler of Notre Dame* or *Alex the Amazing Juggler,* or the poem by George Meredith, *The Last Will and Testament of Juggling Jerry.*

Once juggling has been introduced in physical education classes, there are many follow-up activities you may wish to consider; these are included in the following section.

UPPER ELEMENTARY AND SECONDARY LESSON PLANS

All of the lesson plans that follow assume a 40- to 50-minute class period. The classes should be held indoors in a high-ceilinged gym or multipurpose room, or outdoors on grass or a paved area if bouncing tricks are being taught.

Every class should be preceded by a 5- to 10-minute warm-up period and by stretching to limber the spine. If students normally dress for physical-education classes, they should dress for juggling class. By fouth grade it is possible to teach juggling with beanbags and balls. Your fifth- and sixth-graders can move on to rings and clubs.

Start all your upper elementary students with scarves. You can probably condense Lessons 1 through 4 into one class of about 30 to 40 minutes' duration. Don't forget to use music to establish the sense of rhythm. Lessons 5 through 9 can be consolidated into your second session. Spend the third session reviewing skills, learning balance and playing juggling games. Once all your students feel comfortable with scarf juggling, move on to Lesson 12, the Cascade.

An effective plan with fourth grade and above is to spend five 40-minute sessions on juggling over five consecutive days. This will take your students "over the hump" from bumbling insecurity to self-assurance. At the end of five lessons they should all be able to juggle with scarves. Sixty to 90 percent should be able to complete 10 throws with three beanbags, and a few will have control over the Cascade, the Reverse Cascade and Columns.

Now you can use juggling as a reward. Present your one-week juggling unit at the beginning of the year and plan to hold another eight to 10 juggling days throughout the school year. Juggling is great in those transition days between major sports, or as a station in a volleyball, badminton or games unit.

If you can, build in a reward system using achievement levels or have students write their names on posters as they attain specific goals.

A NOTE ON METHODOLOGY

Each class has an objective. It helps if you tell your students what that objective is. This gives them a sense of purpose. Every lesson is a progression leading from simple to complex. Let your students see the step-by-step process and the additive nature of acquiring skills. Give your students feedback on their achievement by telling them what they are doing right.

When preparing your lessons, remember that you can never over-simplify. For example, some texts and some teachers tell students that after they can juggle three balls, the way to learn three clubs is to substitute one club for one of the balls. This requires the student to use two different methods of throwing and catching, changing from one to the other in midjuggle. Please avoid making something more difficult than it needs to be.

Some instructors start teaching the Cascade by telling their students to "throw in a big arc over your head, back and forth." However, this move has nothing to do with cascade juggling, where you toss with an underhand, infinity-sign throw. Why not toss one ball along the path that three will eventually follow?

Many students have been ruined for juggling by well-meaning teachers who made the mistake of starting them off with two balls in one hand. This creates an almost irreversible bad habit of working in depth, with the balls circling inward in a shoveling motion and the forearm pumping like a piston. Please, if you teach, do no harm! Remember that juggling stays flat in front of you. You work in height and width, not in depth. If you use depth, it is in a controlled manner. If your students do not get this point, they will either run all around the room chasing their beanbags, or they will look as if they were doing a reverse dog paddle with their arms, pumping in and out. First get comfortable with three objects in a nice flat cascade pattern. *Then* work with two in one hand. It can take months to undo the damage if your students learn wrong the first time.

SECONDARY SCHOOL

Because I want everyone to get some degree of success from the juggling program, I often start secondary students off in the following manner:

1. I make certain that I have a co-instructor who can teach scarf juggling.

2. I demonstrate the Cascade with scarves and beanbags and give students a choice of learning with one or the other,

depending on their own level of confidence and coordination.

3. I break the class into two groups, letting those who want to learn "the hard way" get up and go into another space. This leaves those who are less secure with their throwing and catching skills behind to learn with scarves.

4. I start the less confident group off just as I would the upper elementary grades. The more confident group starts with Lesson 12, the Cascade with beanbags.

Whichever way they start, three days seems sufficient to whet the appetite of older students. Once they have been through Lessons 12, 13 and 14, I suggest making juggling an optional activity, which students may continue at their discretion. Some students are "hooked" and want to continue. They will juggle whatever you give them, basketballs, tennis rackets or even shot put balls, so it is best to give them permission to juggle rather than punishing them.

LESSON PLANS

Lesson 12—The Cascade

Equipment   Three different-colored beanbags per student.

Objective   Continuous juggling with three beanbags.

Step 1   (Use the "Basic Cascade" chapter, pages 27 through 32, as your text.) Start students with one beanbag each. Have them toss that beanbag in an infinity-sign pattern until it is smooth.

Teaching steps (May be used as your script.)

1. Start with the beanbag toward the outside, carry with a scoop toward the midline and release.

2. Peaks are about 1 ½–2 feet above shoulders on each side.

3. Don't follow the ball, just notice the peaks.

4. Catch the beanbag as if it were an egg, then scoop under with a U-shaped motion and toss again.

5. Keep your palms up to throw and to catch.

Step 2 Once all the students can toss one beanbag from hand to hand, move on to three. Demonstrate before passing out the equipment. Have students hold one beanbag on the heel of each hand with the little finger and ring finger. Instruct them to throw the third beanbag from hand to hand, using a nest formed by the thumb, index finger and middle finger.

Teaching steps (May be used as your script.)

1. Use your fingertip nest.

2. Catch, scoop, toss, catch, scoop, toss.

3. This is not juggling, it is a warmup exercise to allow you to begin and end your juggling routine. When you start juggling, you throw from the fingertip nest. When you finish, you catch your last beanbag on that nest.

Step 3 Now it is time to begin exchanging two beanbags.

Teaching steps (May be used as your script.)

1. Start with the hand that has two beanbags.

2. When the first beanbag gets to the peak, toss the second up underneath it. They make an "X" across your chest.

3. Catch the first, catch the second. Repeat.

4. As you do this, it helps to say, "Throw-throw-catch-catch."

Corrections   There are several common problems at this point:

1. **Handing across.** Many students have tried to learn to juggle with two objects. They have learned to throw with one hand and hand across with the other. To break this habit, explain to them that this is a very common habit. Have them put two beanbags in their subordinate hand to start. Now the subordinate hand takes the lead and the dominant hand throws second. Since the dominant hand already throws well, it will not hand across. Make sure that they say out loud, "Throw-throw-catch-catch."

2. **Throwing both beanbags at the same time.** Many students rush their second throw. Remind them that they should wait until the first beanbag reaches the top and then throw the second one across and underneath it.

3. **Throwing nonsymmetrically.** Often the first throw is fine, but the second throw is either low or out in front, or both. Remind your students that juggling takes place in two dimensions, height and width, but not in depth. It is like drawing on a canvas in a picture frame in front of you. You should try to hit the corners of the canvas, but don't break out of that flat plane. Go equally high on each side.

4. **Reaching up to catch.** Many students, particularly those with less throwing and catching experience, will reach up and try to catch the beanbags at eye level. Remind them that the beanbags will fall all the way to their hands, and that they should catch them somewhere between the waist and the chest.

Remedial practice point   With very young jugglers or those who are having problems with this step, omit catches. Have them throw both beanbags, but not catch. This eliminates the fear of dropping and gives them the timing of the second throw. Once they can go "throw-throw-plop-plop," have them try to catch the beanbags before they hit the ground.

A note on equipment   In correcting individual errors, it helps to have three colors to work with. You can tell the student, "When the yellow beanbag peaks, throw the red," or "Number 4 is blue, it is number one coming around again," or "Catch your beanbags in the order that you throw them. If you toss a red one first, you catch a red one first."

A note on drops   Remind your students that "A drop is a sign of progress" and let them know that if you touched the beanbag you knew where to catch it, so "A touch is as good as a catch." Self-confidence and persistence are more important than coordination in learning to juggle.

Step 4   Remind your students that juggling is like walking. You alternate your feet when you walk, and you alternate your hands when you juggle. Now that they can exchange two beanbags, they have learned all the moves they need to learn. Now they only have to repeat these moves over and over again.

Teaching steps   (May be used as your script.)

1. Start with the hand that has two beanbags. Throw the first one across from its fingertip nest.

2. When the first beanbag reaches the top, throw the second one up and across, underneath the first.

3. When the second reaches the top, throw number 3. In order to throw number 3, you have to let it roll forward to your fingertips.

4. Number 1 and number 3 end up in your other hand. Just transfer one back, and start again. Say, "One-two-three-stop" as you juggle.

Corrections   Common problems and solutions include:

1. **Running forward.** Often the first two throws are fine, and the third throw goes out in front. Remind your students that there are two peaks, one over each shoulder. Number 1 and number 3 go to the same point.

2. **High, medium, low.** Some students will throw the first beanbag to the correct height, the second about half as high, and the third lower still. The result may be missing the third, or lunging forward to catch it. Again, remind them of the symmetrical nature of juggling and the peaks. Have them count out loud and say, "Two" in a very loud voice, throwing number 2 much higher than necessary. The same for number 3.

3. **Failure to throw number 3.** A few students get stuck at the point where they throw numbers 1 and 2, and refuse to throw number 3. The best way to clear number 3 is to have them throw slowly, without catching. Throw number 1 and let it fall, throw number 2 and let it fall, throw number 3 and let it fall. Now build up by catching just number 1, then catch numbers 1 and 2, but throw number 3. Then throw *and* catch number 3.

4. **Handing number 3 across.** Occasionally a student will throw number 1, throw number 2, and hand number 3 across. If this is the case, have him start with his subordinate hand. Usually this will break the habit. If he still has this problem, stand in front of the student and have him start juggling. At the point where the student hands across, block the receiving hand. This will show him the point in time when he is handing across. Usually students are not conscious of the move. Now they should see what you mean when you say they are "handing across."

5. **Throwing too fast.** A few students try to go too fast. All three beanbags are in the air at one time. They may catch

one of these, or none at all. Have them slow down and pause between throws. Remind them that the cue for each throw is the previous peak. Remind them that they should throw higher and go slower.

6. **Shoveling in toward yourself.** Many people who have taught themselves to juggle with two objects in one hand have developed a habit of "shoveling" their hands in and out. The beanbags are moving in three dimensions—width, height and depth. To eliminate this motion, you must get across the concept that juggling takes place flat in front of you. They may be able to throw and catch successfully but will be stymied in their progress until they can work in a plane in front of themselves. Often you will have to go through all the juggling steps again to get them to juggle flat. Remind them of the two peaks. "Don't just shovel the beanbags up the center, but scoop from side to side." Finally, have them hold their elbows at their sides and juggle. This is one of the hardest habits to break because this student can usually keep three objects going even though the pattern lacks style and precision.

7. **In any case.** If you see a student repeating an error over and over, have him stop and go through correct motions. If he repeats the errors, they will become habits and be hard to break. Remind the student that whenever he drops, he should stop and analyze what happened. Which hand threw? Where was the beanbag headed? Why did he miss it? Where should it have gone? How can he throw it correctly the next time?

Step 5 When students can make three successful throws and three catches, they can progress at their own speed. Have them go on to four throws, then on to five, eight and twelve. They can either count to themselves or go "One-two-one-two" as they juggle. The verbal cues help reinforce throwing.

Teaching steps   (May be used as your script.)

1. Now you can see that juggling is like walking. Just alternate your hands the way you alternate your feet when you walk. When number 3 gets to the top, throw number 4.

2. Number 4 is the second throw from your subordinate hand. It is beanbag number 1 coming around again.

3. To throw number 4, toss number 3 nice and high, then throw the beanbag that is in your other hand. It should go to exactly the same place as number 2.

4. Count as you throw, "One-two-three-four-stop."

5. Once you can do four throws and four catches, you should be able to keep going. Now every time one gets to the top, throw another one. Try for five. Do it five times in a row. Then go for six. Then do eight throws, and finally do 12. Once you can do 12 throws, go for 100.

At this point it is good to put on appropriate music with a good beat. Use something the kids will like. It helps them to develop a rhythm. From this point on, you can use music in all juggling sessions. When you stop the music, it is a signal to stop juggling.

Corrections   Many of the problems students have with three objects recur or are magnified with four. Review the corrections for three. Additional problems include:

1. **Getting "stuck" at three.** Either students feel safe and don't want to take the risks necessary to continue, or they don't see the pattern yet, so they fail to understand that the fourth throw is just like the second. Often this confusion will be expressed by the statement, "Now that I've ended up with two in my other hand, what do I do next?"

   Start by explaining that to juggle continuously, you must never have two in your hand again. So if you see that

477

you're going to have two, throw the one that is already there before you catch the one coming down. Emphasize that there is no "number 4," only a series of "number 1s" and "number 2s." Number 4 is just your second number 2. Don't count "One-two-three-four." Count "One-two-one-two." Whenever you say "two," throw whatever is in your number-two hand.

Finally, if a student is really stuck, you can have him say "one-two-one-two" and shout that last number two. When he shouts it, have him toss whatever is in that hand as far as he can. Then he can tone down his throw until it is correct.

2. **Running forward while juggling.** If they do not have good side-to-side throws, your students may run forward while juggling. There are several corrective measures to take. First, remind them that juggling goes from side to side in a flat plane in front of them and that the peaks are just over their shoulders on each side. Second, have them stand with their toes on a line or kneel erect, and not move forward. Third, have them throw only the exact number of throws that they can do correctly, and freeze as soon as they throw out in front. At this point they may notice that their arms are creeping up, or they are throwing not only in front but too low. Correct this point and go on again, one throw at a time.

3. **Stopping involuntarily.** Some students juggle along and then stop involuntarily. "I just can't get past six throws," they explain. The problem is usually that the sixth throw is so low that number 7 can't fit under it, or they are reaching up higher and higher with every catch, and by number 6 their hands are at eye level. Remind them of two points. First, they should throw every beanbag to the same point. Second, they should keep their hands down to throw and to catch.

4. **Collisions.** As they go on to higher and higher numbers of throws, collisions occur. These are usually a result of breaking out of the juggling pattern. The first few throws are generally underhand scoops with peaks over opposite shoulders, but eventually the pattern breaks down and the juggler is throwing almost straight up or with an overhand arc. At this point, stress consistency and the idea that there are only two throws, a right-hand one and a left-hand one.

5. **Rushing it.** Some jugglers don't get the "beat." They throw too fast and get confused about their catches. Have them focus on the peaks. They should delay each subsequent throw until they have seen the previous peak. Remind them to slow down. Slow down the music if necessary.

6. **Late throws.** Occasionally a student will wait until the previous beanbag is just about to land before throwing the next. Often the throws will either be up the middle, slightly overhand or with almost no scoop toward the center at all. This pattern is usually the result of having practiced on one's own with two beanbags in one hand. To correct this habit, have the student juggle higher than usual with a deep scoop and allow him to make only two throws. Take him on to the third throw, but tell him to imagine he is talking into a microphone, and to throw under the mike every time. Remind your students to throw at the very second the beanbag peaks. Have them focus on those peaks.

Step 6   Continuous juggling is the goal of this step.

Teaching steps   (May be used as your script.)

1. To keep going, you need to be consistent with your throws. Remember that there are two distinct peaks. Throw to those peaks.

2. Once you can throw high and slowly, practice throwing lower and faster. Practice juggling wide and then narrow. Explore the space in front of you.

3. Once you have control, practice looking at a distant wall through the juggling pattern. By changing your focus, you will eventually be able to juggle without looking directly at the beanbags. At this point you see the peaks of the throws only, using your peripheral vision.

Lesson 13—The Reverse Cascade and Columns

Equipment   Three beanbags per student.

Objectives   To learn the other two basic patterns in juggling. (See pages 35, 44 and 45.)

Warm-up   Practice the Cascade you learned in the previous lesson for a few minutes.

Step 1   Have each student put down two beanbags and use only one. They toss that beanbag in an infinity sign pattern with an overhand throw.

Teaching steps   (May be used as your script.)

1. Imagine a small basketball hoop in front of your eyes, about as big around as a circle made by your thumbs and index fingers. Throw your beanbag up and over, so it comes down through this basket.

2. You let go of the beanbag at shoulder level, toward the outside. You catch it near the midline with the other hand. Remember to keep your palms up.

3. Now do the same with the other hand. Now use both hands over and over again. Toss the beanbag from hand to hand in a figure-eight or infinity-sign pattern with this overhand throw.

Step 2 Once you can toss one beanbag from hand to hand, you can switch to two.

Teaching steps (May be used as your script.)

1. Throw the first beanbag. When it peaks and begins to fall, throw the second one over it. They cross and fall into your opposite hands.

2. Remember to throw the beanbags so that they fall down through that eye-level basket.

Step 3 To keep juggling, all you have to do is continue throwing. Every time one beanbag peaks, throw another.

Corrections Common problems and solutions include:

1. **Underhand throw.** The most common problem is that the juggler will revert to an underhand throw. Remind him to catch on the inside, scoop toward the outside, and toss so that the beanbags cross over each other and fall down the center.

2. **Uncatchable throws.** Another is for the pattern to widen out and the throws to become uncatchable. The solution is to remind your students that the peaks are on the same side as the throws, and the beanbags fall down through the center. "Novices make big throws; masters make small throws." Have your students practice juggling smaller and faster.

Step 4 Columns are like elevator shafts, with each beanbag going straight up and coming straight down to the point of origin. Start with the beanbag on the fingertips of the hand that has two. Toss it straight up the middle. When it reaches the top, toss the other two beanbags up the sides. Then catch the solo beanbag and catch the two that went up the sides.

Step 5 Start again. Toss the solo beanbag. When it peaks, toss the two, then catch and toss the one, catch and toss the two, over and over again. Remember to throw to the same height with both hands.

Step 6 Now that you can continuously juggle in columns, start with two beanbags in your subordinate hand. Now your subordinate hand throws first, then both hands, then the subordinate hand again.

Teaching step Often students shovel in toward themselves with these throws, losing the separation between the columns. Remind them that this pattern, too, takes place flat in front of them.

Step 7 Now you can easily see a pattern for two beanbags in one hand. It is the pattern of the hand that started with two. That hand is juggling two beanbags by itself; the other hand is just throwing one beanbag over and over again.

Challenges See if you can keep the columns going, but alternate catching the solo beanbag that goes up the middle with the left and right hands, or with both hands at the same time. Keep the two beanbags going straight up the sides but toss the solo beanbag up outside the path of the other beanbags so that it goes up the right, up the middle or up the left, while the other two beanbags go straight up and down together. Toss the solo beanbag up the center but toss the other two beanbags so that they cross in the center, coming down in opposite hands. Toss the one straight up again, then the other two so that they cross. (*Hint:* to avoid collisions, toss a bit higher with your dominant hand so one beanbag goes over the other beanbag.)

Lesson 14—Transitions and Introduction to Four Beanbags

Equipment Four beanbags per student.

Objectives To learn the transitions from Cascade to Reverse Cascade to Columns; to learn the pattern for four beanbags.

Warm-up Practice the Cascade, Reverse Cascade and Columns for 5 minutes.

Step 1 Students practice the transition from Cascade to Reverse Cascade and back.

Teaching steps

1. Collisions are frequent when you begin to practice these transitions. It is important to learn to avoid collisions by practicing precise throws, rather than compensating by "shoveling" beanbags in toward you.

2. When learning to make transitions, also learn to use the Reverse Cascade just as you did the Cascade, to cover the entire canvas in front of you. Throw low, high, narrow and wide; practice transitions from every variety of pattern. Soon you should be able to juggle below your eyes with all your patterns.

Step 2 Practice the transition from Cascade or Reverse Cascade to Columns and back. Remember to practice with the solo bean-bag coming equally often from your right and left hands.

Special challenges By now, some of your students should have pretty good control over their throws. Issue a series of challenges to them, such as:

1. Walk the width of the room while juggling.

2. Walk up a flight of stairs while juggling.

3. Sit down on the floor and stand up again while juggling.

4. Climb up on a chair and climb or jump down again while juggling.

Four beanbags This trick is introduced early because as soon as you can handle three, the pressure is on to learn four.

Step 1 Demonstrate or diagram the three patterns for two in one hand, Outside Fountain, Inside Fountain and Columns. (See pages 90 through 93.) Students practice each move in each hand separately.

Teaching steps Keep the pattern flat in front of you. Get good scoops to avoid collisions. Use your elbow as well as your wrist to move the hand back and forth. Practice your weak hand more than your strong one.

Step 2 Toss two beanbags simultaneously in an Outside Fountain. When they peak, toss the next two, and so on. Practice Outside Fountain, Inside Fountain and Columns in that order.

Lesson 15—Clawing

Equipment Three beanbags per student.

Objective To be able to catch and throw with palms down consistently. (See pages 36 and 37.)

Warm-up Practice juggling to music for one song.

Step 1 Start with one beanbag. Throw it from hand to hand with palm down, tracing infinity signs in the air. High throws are best, about 1½ to 2 feet over your shoulder on each side. Good advice is, "Throw as if you are waving goodbye and claw to catch, straight down, like a lion."

Step 2 Toss one beanbag across with palm down. When it peaks, throw the second one from the other hand. Now claw the first and claw the second. Resist the temptation to turn your palms up.

Step 3 Move on to three beanbags. Use the moves you practiced above and keep going in a cascade pattern. Practice gradually bringing the pattern down until it is below your eyes. At this point it will be very fast, and you will touch each ball for only a second. Resist the temptation to turn your palms up.

Now that you can juggle with palms down, there are a number of tricks to practice. The most common of these is often called "The Tax Collector."

The Tax Collector, step 1 (1960s)   While juggling the Cascade, tell your audience that you are going to demonstrate the tax collector in the 1960s. Let's imagine that you have three beanbags, red, yellow and blue. Every time the red beanbag comes to your right hand claw it, turn your palm up, and toss it back across. Let the class learn this move.

The Tax Collector, step 2 (1970s)   You are now clawing every right-hand catch while your left hand simply catches with the palm up. This is the tax collector in the 1970s. Everyone practices this move.

The Tax Collector, step 3 (1980s)   Now practice clawing every other ball with both hands, right and left. The hard part is returning your hands to the palm-up position. This is the tax collector in the 1980s.

The Tax Collector, step 4 (1990s)   This is simply a fast low claw with both hands. You can stop by clawing all three beanbags into your right hand and saying, "By the year 2000, they'll take it all."

The Escaping Ball   Another clawing move is to juggle in a small, tight cascade pattern. Then suddenly toss one ball out of the pattern to the side, reach out quickly, claw it, and continue juggling in a small, tight pattern.

If time permits, urge your students to practice clawing with the Reverse Cascade and Columns as well. The clawing move is helpful in many situations to accent a move or to retrieve an errant object. It should become as comfortable as catching palm-up.

Lesson 16—The Shower

Equipment   Three beanbags per student.

Objective   To be able to complete 10 consecutive throws in the shower pattern from right to left for right-handed students and from left to right for left-handed students. (See page 39.)

Step 1   "Throw-throw-catch-catch." Start with two balls in your dominant hand. Toss them rapidly, one at a time, in a high arc to your subordinate hand. The second ball is well on its way when the first one lands. Say, "Throw-throw-catch-catch" as you practice.

Step 2   "Throw-throw-pass—throw-catch-catch-catch." Start as above but put one ball in your subordinate hand as well. Throw the two from your dominant hand in rapid succession and, just before the first ball lands, hand the third one across and toss it as well. The problem at this point is speed. The first two throws must be very fast to give you time to pass number 3 across before number 1 lands. Also, accuracy is important. Every throw should be identical to the previous one.

Students will often revert to the Cascade at this point because it is familiar. Learning to be a good juggler is a matter of learning moves until they are habits and then breaking those habits by learning variations or new moves. Remind them that what seemed difficult before is now easy and urge them to repeat the moves over and over until they are easy too.

Step 3   Start the same way, but now it is time to keep going. Every time a ball lands in your subordinate hand, immediately pass it across to the dominant hand and throw it in that same high arc. The keys are speed and precision.

Step 4 Once students can maintain a Shower, have them vary the height and speed. Higher and slower is easier. Lower and faster builds up your reflexes. Hold a contest at the end of the period to see who can maintain a Shower the longest.

Step 5 Reverse the Shower. Because the Shower is a move that emphasizes your dominant hand, it is a very humbling and edifying experience to go through the steps above for your other hand. It will be several times as difficult, but worth the effort.

No matter which way you are going with the Shower, try to keep the palms of both hands up. Don't claw the ball that is handed across. Also, keep as much separation between your hands as possible, so that you can eventually throw the ball across, rather than handing it.

Step 5 For homework, challenge your class to learn the Seesaw, a series of shower throws, first from one side and then from the other. (See pages 46 and 47.)

In all of the subsequent classes it is assumed that students will warm up before class and will run through their repertoire of tricks for at least a few minutes at the start of the lesson.

Lesson 17—Pauses, Fancy Catches and Recoveries

Equipment Three beanbags per student.

Objectives To learn three pauses and two recoveries. (See pages 54 through 61.)

Step 1 Start with one beanbag and practice catching it in a variety of locations: on the forearm, the back of the neck, the foot or the back of the hand. Wherever you catch it, the principle is the same: you should absorb the shock of the beanbag.

Step 2 After you can catch the beanbag in this special way, move on to step 2. Now throw one beanbag in a cascade pattern, then throw the one you are planning to catch in a special way. Once you can do two beanbags, move on to three, and try your special catch while juggling.

By giving general instructions you will give your students a chance to experiment and to practice the process of breaking each move down into the smallest possible steps, building back up again to a completed move. You may find that they will think of some pretty fancy pauses, such as the forehead, top of the head, temple, small of the back, crook of the knee, etc.

Step 3 Whether you drop or pause, the trick is to resume juggling in a smooth and natural way. Describe, demonstrate or have one of your student "hotshots" demonstrate the kickup, where you pinch the fallen beanbag between your heels and kick it up over your shoulder. There is no better time for experimentation. There is no "school solution" for a drop. One student may even be able to turn a cartwheel, picking the beanbag up on the way around and resuming the juggle.

For extra credit Learn body bounces. Start with one beanbag. Toss it to your knee, bounce it off and catch it. Now try two beanbags. Toss the one from your right hand in the Cascade, toss the one from your left hand to your knee and bounce it up to your right hand. Now try three. Every throw from your left hand bounces off your right knee. Where else can you bounce? Off your foot, forearm, elbow, back of the hand, shoulder, forehead or even a wall. With practice, bounces will become part of the natural flow of your juggling.

Lesson 18—Yo-Yo and Oy-Oy

Equipment   Three beanbags per student.

Objective   To learn the Yo-Yo and its variations on one side.

Step 1   Review two in one hand. Practice with the subordinate hand doing Columns.

Step 2   Hold your subordinate hand up where you can see it, but don't move it yet. Just get used to seeing it there, while juggling two in the other hand.

Step 3   Begin moving the subordinate hand around randomly, but don't let it bother you. Just keep juggling two in your dominant hand.

Step 4   Now start moving your subordinate hand up and down at the same time one of the balls you are juggling goes up and down. Parallel the movement of this one ball with your empty hand. Hold that ball between two fingers so it can be seen from the front and go up and down with one of the thrown balls.

Step 5   Now do this same move, but hold a ball in your subordinate hand between two fingers so it can be seen from the front and go up and down with one of the thrown balls.

Step 6   Now do the same move, but with the ball you are holding above (Yo-Yo) or below (Oy-Oy) one of the balls in the air.

Step 7   Turn these directions around and do them with your other hand. This may be your most challenging lesson so far in juggling. However, learning the Yo-Yo on both sides is a strong step toward ambidexterity.

Lesson 19—Under the Leg, and Behind the Back

Equipment   Three beanbags per student.

Objective   To learn to continue the juggling pattern even if one beanbag is out of your field of vision for a period of time, blocked by part of your body. (See pages 65 through 69.)

Step 1   Stand on your left leg with the right one raised and two beanbags in your right hand. Now begin juggling by tossing your first beanbag under your leg. Lower your leg. Stop. Repeat.

Step 2   Now that you can start under the leg, start with the right leg raised and with two beanbags in the left hand. Throw your right-hand second throw under your right leg. Lower the leg. Stop. Repeat.

Step 3   Now start with two in the right hand again. Toss your first right-hand ball, and, as you throw with the left hand, raise your right leg, throw under it and put the leg back down in time to catch the second ball. Your right leg goes up and down in the time it takes to throw with the left hand and catch with the right.

Step 4   Now you should be able to raise your right leg up and toss under it at will. It may help to throw the previous toss a bit higher to give you more time. Now work through the steps from the other side using the left leg.

Step 5   You should eventually be able to toss successive throws under one leg or toss under both legs in turn, jogging in place and throwing under your knees.

Step 6   Now you have the principles for learning to throw behind the back. Start your juggle by reaching way back and throwing the first ball up and over your opposite shoulder. Then put that special throw in the number 2 position, starting with two beanbags in your subordinate hand. Reach high up behind your back with your right hand to throw.

When you throw behind your back, the path of that ball is longer, and you must pause before your next throw. If you throw with your right hand up over your left shoulder, turn your head to the left, and as soon as you catch a glimpse of the ball coming over, toss your left-hand throw. Eventually you should be able to toss successive right-hand throws up over your left shoulder, in which case you can keep looking to the left. Now work on the other side.

Step 7 To learn to alternate throws behind the back, start with two beanbags. Throw with the right hand over the left shoulder and immediately throw with the left hand over the right shoulder. Look to the left and catch; look to the right and catch. Add a third ball. Now practice: number 1 ball behind the back; number 2 ball behind the back; number 3 ball, resume the Cascade juggle. Eventually you should be able to be juggling along and toss a right and then a left behind the back, resuming the Cascade as they come in.

Lesson 20—Juggler's Tennis and Two Fancy Starts

Equipment Three beanbags (at least one of which is of a different color) per student.

Objectives To learn to do the Cascade and Reverse Cascade simultaneously.

Step 1 Practice the Cascade with your left hand and the Reverse Cascade with your right simultaneously. This is called the "Half-Shower." Now practice the Cascade with your right hand and the Reverse Cascade with your left. (See pages 26 through 41.)

Step 2 Start juggling the Cascade, but every time the different-colored beanbag comes to your right hand, toss it over in a high throw to your left. Now do the same move from the left hand with that ball.

Step 3 Every time the marked ball comes to either hand, toss it over the top to the other side. The other two balls simply follow a cascade pattern.

Step 4 Practice juggling small, with little hops by the odd ball back and forth over the "net." Then take longer shots "into the back court." Eventually you should be able to toss that "tennis ball" 15 or 20 feet back and forth, while the other two balls continue to cascade underneath.

Now for those fancy starts. Your steps are outlined on pages 81 and 82. No additional description should be needed.

This is the last formal lesson on solo beanbag juggling. By now you and your students should have facility with three and four beanbags. Let your students know that each new trick should take from 10 minutes to an hour or more to learn. You can work together to continue this process, going page by page through the book. The only "secret" is to break each move down into its smallest parts and then build it up again step by step. Now let's move from beanbags to rings and clubs.

Lesson 21—Rings

Equipment Three rings per student. (Use mats, carpet, padded floor or grass to cut down on noise.)

Objective To be able to juggle continuously with three rings.

Teaching steps   (See pages 156 through 162.)

1. Demonstrate how you throw a ring from hand to hand. Pass out one ring per student. Advise students to throw higher than normal.

2. Demonstrate two rings. Pass out a second ring per student and let them practice for a few minutes. Peaks should be equally high on both sides.

3. Show students how to hold three rings and how to start. Pass out the third ring and give them plenty of time to practice.

4. Demonstrate spinning a ring on a ring, pancake flips and color changing.

5. Rings are ideal for learning to pass five objects as outlined on page 164.

Lesson 22—Clubs

Equipment   Three clubs per student. (Use mats, carpets, padded floor or grass to cut down on noise and breakage.)

Objective   To be able to juggle three clubs for 20 throws and stop cleanly.

Teaching steps   (See pages 170 through 199.)

1. Demonstrate throwing one club from hand to hand. Pass out one club per student. Students should be reminded to "choke up" on the club and to scoop the butt under to throw.

2. Once they are comfortable with one club, demonstrate two. Now both hands scoop and the clubs go equally high on both sides.

493

3. Show students how to hold three clubs, how to start juggling and how to catch the last club. Give them an objective of four throws and four solid catches. Emphasize side-to-side arm movement so clubs do not travel forward or collide in front.

4. Challenge students to make as many throws as possible. Eventually they should be able to juggle three clubs indefinitely.

Lesson 23—Stations

Equipment   Whatever sports balls you may have, plus all of your juggling equipment. May also include cigar boxes, devil sticks, diabolos, spinning plates or hats.

Objectives   Each student moves as far along as possible with one, two or more items of equipment of his or her own choice.

Teaching steps   First set out equipment neatly around the room at separate work stations. Print posters with instructions at each station.

1. Students sit in the center of the room as the instructor goes around the room demonstrating the activity at each station.

2. Students are divided according to interest. Once they are at a station they should stay for a designated amount of time. At that time (approximately 10 minutes) the instructor signals that they may move to any other station.

3. Stations may include the following:

   · Basketballs or volleyballs to work on juggling 3 and 5 between two people

   · Stage balls or softballs to play Jollyball

- Hula Hoops, quoits, Frisbees and other common gym items to get a feeling for juggling with a variety of shapes and sizes
- Any other juggling items

MAKING MONEY

WITH

JUGGLING

Everyone who juggles eventually considers performing professionally. Few who start out of the gate stay on for the ride. Most bite the dust and end up getting "real" jobs. The same skills you used in learning to juggle—planning and persistence—can serve you well as you plan for and pursue success as a performer or teacher of this coordinative craft. In this chapter we will look at some of the markets you can enter and the marketing methods you can use to turn right action into right livelihood.

THE PROCESS

I assume you already know how to juggle well enough to present a show of 20 to 30 minutes' duration. You may also have business cards, publicity materials, an answering machine and a costume. Why isn't the telephone ringing? Let's look at two areas you can control: the product (you) and the packaging (how others see you), and let's relate them to the potential buyers. If you do this properly in an organized fashion with focus on the bottom line, you should have plenty of work.

THE PRODUCT

The product is you. Are you a hobbyist or a dabbler who knows a dozen moves, or are you ready to commit yourself fully to juggling? Here's what it takes:

1. You must be willing to invest two or three years of hard work before you begin to see success. Don't quit that day job yet.

2. You will have to make some decisions about image and invest money and energy in props, costumes, music, photos and printing, video, promotion, grooming and the development of a unique and marketable style. You have to spend money to make money.

3. You must learn to talk in a businesslike way about yourself and make numerous phone calls and business calls to sell yourself.

4. You must constantly review potential markets, staying open-minded about places to play and people for whom you might perform.

5. You must decide how much you are willing to travel and realize that you limit your potential market by putting restrictions on your movement. Entertainers are travelers.

6. You must stop wasting time, especially watching television, making small talk and hanging out with unproductive and negative people.

START BY SELF-ANALYSIS

The kind of person you are determines your performing image. Are you lean and lanky or short and stocky? Are you a lyrical technician with an easy, flowing style, or are you a buffoon with an infectious grin? Your body type and offstage personality will determine your style. Now focus your practice on accentuating that style. Rehearse your moves over and over so they come comfortably and your lines sound natural.

Are you open to coaching and to criticism? Few of us have an easy time with the critical comments of others. Learn to listen, not just to doting relatives but to those who have no reason to salve your ego with flattering words. Find a friend whose judgment you trust and ask him or her to critique your shows. A separate but equally effective means of gaining perspective is to videotape your performances. Then look at the tape, asking questions like: Could I have gotten a stronger laugh if I'd paused and turned slowly at that point? Did I lose a line during the burst of applause? Were my moves sufficiently dramatic, yet believable? Did I use my eyes and smile effectively, or did I forget the audience and get caught up in the furious welter of activity? What does my body say at this moment about my level of involvement and excitement?

Once you have developed a unique style that works in a variety of settings, don't worry that others may steal your moves, your material or your bookings. Quality stands out. There are no shortcuts, and those who would undercut your price or copy your style simply hurt their own credibility.

Conversely, don't gossip about or undercut fellow performers. If you have nothing good to say, say nothing.

Once you have tested your moves and material on friends, family and the video camera, set and maintain your own high standards of quality. Never be satisfied with a lackluster performance. At the same time that you are severely self-critical, do not fall into the pattern of constantly changing your material and searching for some magic formula. Instead, polish your performance.

DEVELOPING A "PERSONA"

You will need to be a character or develop a character to be successful. If you are an outgoing person with a strong voice, self-confidence and "presence," you can turn up the volume on your basic personality and turn that stage presence into charisma.

If you are a shy, bashful introvert, the job is harder. You have to create a personality that is far larger than life. It might help to take acting classes and assertiveness training. The very best school for developing stage presence is street performing. On the street, if you don't have control of your crowd, it will disappear. You hold it with your commanding voice, your direct gaze, your winning smile, your unique juggling style and your ability to create and sustain a feeling of dynamic tension.

Practice taking risks. Call up a volunteer, work with him and send him back a hero. Practice snappy patter and witty rejoinders. Jugglers must be as fast with their minds and tongues as they are with their hands.

The personality traits that help a person to become a great technical juggler may not be the same traits that make for a great performer. A superior technician is more likely to be able to concentrate on detail, work under controlled circumstances, criticize his own work, demonstrate patience and persistence and keep a detailed mental or written record of his progress. On the other hand, a great performer is more likely to be an enthusiast with a fertile imagination who is good at taking control of situations, thinking on his feet, generating enthusiasm in others and verbalizing easily. In charting your course as a juggler it is good to undertake a personality assessment and look in a dispassionate manner at your strengths and weaknesses. You may find you need help with any of the following factors:

- Technical juggling skills

- Putting together a show that has continuity and strength

- Presentation skills

- Booking and scheduling

- Office management

- Time management

When looking for people or agencies to assist you, it is important to understand your own deficits and to seek out people with skills to fill in the gaps, rather than people who share your own strengths and weaknesses.

PROMOTION

Now that you have a product of which you can be proud, it is time to shift from show to business. Once you can perform and can successfully market that performance you are in "show business."

It is time for a note on "freebies." When you're first getting started, you may have to do a few performances for free. Use these as opportunities to test material; if you do a good job ask for a letter of recommendation as payment.

Once you've developed a complete, self-contained show, don't give it away, except to your favorite charity. You can always say "No" to the request for a free performance and refer the caller to your local IJA affiliate or recreational juggling club where some struggling neophyte would love the opportunity to try out his or her show. If you're capable of presenting a professional performance, you should be able to work constantly and should be compensated well.

PUBLICITY KITS

Be businesslike. You are designing a sales tool. Don't simply send your potential customer a pile of xeroxed letters of recommendation in any envelope that happens to be on your shelf. Here is what experience has shown me works best.

· Get a supply of envelopes that exactly fit your kit and have them imprinted with your logo and address, or have labels printed with your logo and address.

· Get a supply of glossy folders with flap pockets and either have your logo imprinted on them or use labels.

· Get a single sheet typeset for each market, giving your experience in that market and explaining exactly what you will do. Use bold type and various font sizes to stress key points. Keep it short.

· Have a professional studio photographer shoot several black-and-white action photos of you in several costumes. Include one in each mailing.

· Send a short cover letter of no more than two paragraphs explaining what exactly you want the recipient to do.

· Include a price sheet that is typeset and gives your latest quotations. If it is typeset it shows you are serious about these prices.

· If you do not yet have a personal logo that represents you, seriously consider having one drawn by a graphic artist. Don't let it be too "cute" or you will become a birthday clown. Put that logo on every letter and/or piece of publicity you send out. Use the finest quality paper, envelopes and printing you can buy.

· Whenever you send out a packet, call the prospective employer and let him or her know who you are and that the packet is on the way. Call him or her back a few days later to see if he or she has received the packet and quite forthrightly ask for the booking.

This process, including preparation of the mailing piece, postage, and follow-up phone calls, should cost you no more than $5.00 per contact if you do the work yourself. Figure twice that amount if you hire someone (on commission, I hope) to do your booking for you.

VIDEOTAPE

It is essential in most cases to have a professional-quality videotape made on 1-inch or ¾-inch equipment. This will cost you from $500 to $1,500 for a tightly edited 7-minute program. Use upbeat non-rock music, colorful costumes and your best material. The tape should be aimed at a conservative audience. Studio recording is acceptable, but recording in front of a live audience is preferable.

Get a dozen or more VHS copies of your program and three or four ¾-inch copies. For European and Australian customers you will need conversion to the PAL system. When you mail out a video, send return postage or a self-addressed, stamped return envelope. Keep a record, by date, of videos you send out. If the video is not returned, do not hesitate to ask for it back.

For best rates on video reproduction check the Yellow Pages of the telephone book. Shop around; video prices vary enormously.

After you have booked the show, ask the customer how she/he heard about you. This will help you to decide which of your advertising strategies works best. Whatever telephone number you use in your publicity should be one that is well-monitored by a secretary, answering service or answering machine, preferably around the clock.

Set up a card file (or a computer file) of customers. Every time you book a program, put the customer information in your file. Then call back one or two years later and remind them of the great times you had together.

You should be making 20 out calls every day to companies and businesses. If you are booking school programs, you will be making 40 to 50 calls per day during certain periods when the schools are setting up their annual assembly schedules.

Look in the Yellow Pages for your own town and nearby cities under "Entertainment Bureaus," "Agents" and "Party Planning Services" to find the numbers for booking agents in your area. Call, make an appointment, visit and show them a sample or a video of your work. Agents work hard for their money. If they get bookings for you, do not begrudge them the 10 to 15 percent cut they take. You generally get paid on the day of the performance by the client and then send the agent his commission. Be prompt in your payment to your agent and put a thank-you note in with the check.

If you are in the happy quandary of being overwhelmed by work at certain seasons, don't turn down engagements; instead, hire a protégé. You will keep the client and develop a reciprocal relationship with your fellow performer.

GOOD GROOMING IS GOOD BUSINESS

If you look like a hippy, you will get a hippy's wage and treatment. This is a difficult dilemma for those of us who survived the sixties and see in juggling an alternative lifestyle. The impression you make when the curtain parts is how you will be perceived. Baggy pants and bright colors label you a clown. Tailored suits or a fitted or stylized tailcoat tell your audience you are a "gentleman juggler." Wearing a T-shirt and jeans will cut down on your credibility and your cash flow by 90 percent. Once you find an outfit or style that suits you, stick with it.

Whether long or short, hair must be clean and well kept. If you wear a beard, keep it neatly trimmed. Because we work out vigorously as part of our daily grind, we may not realize that even jugglers need a deodorant to stay fresh. Wash your hands, trim your nails and carry and use a breath spray. Also, don't forget to keep your teeth brushed and flossed. A sparkling smile is essential.

If you go to an engagement and are offered a drink, ask for a soft drink or fruit juice. And while we are on the subject of health, juggling may be great upper-body exercise but there is no excuse for letting your waist sag and your hips spread. Stay in shape.

Jugglers tend to be healthy people, nonsmokers and more likely to eschew red meat, sugar, artificial colors and flavors, additives and other harmful and addictive substances. Because we are so in touch with our bodies and our reflexes, we can feel the effects of overindulgence immediately. Remember, not only are you representing yourself, you are often the only representative your audience will ever meet of our often maligned ancient profession.

YOUR OFFICE

If your office is set up efficiently from the start, you will be able to cut your workload considerably. Each task will be new only once, the first time you do it. After that, it becomes routine. Essential tools include:

- A room dedicated to your business. When you are in this space, you are a business person.

- Access to a computer system that is capable of sending out form letters, such as a word processor with software enabling you to do a "merge" of your mailing list with form letters; or a typing/secretarial service that will handle this for you. If you use a computer yourself, have the final letters printed on a "letter quality" printer, rather than on a "dot matrix" printer.

- A filing cabinet stocked with plenty of manila file folders.

- Lots of shelf space and a tabletop to work on. Your desk need not be fancy. Check garage and moving sales for used desks and tables or place a sheet of plywood or an old door on two sawhorses to serve as a large work surface.

- Two telephones with two separate lines. You can use your home phone number for calling out; use your business lines for inbound calls.

- An answering machine, answering service, or, better still, a secretary to take calls while you are out performing.

- Promotional materials, letterhead paper with your logo and address on it, a stapler, paper clips and other office supplies.

- A simple business bookkeeping system that you can get from your bank.

You may be required to get a business license or home-occupation permit as well. Check into this by calling City Hall.

POTENTIAL BUYERS

Your market is vast. I will list those areas that come immediately to mind as the most open or lucrative. These are markets I have personally worked, but the guidelines that follow should work in any market you might develop. Whatever markets you enter, remember the four "P's": Politeness, Patience, Perseverence and Promptness. They lead to our favorite "P": Payment.

SCHOOL SHOWS

Unless you live in the wilderness, there are hundreds, perhaps thousands, of schools within range of your home. Every one of them has school assemblies. Some are in the habit of paying for these, usually with PTA or student-activity funds. The range is from $100 to $300 (1986 prices) for a 40-minute performance. If you are a good teacher as well, you may be able to conduct workshops after your show for $50 each. A full day of work in a school can net you $400 to $500, and you should be able to do about 100 days of work per year.

The following are suggestions for reaching the people who book school programs:

- Attend conventions of cultural-arts coordinators, PTA officers, principals and vice-principals, activity coordinators, student council members and physical educators. Generally speaking, you will need to rent a booth or table, decorate it appropriately and stay in that booth for one, two or three days. If you can, get on the program as the banquet entertainment, present a juggling teaching session or give a sample show. Call your state education association to get names and addresses of these associations.

- Attend showcases and booking conferences. In some states or large school districts the cultural arts office will hold an annual event where potential purchasers can review available programs. Go to these and present your very best material.

- Send a very specific mailing to every school, addressed to "The person who schedules assembly programs or special activities." Follow up with phone calls. Expect to make four to six calls before you locate and can speak with the key person. Expect to call back at least twice to schedule and confirm. Only after you have been in the school marketplace for several years will they call you. This is generally a buyer's market.

- The "booking window" for school programs generally opens three times a year. It opens for three weeks from late August to mid-September, when the fall assembly schedule is being finalized. It opens again for three weeks after the winter holidays, starting in January, when spring programs are booked. The window is opened again in May for some schools who make their assembly-scheduling decisions in advance of the upcoming fall semester. Then again, some schools book year-round, and it is important to keep scrupulous notes indicating when those particular schools traditionally book programs for the year.

If you want help with entering the school market, the Juggling Institute (c/o Jugglebug, 7506J Olympic View Drive, Edmonds, WA 98020) may be able to help you get started. The institute conducts training programs from time to time and then helps graduates in presenting assemblies and teaching programs in schools.

PRIVATE PARTIES

Private parties run the gamut from birthday bashes with 24 screaming eight-year-olds to fashionable holiday feasts at country clubs. Fees range from $100 (or less) to $500 for local work, more if you have to travel.

· Start close to home. Put up flyers in your neighborhood and work outward in ever-widening circles, pinning a poster up on every bulletin board you see.

· Put ads in the Yellow Pages under "Entertainers," "Jugglers" and "Magicians." Design and pay for a display ad that stands out and tells the person who is looking for an entertainer exactly what to expect.

· Test your local shoppers' papers and see if an ad yields results. You will have to let it run for a month or more to measure the response.

· Use word of mouth. Treat everyone you meet as a potential customer. Give out cards at the finale of every party to let your audience know you are available. Your host won't mind, and today's audience member is tomorrow's client.

- Get on the phone and call every local business of decent size. Ask to speak to their entertainment coordinator. If they ask "Who?" tell them "the person who plans your annual company picnic."

- When you get a party booking, find out about the event. If it is a birthday, plan something special and personal for the celebrant. Use your imagination to come up with a tie-in to the event. When John invites you to entertain at his 20th wedding anniversary with Marsha, why not put "Happy," "20th" and "Anniversary" on one side of your cigar boxes, and "John," "Loves" and "Marsha" on the other side. This can spell out "Happy 20th Marsha," "John Loves Marsha" and "Marsha Loves John".

PARKS, RECREATION DEPARTMENTS, EXPERIMENTAL COLLEGES AND HEALTH CLUBS

Take advantage of fitness consciousness by teaching juggling for groups from the YMCA to executive health clubs.

- Go to the facility in athletic attire during a slack time of day. Teach the decision-maker how to juggle and let her see how this activity could be turned into a series of weekly classes. Take your publicity kit with you. Charge a fee of $3 to $5 per person per session. Collect the fee before the first session. Don't give the first class away for free.

- Caution your students that there is a terrible attrition rate in juggling classes because students begin comparing themselves with each other. Urge them to return each week whether they have practiced or not.

- Distribute an outline of the material you will cover in the course. Give specific instruction and spend some quality time with each student every session in a one-on-one relationship.

- At the first session, let your students know where they can go to buy their juggling equipment and urge them to invest in "the real thing."

- Spice up your classes with guest jugglers, miniperformances, juggling games and relay races, pleasant background music and at least one "video night" when you show the most inspiring footage you can find.

- Hold ceremonies to commemorate significant accomplishments by your students, such as the first in the class to complete 20 throws, juggle four beanbags or pass "3-3-10" with a partner. Give a weekkly award for the "most improved."

- Ask students at the end of each session what they want to learn the next week. At the beginning of each session ask them to share the juggling events of the past week.

- It helps maintain interest to focus the class on a goal. The recreation center may want them to perform at its annual Christmas party, march in a parade or entertain at new members' night.

STREET PERFORMING

The street is the ideal venue for a juggler. The worldwide renaissance of street performing is due in large part to the efforts of jugglers.

- Your job is to attract a crowd, entertain them for 15 to 20 minutes and collect your fee. Wits and guts are as important as tricks and props. Snappy patter is essential.

- You can attract a crowd gradually by beginning to lay out your props. Once a few people have stopped, make friends. Tell them you are about to start the show and ask them to be your front row. When you need a volunteer, use one of them.

- Start with a big trick. Fire draws people like moths. Make noise, blow a whistle, get the audience to join in. Now you have your crowd. If feasible, get the first five or six rows to sit down.

- Use big props, a big voice and moves that can be seen from the back of the crowd. Get audience involvement by asking questions of the crowd and by using volunteers. Don't let the show lag, or you will lose the audience.

- At least twice in the show, refer to your spectacular finale. People will stay around to see it if it sounds exciting. Keep tension in the air. Break it with spectacle or humor.

- In Europe every street performer has an assistant who moves through the crowd during the show collecting coins. In North America it is customary to pass the hat at the end of the act. As you pass the hat keep up your patter with lots of "thank you's" and remember to look everyone straight in the eye.

- There are hazards in the street. Drunks shout abuse at you and the police may ask you to move on; but it is a great training ground and the pay can be quite good. Don't be intimidated; it's your stage. Work on the snappy comeback. Stay alert.

- Selecting an appropriate spot may mean the diifference between coins and dollars. Some enlightened cities, like Baltimore, Boston and San Francisco, have designed performance spaces where crowds can gather with small stages and some benches for seating. However, all you need is a large space where your audience can gather and a crowd of people with time on their hands.

- Musicians and close-up magicians can work with far smaller groups than jugglers. They can set up in doorways or on the curbsides of alleyways. Because juggling takes space, jugglers generally need a plaza, the steps of a public building or a park. A good street juggler in a well-designed location can entertain 300 to 500 people at a time with no sound amplification. This is significantly different from guitar players or even mimes and should be explained to the authorities who control the space. In many locales, if you are good, you draw a crowd; if you draw a crowd, the people block the sidewalk and spill out into the street; and if you block the sidewalk you may be told to move on.

- In the United States, keep in mind that we have in our Constitution and Bill of Rights guarantees of freedom of speech and assembly. Remind your local police and municipal authorities of this if you get into trouble. For legal precedents contact Stephen Baird, Street Performers Newsletter, P.O. Box 570, Cambridge, MA 02138.

SHOPPING MALLS

Every town now has one or more malls, and every large enclosed mall has a promotions manager. Her job may include getting out the monthly shoppers' newspaper, planning holiday events, decorating and designing as well as bringing acts to the stage.

- Send your publicity kit to the promotions manager and follow up with a phone call. She usually plans things at least 4 to 6 months in advance and is often under the gun to: (1) Keep something going every weekend and (2) spend as little as possible by letting local dance schools, gymnastic classes and beauty pageants use her stage for free.

- Be flexible. Sure you can do a stage show in the center of the mall, but you could also do a roving act with smaller audiences, less elaborate tricks and additional skills like balloon sculpture, magic or face painting. Realize, though, that as soon as you tie one balloon or paint one face, the line will start forming. Hyperventilation from inflating hundreds of balloons may be a real hazard on a busy Saturday.

- By booking well in advance, you can become a drawing card for the mall. They can send a press release and your photo to the local paper, include you in their newspaper ad or feature you in the shoppers' news.

- Don't expect to get rich on mall work alone, but do expect to make $100 to $250 for a schedule of four shows or for five to eight hours of roving work.

CRUISE SHIPS

You can earn from $500 to $2,000 per week on a cruise, depending on the clientele and your experience.

- You start by calling and asking for the names of the entertainment directors of the dozen or so cruise lines found in the travel section of your nearest big-city newspaper. Then send each of these people a promotional package including a cover letter, photos, letters of recommendation, and a tightly edited one-page description of your program.

- Call the person to whom you addressed the package and alert him to the fact that your kit is on the way. Several days later, call to make certain he got the kit and ask whether he has had a chance to look at it. Ask if he would like to see your video.

- To work a cruise ship you need two, three, or even four complete 30-minute shows. Remember, you will see the same people several times, and they won't go for the same gag twice.

- Ship ceiling height is no more than 8 feet, so there goes the fancy four- and five-club juggling. Leave the torches and machetes at home. What you need are 1 ½–2 hours of material that can play to any crowd of any age.

- Plan to use plenty of audience volunteers. This can involve half juggling, scarf juggling, feather balancing and other easy tricks that audience members can do. Brush up on your mime, musical ability, magic or standup-comedy expertise.

- Expect to dress well and eat well on the ship. You will be expected to show up for social events and meals and to be a congenial person. Keep your behavior totally above-board, since word travels fast on a ship.

THE COLLEGE CIRCUIT

If you have 50–60 minutes of sophisticated material with lots of laughs and plenty of flash, you may be able to work the college circuit.

- This job requires stamina and a love of travel. Your life is a succession of one-night stands at about $1,000 per engagement, plus transportation. Expect to work three or four days a week.

- Booking is through the National Association of Campus Activities (NACA), P.O. Box 6828, Columbia, SC 29260, which holds an annual showcase for all sorts of variety acts. You pay a fee and your own expenses and present a sample performance. Student body representatives from hundreds of colleges attend this event.

- After auditioning, you hand out your promotional material to student representatives, who generally contact you at a later date for bookings.

- You will need a poster for this work. It goes up all over campus to let students know you are on the way. You can even sell posters and T-shirts after your performance.

- Performing spaces vary. At best you are in a small theater in the drama department. More typically, you are on a raised area adjacent to the cafeteria or in a large lecture hall or "multipurpose" room.

- College crowds love zany humor, audience participation, wild costuming and that one spectacular trick they can tell their friends about. Expect hecklers, audience repartee and surprises.

NIGHTCLUBS AND CASINOS

You need 10–15 minutes of fast, high-intensity juggling to play in this league. I will assume that you have already developed such an act and that it includes hot music, flashy costumes and immaculate props which are kept on a custom-built rack or are handed to you by an attractive assistant.

- Bookings for these engagements come primarily through variety or novelty agents. Lists can be found under "Entertainment Bureaus" or "Theatrical Agencies" in the Yellow Pages. You can be handled by several entertainment bureaus at once, but if you are picked by an agency, stay with them as long as the work keeps coming.

- Your video is a vital element in this process. Even so, you may be asked to present a live audition, for which you may or may not be paid a fee.

- You may be able to book yourself into smaller clubs, discos and review shows. Send in your promotional kit and call immediately to let the entertainment director know it's on the way.

EVERYTHING ELSE

Aside from the major markets listed above, there are the following minimarkets to explore:

- **Commercials and movies:** Here an agent is essential. Don't expect much and you will be surprised if anything turns up. You will usually receive money up front (four figures) plus the residuals.

- **Trade shows:** These are a potential source of big money. You attract people into a room or booth, you make a tie-in between juggling and the product or service being offered and create a festive atmosphere for potential customers.

- **Theme parks:** Almost every theme park hires jugglers. It is steady work with steady pay, and with five to eight 20- to 30-minute shows per day six days a week, you get lots of practice. Call the entertainment department and ask about auditions.

CONTRACTS

Except for street performing, you should expect to sign a contract for every program. On the day you book your program over the telephone, send out three copies of a signed contract and ask the client to return two of the copies with his or her signature. You can keep one on file and take the other copy with you to the event. (A contract may also be initiated by the client, and copies may be sent to you for your signature.)

JUGGLING

AND

HEALTH

This book is not intended for someone who needs to be convinced that juggling is a worthwhile endeavor. No one ever hiked to the top of Mt. Everest because he or she read about the "benefits" of mountain climbing. If you have come this far, you may not know why you juggle, but you do know that juggle you must. You couldn't quit even if you wanted to.

You may, however, have to convince other people that juggling is either harmless or good for you. Concerned relatives, a boss who worries about image ("Who's that bozo in accounting?") or the PTA you are hoping will fund a juggling class may need convincing. This chapter provides you with ammunition to use in convincing others, or yourself, of the benefits of juggling.

Juggling is not just a metaphor for life, it's a model. Practice juggling and you practice simplifying complexity. As your juggling improves, your ability to handle physical, mental and emotional complexity improves.

To learn to juggle well, you must break each complex move down into its smallest possible components and build it up again, step by step. Juggling requires, rewards and reinforces patience, persistence and self-analysis. You bring ever-increasing order to the chaos of hands and objects. You can see it, and so can your admiring kinfolk. What seemed impossible only a short while ago has become mundane. The horizon retreats endlessly before you, and you become more adept as each milestone is reached.

Amazingly, with practice, your juggling pattern seems to slow down. You gain time as you gain agility, poise and balance. You have earned a measure of self-confidence that is transferable to the next seemingly chaotic situation in your life. You are becoming a master at simplifying complexity.

IF YOU ARE A THERAPIST OR WORK IN MEDICINE, HEALTH OR REHABILITATION

Because of the precise nature of tasks in juggling, it is feasible to use them as assessment tools to determine whether neuromotor impairment exists and the extent of the problem. Often while teaching younger elementary students with scarves, the author has been able to identify students whose gross and/or fine motor skills were far below their peers. Research should be undertaken on this topic.

Juggling is also an activity that can be initiated as therapy. For some youngsters and disabled adults, nylon scarves may provide their first successful throwing-and-catching experience. In recovery from trauma, rehabilitation from illness and work with the aged or chronically infirm, scarf juggling can provide a successful experience and positive reinforcement of self-esteem.

IF YOU WORK IN AN OFFICE

Juggling provides an ideal break from the pressures of office work. When you juggle, you are in the present moment. The past and future do not exist for you, or you cannot maintain the pattern. But the moment you stop juggling, you are back at work with the attendant tensions, deadlines and problems. Juggling sweeps the mind clean of tensions and brings you a sense of peace and order.

A coffee break can pep you up artificially. A juggling break wakes up your body and gets your circulation moving. You become alert and sharp and maintain that condition of clarity long after the beanbags are back in your desk drawer.

IF YOU ARE A HIGH SCHOOL OR COLLEGE STUDENT

If you would like a break from your studies that is inexpensive and neither mind-numbing like TV nor physically debilitating like drugs or alcohol, juggling may be just the thing. It lets you disconnect from the workload without going to a gym or tavern. It can provide you with friends who will want to pass beanbags or clubs; and, who knows, you may be able to work your way through college doing shows and giving juggling lessons. If you can combine your hobby with your work, you will have a more satisfactory life. The author has certainly discovered that.

IF YOU PRACTICE MEDITATION

Some jugglers experience what Zen novices and yoga students struggle for years to acquire. I know. For one full year I chanted a mantra day and night, working my way toward the condition of Samadhi, where the senses are disconnected and only one thing exists, your connection with the infinite. Then I discovered that once I could juggle smoothly and without trying, I achieved Samadhi. Now to go to that peaceful place, I need only get out three beanbags and start weaving infinity signs in the air.

Unlike the martial arts, which are linear and outer-directed, juggling is curvilinear and directed inward. I call it an "impartial art" because it is not aggressive or intrusive. It is a peaceful, nonverbal prayer that you perform, and in the process you may find yourself gaining focus.

IF YOU WORK WITH YOUR HANDS

Pilots, dentists, surgeons, heavy-equipment operators, assembly-line workers, keyboard operators, drivers, repairmen, and others who work with their hands can use juggling to improve dexterity and endurance, and as a break from the tedious nature of hand-work.

Juggling requires and rewards precision. If you do precise work, you may find the following take place:

- Improved fine and gross motor skills
- More accurate throwing and more reliable catching
- A keener sense of rhythm
- Better visual discrimination, particularly tracking and peripheral vision
- Ambidexterity
- Faster reflexes
- Improved ability to concentrate
- More patience with yourself

IF YOU WORRY OR HAVE STRESS IN YOUR LIFE

Juggling, once mastered, cuts through stress like a hot knife through butter. When you are first learning to juggle, it is important that you learn with scarves so that the frustration of acquiring the skill will be minimized. When you first approach juggling, your stress level may rise because the first few steps are left-brain activities requiring verbalization, counting and worry. However, continuous juggling is a right-brain activity in which you simply get lost in the flow of the whole pattern.

The transition from worry to mild concern to elation is swift and may be marked by a "Eureka" experience, that wonderful moment when it all falls into place. Once you can juggle effortlessly, if a problem arises in your life, you can just juggle it away. The problem is still there, but you don't care as long as you are juggling. And when you stop juggling, the perspective you have gained makes the problem seem a lot less important.

IF YOU ARE AN ATHLETE OR ASPIRING ATHLETE

Juggling can be good conditioning as well as being good for your eye-hand coordination. Professional basketball players should learn to juggle three basketballs, and football players should learn to keep three footballs going. In each case, ball-handling skills will be improved.

To improve strength as well as agility, you can build up the weight of your juggling implements until you are getting a good workout. By mixing various objects and working to learn new tricks, you can improve your ability to improvise and act quickly and appropriately at critical moments.

Juggling with heavy objects can be a great workout. If you toss three 4-pound beanbags for 10 minutes, you will be doing thousands of foot-pounds of work, gaining strength and coordination at the same time.

IF YOU ARE INTERESTED IN MUSIC
OR THE THEATER

Juggling is rhythmic in nature and can assume any tempo, depending on the objects juggled and the size of the pattern. It lends itself to composition and provides "music for the eyes." It is learned by the same step-by-step system you use when you are learning a musical instrument. With every practice session you improve. The product is an orderly progression of throws and catches leading to a visual symphony. Combined with music, juggling can be a truly satisfying synergy of the arts.

Because juggling gives you an ability to get up in front of others and perform, it can improve your stage presence and self-confidence. It is, like fencing, a traditional tool for gaining body awareness.

IF YOU ARE A RUNNER

Running is a positive addiction. So is juggling. Put them together, and you have joggling. Your hands and arms are kept as busy in joggling as your legs. The challenge is to minimize drops and improve your time. While joggling, if you drop an object you simply stop, pick it up and keep going. You can use beanbags, balls or clubs. Look for more jogglers in major races and fun runs as time goes by.

IF YOU ARE IN THE MILITARY OR WORK
WITH INCARCERATED PEOPLE

Certainly juggling should be part of prison recreation programs. It is nonaggressive and requires complete concentration. The only difference between a good juggler and a great one may be the time spent practicing, and in prisons time is an abundant commodity.

The military might do well to consider juggling for all recruits. It quickens the reflexes, improves coordination and may sharpen visual acuity as well as peripheral vision. One added benefit is the relatively small amount of space required. Even in a submarine, there is room to juggle beanbags or scarves. The post exchange system might consider carrying a good juggling book and a limited line of equipment for military personnel and dependents.

JUGGLING INJURIES

As with any other sport, there are hazards in juggling to which practitioners are prone. Least among these, but first in the minds of parents and principals, are impact injuries or traumas. Unlike football or basketball, no one is going to run smack into anyone else intentionally, nor is anyone hitting an object horizontally, running pell mell toward a base or racing someone else toward a goal or finish line. So the worst traumatic injury in juggling might be a bruise from the knob of a club, a contact lens dislodged by a beanbag or a scratch from a neighbor clawing for a scarf.

However, there are some conditions to which jugglers are prone. What do jugglers do all day? They stand in one spot and throw things up in the air. Often they simply tilt their heads back and begin to toss, particularly if they are trying to keep four, five, or more things going. So stiff necks are possible, and many a juggler has to check in periodically with his local chiropractor for an adjustment of shifted vertebrae. To prevent this, we suggest a warm-up before juggling which includes stretching and limbering the spine. Also, during practice sessions, vary your position, turn your head, bend over slowly from the neck to your waist and straighten up just as slowly, one vertebra at a time. Arch your neck both forward and back.

If you pass clubs back and forth or practice club juggling for hours on end, you may develop an impact bruise on the first knuckle of your left hand from repeated pounding by the club handle. Pain may radiate throughout your palm, making club-juggling difficult. As with any bone bruise, this condition may last for months. The only solution may be to stop club-juggling altogether for some time.

To prevent this condition, buy a set of soft-handled clubs, get a racquetball glove for your catching hand or pad that area with foam tape before extensive practice sessions.

If you are working on four, five or more rings, the surface between your thumb and first finger and the backs of your knuckles may ache. Racquetball gloves help, as will A & D ointment to soften your skin. You might want to tape your finger joints and knuckles.

Strains and pains from pulled muscles are common with jugglers. It is imperative that you warm up in advance of a juggling workout. Twenty minutes of stretching and bending exercises are recommended if you are going to be working out for a few hours straight. Typically you are eager to practice and have been looking forward all day to the opportunity to try a new trick or work on your latest pattern. Resist the temptation to tip your head back and get to work. Start every practice session with bending and stretching. At the International Jugglers' Convention, there is a well-attended stretch-out session every morning to help jugglers get into the habit of limbering up.

Juggling is work, but it is generally light work. The muscles it develops are long and slender, not bulging and knotted. Many jugglers who have concentrated on juggling to the exclusion of other activities appear stoop-shouldered and hollow-chested. If you want to add bulk to your frame, strengthen your body and improve your posture, it is suggested that you balance juggling with weight-training or body-building. This is true at any age but particularly during your growing years.

Jugglers usually don't get sufficient exercise below the chest. There are two fine juggling exercises to add to your repertoire which should be repeated daily. One is the under-the-leg toss. Get to the point where you can throw successive tosses under your legs, alternating them and running in place. This is great for balance, endurance, leg strength and maintaining your stomach muscles. The other exercise to consider is joggling, juggling while running. Give it a try; it builds stamina.

Of course, if you juggle dangerous objects, you run the risk of injury. Torches generally have screws and metal parts at the wick end which get hot. When you catch a torch backward, let go as quickly as you can. Don't try to give it a half turn and keep juggling. For safety's sake, you should keep your fuel source tightly capped and far away from the stage or your practice area. Needless to say, you should keep a blanket and a fire extinguisher handy and carry them with you when you do any fire-juggling.

Knives, machetes and axes are a different story altogether. Very few performers use really sharp blades. Even a dull knife can be shown to be "sharp" by chopping an apple, cabbage or carrot in two. The audience thinks that a shiny blade is a sharp blade, so if you must juggle "sharp" implements, file off the points and edges and keep the blades clean and shiny. Better still, avoid sharp instruments altogether.

SPREADING
THE JOY
OF JUGGLING

So now you know how to juggle. What's next?

Juggling alone is fun. Juggling with others is more than twice as much fun. If you are like me, as soon as you learned to keep three objects going, you said, "Why doesn't everybody know how to do this?" With your help, pretty soon everybody will get the opportunity to learn. There are lots of ways to build up momentum.

If you've gotten this far in the book, you've probably already started showing off your skills and teaching other people. Why not build a network of jugglers in your town or school? Teach your friends to juggle. Tell them to teach their friends. Then see how long it takes before the whole town or the whole school knows how.

Challenge everyone in your school to learn how to juggle. You could write and submit an article stating your challenge for the school newspaper. Teach eight friends. Put up a sign-up poster in the school cafeteria with your names on it and leave room for everyone else to sign up. As soon as someone learns, he or she can sign the poster and get a sticker that says:

I KNOW HOW, AND I'LL TEACH YOU!

Now see how long it takes before everyone in the school learns.

If there are people who would like to learn but are physically unable to, make special labels that say:

I DON'T KNOW HOW, BUT I'M A FAN

That way nobody feels left out. Once your whole school can juggle, write me and let me know how fast juggling swept through your school. I'll see that the current record is published in *Jugglers' World* magazine. We may even make *The Guinness Book of Records*.

Now that you've got a bunch of juggling friends, how do you keep them going? It's easy to say form a club, but how do you do it? There are about 100 juggling clubs around the country registered with the IJA. Some are very active, and some are the pits. Let's see what makes the active ones successful.

1. One person or a small core group must take responsibility to set up a time and place for regular meetings. Then someone has to be there every time and "run" the meeting. Forget the idea that anarchy and apathy are fashionable. You should be as enthusiastic about your juggling club as you are about juggling.

2. At every meeting there is a time when everyone stops juggling and sits down to talk about plans and events. Otherwise the meeting is just a big weekly practice session for your juggling clique.

3. You need an education coordinator to be in charge of teaching new people. Nothing is more intimidating than walking into a room full of club passers if you can only juggle the Cascade. Greet visitors and guests at the door and offer to show them something new.

4. You need an event coordinator whose job it is to help you focus on an event or an activity. For instance, you can plan

to be in a parade or talent show. You can present your own gala public juggling show, or you can offer to do a halftime performance for a local basketball team.

5. Elect a treasurer, collect dues and get out a monthly newsletter to keep everyone informed of activities and events.

6. One person should be in charge of publicity. Send out press releases to the local papers and radio stations telling them when and where you meet, and that lessons are available. Don't forget the high school papers in your town.

7. Get as many members as possible to join the IJA, and bring copies of *Jugglers' World* and any other juggling publications you own to your weekly meetings.

8. Plan to send a delegation to the annual IJA convention and inspire one another to work on getting money or transportation together for that purpose, or go to regional mini-conventions.

9. Elect or appoint a games master to organize juggling games at every weekly meeting.

10. At least once a month, hold a video session to show your latest juggling videos to one another.

11. Elect or appoint a workshop director and have him arrange a workshop each week on something new.

12. Select a competitions director who can organize ongoing contests such as a Jollyball ladder or an annual competition modeled on the IJA championships.

13. Select an achievement committee to review members for awards on a regular basis and give out awards at your weekly meetings.

14. Organize a charity event like a "juggle-a-thon" to raise money for a worthy cause; or offer to provide a free show for a hospital, prison, retirement center or telethon.

15. Get a local sporting goods, toy or magic store to carry juggling equipment. Put up a sign by the juggling-equipment displays that tells where and when your club meets.

16. Challenge a nearby club to a juggling contest, an endurance juggling event, a joggling race, a Jollyball match or a game of Field Juggling.

17. Check *The Guinness Book of Records* and hold an event to break an existing world record in juggling. Get sponsors and give the proceeds to charity.

18. Sponsor a juggling show and invite one of the several well-known juggling troupes to town as your headline act.

19. Offer to have your club teach your local professional or college sports team how to juggle as a form of eye-hand coordination training.

20. At least once a year, sponsor a juggling festival in your community with contests, workshops, games, a parade and a public show. For details, see the next section, "Holding a Juggling Festival."

Not all contests have to be serious. What about these?

- Three-legged joggling race
- Endurance water-balloon juggle
- Egg-juggling relay race
- Bowling-ball juggling contest
- Follow the leader while juggling
- Apple-eating while juggling race

HOLDING A JUGGLING FESTIVAL

You can sponsor a juggling festival in your community. If you follow these guidelines, results are assured:

1. At least six months in advance, choose a weekend when there are no conflicting community events, and find a facility that has a gymnasium available. It helps to have an auditorium or stage also, for performances and competitions.

2. Prepare a press release on your event and send it to newspapers, TV and radio stations and organizations like the YMCA, recreation and parks departments, public schools and the chamber of commerce. Follow up with phone calls to make sure they take your event seriously. You should arrange for interviews, articles and public service announcements in advance. On the day of the event you will want on-site coverage.

3. Prepare a sponsorship proposal and send it around to businesses to get contributions in cash, products or services. You may be able to get a radio station to bring its sound system and businesses to contribute T-shirts, trophies, programs or name tags.

4. If you expect to hold a "juggle-a-thon" for charity, identify your cause early and ask for volunteers to man your registration table.

5. Print a program that includes a schedule of events for the day or days of the festival. You can send this out as a reminder to the people who got your press release. You can often get display ads or some help with printing costs from sponsors. Try the store where you buy your juggling equipment.

6. You will need a sound system with microphone and cassette player to announce events and play music. Bleachers for spectators are helpful. You will need access to restrooms. On-site or nearby food service keeps people at the event.

7. One person should be assigned to oversee each of the following tasks:

- Preprogram publicity

- On-site press relations

- Information/registration desks

- Announcements, music, general-event coordination

- Workshops for jugglers

- Classes for the general public

- Competitions (staging and judging)

- Stage show

- Games and races

- Sponsorship

- Housing for visiting jugglers

- Dealers and equipment vendors

- Concessions

- Parade

- Picnic

- Awards banquet

8. It is important to hold a ceremony to give awards to winners of competitions, games and contests. Ask community sponsors for prizes. Give at least a T-shirt to every volunteer worker if you can.

9. Charge an overall registration fee; if you need to buy trophies and can't find a sponsor, charge an entry fee for competitions. Sell an event T-shirt.

10. To draw out-of-town performers, you might want to sponsor a public show and charge admission, then split the gate among the performers. It might also help to have the city sanction a street-performing location just before or just

after the event, where visiting performers can pass the hat to make money without fear of police hassles.

11. Don't forget to invite allied arts and sports like your local Footbag and Frisbee players, jump-rope teams, baton twirlers and cheerleaders, physical educators and mimes or other variety performers. They may want to learn more about juggling and can be a great addition to your public show or workshops.

12. To make registration flow smoothly, you need several people on the desk on the first day and if possible a preregistration system where those who have paid in advance automatically get a badge and a program.

13. Workshops can start early in the day and run back to back. To be effective, they should include a *short* demonstration by the instructor followed by lots of practice time for participants. The workshop space can be a separate room or a corner of the gym. Many workshops should be held on two levels at once, for those new to the apparatus and for those who already know how but just want to polish their skills. Participants choose their own levels.

14. Juggling games, contests, joggling events and relay races can take place outside on a field or in a park. A parade adds spice and attracts families. A picnic and outdoor performances can make your festival a true community event.

15. Invite local juggling-equipment dealers and prop makers to set up shop right in the gym. Provide them with tables and chairs if needed. Charge them a flat fee for participation.

16. Hold a general meeting at least once during your event. At this meeting you can strengthen your organization, hold elections, pass out information and give out awards. If you hold it just before your parade, you can give out marching orders.

17. Each day at around noon, or whenever your attendance is highest, stop all activities in the gym. Welcome the jugglers

and thank them for coming. Introduce various volunteers. Thank your sponsors and any vendors. Review the day's schedule, reminding the jugglers of important events. Make all announcements. Resume activities.

18. Miscellaneous ideas include:

- Posting the daily event schedule on entry and exit doors

- Providing shower or pool facilities on site

- Providing a blackboard for messages

- Having one person on call who is a paramedic or has first-aid training

- Getting video and photo releases signed by performers and workshop leaders

- Arranging for pre-event publicity stunts which could include world record attempts at a local shopping mall, teaching your mayor and city council to juggle, or getting one day designated as "Our Town Juggling Day" by the mayor

- Going to all the local schools with a "teaser" show or with juggling lessons for physical-education classes before the event

- Securing a storage area for your equipment, for visitors' gear and for vendors

- Making a schedule for people to sit at the registration/information table

- Designating an official event video team and a photographer and agreeing to pay for their tapes and film if they will make copies available to members

- Scheduling your event just before or just after a major community festival and making it part of the larger event

- Keeping a complete record of what each of your volunteers or officers does and passing that record on to the people in charge next year
- Scheduling plenty of time for small informal performances, using them to qualify for achievement awards

PUBLIC SERVICE ANNOUNCEMENT/PRESS RELEASE
Our Town Juggling Festival
Fact Sheet

Dates: Friday, June 12–Sunday, June 14

Location: Community College Gym and City Park

Activities: Friday 9 A.M.–8 P.M. Registration and Open Juggling
  8 P.M. Our Town Juggling Championships
  Saturday 9 A.M.–6 P.M. Workshops and Games
  8 P.M. Gala Public Show, $5 Adults, $2 Children
  Sunday 9 A.M.–1 P.M. Workshops
  2–3 P.M. Parade Down Main Street
  3–5 P.M. Juggling on the Green at City Park
  5 P.M.–Dark, Picnic and Performances

Admission: Free to spectators, $5 for participants.

Special Attractions: The Frying Burrito Brothers will headline the public show. Free lessons for the public at the city park on Sunday. Workshops for jugglers of all ages and abilities.

Competition: Friday 8 P.M., Our Town Juggling Championships, featuring the finest jugglers from this area.

Sponsors: Papa's Pizza, Station KJUG, Our Town Ice Cream Parlor

Contact for more information: (Your name)
(Your address)
(Your telephone number)

MINI POSTER

JUGGLING FESTIVAL

JUNE 12–14

COMMUNITY COLLEGE GYM

**Classes and Workshops
Games and Contests**

**City Juggling Championships
Gala Public Show
Parade and Picnic**

Schedule:

FRIDAY

9 A.M.–8 P.M.	**Registration and Open Juggling**
8 P.M.–10 P.M.	**Competition followed by open juggling until midnight**

SATURDAY

9 A.M.–3 P.M.	**Workshops:**
9–10	**Stretching and warm-up**
10–11	**Three-ball tricks**
11–12	**Four- and five-ball juggling**
12–1	**Rings**
1–2	**Cigar boxes**
2–3	**Club passing**
3–6 P.M.	**Field Events:**
3–4	**Joggling races and relay races**
4–5	**Jollyball championships**
5–6	**Field Juggling**
8–10 P.M.	**Public Show**

SUNDAY

9 A.M.–1 P.M.	**Workshops:**
9–10	**Stretching and warm-up**
10–11	**Devil sticks**
11–12	**Diabolo**
12–1	**Club passing formation and configurations**
1–2:30 P.M.	**Awards luncheon and annual meeting in cafeteria**
3–4 P.M.	**Parade from community college to city park**
4–5 P.M.	**Juggling on the green**
5 P.M.–Dark	**Picnic and open air performances**

VISITING A
JUGGLERS'
CONVENTION

S tanding in the middle of the gym at an International Jugglers' Association annual convention surrounded by 1,000 or more jugglers, it is easy to see our roots and look back at our history.

In one corner Albert Lucas, Tony Duncan, Sue Kirby, Demetrius Alcarese, Matt Cantrell, Dan Bennet and Robert York are working with their colleagues to see how many objects they can keep aloft, and for how long. Lucas has equaled or bettered all world records with 10 balls, 12 rings and seven clubs; and his run of 37 minutes, 10 seconds with five clubs, set in 1984 in Las Vegas, eclipsed the previous record of 16:20 set by Serge Ignatov of the Moscow Circus.

This is one of the most challenging areas in juggling: the numbers quest. In the 1930s Enrico Rastelli, Russian-born Italian performer and third-generation circus star, set records with 10 balls and eight plates.

Although Rastelli set the modern standards, numbers juggling goes back into antiquity. A popular juggler of ancient Rome, Septimus Spika, was represented with seven balls in motion. Rastelli is a name every juggler should recognize, not just for his numbers work but for his incredibly skillful manipulation of sticks and inflated balls. In turn, Rastelli was greatly inspired by the dextrous work of the

Japanese juggler Takashima, who toured Europe in the late nineteenth century. The skill of balancing large balls on various parts of the body and rolling them from point to point was largely developed and also presented by Moung-Toon, a Burmese juggler who toured Europe in the 1890s. Rastelli spent his formative years, from 1912 to the early 1920s, in Russia and "in the midst of the turmoil, he found refuge in circuses and theaters where he practiced without interruption."* He toured the United States in 1924 and again in 1928, playing vaudeville theaters from coast to coast.

In 1931, at the age of 34 and at the height of his career, Enrico Rastelli cut his gum on his mouthstick. The cut became infected, and he died suddenly. By this time his work with sticks and balls had become an inspiration to an entire generation of performers such as Serge Flash, Bob Ripa and Trixie, to name a few who carried on in his footsteps.

In another corner of the "Great Hall of Jugglers," we find that practitioners of the gymnastic style of the great Rastelli, jugglers like Michael Chirrick and his mother, the inimitable Lottie Brunn, are holding a practice session. To the Brunn family, practice is a way of life. Lottie and her brother, Francis, were schooled in juggling by their late father, who loved to watch them practice and continually inspired them to excel.

Francis has said, "To be a great juggler, don't look at other jugglers, look at other art forms." Following his own advice, he learned to use a flamenco style in his act, taking full advantage of his lithe body and piercing gaze. Bouncing one or two balls on his forehead with perfect control is Francis' forte. Raising his leg and bending at the waist, this incredibly elastic performer permits a large inflated ball to roll from his extended foot along his leg, across his torso, past the nape of the neck and out the extended

* *Juggling—Its History and Greatest Performers*, by Francisco Alvarez, 1984, P.O. Box 8795 Albuquerque, NM 87108.

arm, where it comes to rest on the back of his outstretched hand. Like Rastelli, Francis Brunn is a master of the mouthstick, upon which a ball is balanced. With incredibly rapid speed and the delicate touch that comes from years of practice, Francis whips the mouthstick out from under and all the way around the stationary ball, balancing it once more.

The Brunn family always finishes its act with "the big trick," as do many of the great stage jugglers today. The classic "Brunn Finale" might include balancing spinning balls on a mouthstick and on a pedestal on the forehead and spinning two rings around the right leg, while standing on the left leg. Meanwhile, a ball is spinning on the extended index finger of the right hand while two rings turn in opposite directions around the right arm between shoulder and elbow. All the while the left hand juggles three rings.

Following in this tradition, jugglers today may finish with a classic combination move, or one that is a bit bizarre. Anthony Gatto, under the tutelage of his most devoted fan, best friend and father, Nick, practices with the classic tools of the trade—balls, rings and clubs—all the while balancing a long pole on his forehead with a stuffed animal on the top. Ernest Montego, stepbrother of Francis and Lottie Brunn, executes the same combination move as Francis, all the while pedaling a 6 foot unicycle with one foot. Larry Vacksman finishes his routine by spinning four Hula Hoops around his knees and three around his waist, juggling a basketball and a club in his left hand and three balls in his right.

Go out a door and down the hall to a padded room used for martial arts, wrestling and gymnastics, and there you will find the heavyweight jugglers, Larry Merlo, Toby Twist and Bob Nickerson in a friendly competition to see who can keep three bowling balls aloft for the longest time. Most recently, this specialty has been adopted by the Dallas Cowboys and other professional sports teams who want to combine the dexterity and speed of juggling with strength training and conditioning. The Cowboys, however, use heavyweight beanbags made of tough Nylon stuffed with gravel, sand or lead shot.

These feats of agility and strength are reminiscent of a school of juggling popular around the end of the nineteenth century perfected by Severus Schaffer and Herr Holtum in Europe and brought to North America by Paul Spadoni and Paul Conchas. Spadoni launched the barrel of a cannon from a springboard, and caught it on his shoulders. Conchas balanced an entire cannon, including the wheels and mount, on his forehead. Both juggled incredibly heavy metal objects like cannon balls and artillery shells.

The manipulation of military hardware, guns and bayonets was the signature trick of Signor Antonio of the P.T. Barnum Circus in 1836. Long before, in ancient China, soldiers had developed ways to manipulate their spears and tridents while idle in camp, and vases weighing up to 20 kilograms were balanced, tossed, rolled and spun on the forehead, neck and chin. These same moves can be seen today in circuses from China and Taiwan.

At the jugglers' convention we are eager to participate in one of the most popular workshops, the one on club swinging conducted by Allan Jacobs, who is assisted by Sandy Brown, Karen Rothstein and Robert Nelson, "The Butterfly Man." Through their efforts, an entire art form has been revived, rivalling toss-juggling in popularity. Club swinging was a common form of exercise in the late 1800s, using heavy wooden Indian clubs available in every gymnasium and sold in sporting goods stores around the world. In the post—Civil War period, club swinging was popularized by Gus Hill. Some of Hill's clubs were very large and heavy, with huge bulbs and short handles. One of the first to juggle with clubs was DeWitt Cook, and two of the first vaudevillians to juggle clubs smoothly in their acts were Morris Cronin and James Darmody, both of whom played the circuit around the turn of the century. Darmody actually juggled five of these heavy wooden clubs.

As we look around the room, we see hundreds of club jugglers. To own a set of clubs today, one has only to go to the local sporting goods store. There you can find a set of three durable, lightweight plastic juggling clubs for less than the cost of one wooden juggling club in the 1930s. The history of juggling is paralleled by a history of equipment manufacture. Around the beginning of the twentieth century, painted sticks turned on a lathe, tennis rackets, battle axes and banjos were passed just as clubs are passed today. Since at least the beginning of the nineteenth century, Asian and European jugglers were making their own clubs laboriously, by hand. A central dowel ran the length of the club with a basket of bamboo strips forming the bulb. The bulb was then covered with papier maché to give it the characteristic shape. Edward Van Wyck is credited with the development of a hollow-bodied wooden club, which he manufactured for other jugglers. He sold his patterns and manufacturing methods to Harry Lind, who continued to make hand-turned wooden clubs until his death in 1967. Lind's designs were adapted to fiberglass by Stu Raynolds and are the basis for the modern one-piece plastic juggling club of today. Plastic clubs are lighter, stronger, more durable and far less expensive than those of wood or fiberglass. As a result, today's club jugglers are performing tricks never thought possible by our predecessors.

Boulder, Colorado, has become a training ground for serious club jugglers, passers and performers. Kezia Tennenbaum, Peter Davison and Jon Held, collectively known as Air Jazz, and Barrett Felker and Jim Strinka, the Dynamotion Jugglers, have set the pace in this mile-high mecca. Their individual juggling moves, showmanship and choreography were nurtured by one of the finest "products" of the IJA, Dick Franco, and reflect the legacy of two grand old men of vaudeville, Homer Stack and Bobby May.

Bobby May made his stage entrance in a casual style with a pixie grin and a dancer's grace. Picture a juggler with the savoir-faire of Fred Astaire and the dynamism of Gene Kelly and you have Bobby May, known as "The International Juggler" during a career that spanned four decades in 35 countries. Bobby was gentle, modest and the originator of numerous tricks and moves. He developed a fluid club-juggling style, reflected in the work of today's solo club masters, Peter Davison, John Webster, Ken Falk, Andrew Head and Michael Kass.

Bobby used the entire stage, turning, running back and forth, lunging (gracefully, always gracefully) after an "errant" club and seeming to be blessed with an "extra second" before having to make a catch. His control over three and five lacrosse-style balls is still legendary. Two tricks stand out in the minds of his many admirers. Bobby bounced five balls off a drum as stood on his head. For a finale, he juggled five balls in a variety of bouncing and aerial patterns, ending up with a deliberate drop of all five from a shower pattern to the floor. Then as each ball bounded, Bobby scooped it up with his hat, bouncing the last ball off his forehead to the nape of his neck. From there it rolled down his back into the hat held between his legs. From this position, he did a forward roll, smiled, waved and walked off the stage.

Homer Stack, who downplays his own vaudeville career, has made an avocation of assisting young jugglers in the creation of first-rate acts. This transfer of skill was haphazard process in the past, with vaudeville and circus families passing along closely guarded bits of lore to their children, along with admonitions to keep the routine a secret. In the early 1900s, American jugglers went so far as to write out their routines and send them to a central repository, where they were kept on his file in case a copyright dispute arose. Some performers would purposely omit their best material from their acts if they knew another juggler was in the audience, and some threatened to sue over the alleged theft of bits of "business."

In the end, however, the major difference between juggling and magic is this—with magic the trick is concealed, but with juggling it is revealed. Since attempts at secrecy are bound to fail, jugglers are now known for their open and sharing nature. Like Homer Stack, many older jugglers now seek protégés.

In the Soviet Union, some Eastern European countries and China, the state has taken over from the circus family as the repository of lore, and these state-sponsored troupes come as close to human perfection as anyone has in recorded history. The masters of one generation become the teachers of the next, and their pupils are selected for interest, ability and the ease with which they take coaching. Every generation is urged to outdo its predecessors.

Modern juggling coaches and teachers like Randy Pryor, Kit Summers, Mike Vondruska and the author have broken with the tradition that used to keep our art a secret to be passed on from parent to child, or from mentor to protégé. In order to make juggling accessible to everyone, the Juggling Institute was founded in 1977. It is a network of professionally trained and certified instructors who are prepared both as performers and teachers. Juggling Institute teams present first-rate all-school assemblies and teach juggling in classes of up to 100 students each. This growing network includes teams covering the West Coast, the Midwest and the Southeast. The goal of the Institute is eventually to have teams available in every major metropolitan area.

Meanwhile, back at the IJA convention, if you arrive at the gym early in the morning, you are likely to find an instructor from the Juggling Institute surrounded by 50 to 100 preteens flinging scarves and beanbags with exuberant abandon in patterns that grow in order day by day. The Juggling Institute tries to connect with a local day camp at each convention site to help conventioneers learn to work with youngsters, and to pass on the skill formally.

Physical educators have long been aware of the value of juggling. From about the time of the decline of vaudeville, juggling was used as a model to show physical-education majors how a complex skill is learned. Prior to that time, many physical-education programs incorporated club swinging, using heavy wooden Indian clubs.

In fact, in the early 1900s, it was not at all rare for juggling to be a schoolyard game, learned by virtually all the youngsters on the playground, using stones. In the Netherlands and Scandinavia, a particular type of bounce juggling was played off walls and stoops, and in Japan every girl learned "Otedama," a game played like jacks using small beanbags which were juggled in a circular or "shower" pattern. These playground games almost disappeared during the mid-20th century but are still available if we will just ask our grandparents to show us how they used to be played.

When we focus our attention on club passing, there seems to be only one rule: keep going no matter what. Inventive duos like Waldo and Arsene, Bryan Wendling and Scott Burton, Benji Hill and Dana Tison, teams like Gravity's Last Stand, the Cabangahan Jugglers from the Philippines, the Jongleur Jugglers and Manic Expressions are all eager to demonstrate the new moves they have invented over the past year.

Major contributions to the art/recreation form of club passing have been made by imaginative teachers like Joe Buhler, Hovey Burgess and Richard Dingman. Thanks to the lighter, more durable and more manageable clubs, and the openness of today's jugglers to share even their most difficult moves with one another, these contemporary club-passing technicians far surpass even the most skilled teams of vaudeville days, such as the Three Swifts, the Elgins, and the Juggling Jewels. Parallel developments have taken place in Western and Eastern Europe.

As we look around the gym, we see a knot of spectators gathered around curly-haired Daniel Holzman. As he completes a particularly intricate three-ball sequence, the assembled throng bursts into spontaneous applause. One by one, other "three-ball wizards" get up to exhibit their skill. Robert Peck, Edward Jackman, Steve Mills and Craig Barnes can all trace their style back not just decades but centuries, to the wandering troubadours of the eleventh century and beyond.

The first graphic representations of three ball jugglers that have been preserved appear on the wall paintings of the Beni-hassan tombs on the east bank of the Nile, dating from 4600 B.C. Later, but still in the pre-Christian era, a Roman legionnaire, Sidonious Apollinaris, was renowned for entertaining his troops by performing with three balls.

By the sixth century A.D., the wandering "jongleur" was a mainstay of the French and English countryside. He provided varied entertainment, recited poems, sang, danced and played musical instruments. Juggling was usually performed with balls and knives. The balls were carved from wood, made of clay, or sewn from leather, much like today's popular beanbags.

Around 1100 A.D., poets of the wealthy class began to tour, particularly in France, as the first "troubadours." They joined with the jongleurs, and eventually schools of minstrelry developed. The first organization of jongleurs was established in Fecamp in the tenth century. From the time of William the Conqueror (1066), the title "King of the Jugglers" was conferred by statute on the most esteemed palace entertainer in England. This custom persisted for four centuries.

The image of the wandering juggler has persisted until this day. At any Renaissance fair, one is likely to find a solo performer with a small bag of props and the quick wit of a jester. These artists seem to have stepped from the pages of an illuminated manuscript or a tapestry of the Middle Ages. They may or may not appear at our convention, since the midsummer dates often conflict with their busiest season. But we look forward to visits from our own medieval minstrels, Moonbeam, Lynn Thomas, Stewart Fell, Roberto Morganti, Crazy Richard the Mad Juggler, Jim Ridgely, Turk Pipkin, Paul Zimmerman or Kaj Fjelstad.

Of course the legacy of the jongleur and of the vaudevillian becomes the heritage of the street performer. At our annual Street Performers' Workshop, the secrets of the street are shared by Robert Nelson, "The Butterfly Man," Laura Mae Greene, "Miss Tilly" and Bounce, Murph and Benji, as well as dozens of performers who appear in public parks and on street corners throughout the world. The legal hassles and latest regulations are shared, and neophytes are encouraged to try their wings in friendly spots.

Street performing is felt by Ray Jason, one of its proudest practitioners, to be one of the most honest ways to earn a living. The audience pays an admission fee only after having been entertained and in direct proportion to its enjoyment. It is free to walk away at any time and can always refuse to donate. One might wonder how street performing came to be so widely disparaged.

The radio, long-playing records, and movies put an end to vaudeville. Television drove the final nail into the coffin. From 1875 to 1925, this marvelous entertainment form flourished, producing work for thousands of acts and joy for millions of theatergoers.

It was in this era of the decline of vaudeville that eight jugglers got together in June 1947 and founded the International Jugglers' Association. The founders were Harry Lind, Bernard Joyce, George Barvin, Jack Greene, F. R. Dunham, Eddie Johnson, Roger Montandon and Art Jennings. They stayed in touch with one another through a Jugglers' Bulletin which has evolved into a glossy magazine, *Jugglers' World*. Membership now numbers in the thousands. The organization holds annual conventions, and, through local affiliates, sponsors regional miniconventions.

The demise of vaudeville forced literally thousands of people to look for other work or other venues for their performance. The street corner became the only stage upon which an emerging act could develop. But throughout Europe and North America, Depression-era governments and their austere World War II and postwar successors passed laws severely restricting or banning street performing.

During the 1960s, '70s and '80s, local regulations restricting street performing have been loosened throughout the United States, where performers can stand on their rights to freedom of expression and freedom of assembly. In countries where these freedoms are regarded as privileges, rather than rights, jugglers still risk arrest or an order to move on. Some more enlightened cities such as Boston (Quincy Market), Baltimore (Harbor Square), New York (parks in general) and San Francisco (Fisherman's Wharf) have gone so far as to welcome street performers, hold competitions among them or erect stages and designate areas where performing is welcomed. Often enlightened merchants have led the way, once they see that street performers draw audiences, and audiences are composed of shoppers.

As we look around at this year's convention we see groups of jugglers who specialize in particular types of apparatus exchanging tips on their latest moves. We may find Bruce Block patiently building a stack of 40 or more cigar boxes and balancing that stack on his chin. Master manipulators like Charlie Brown, Steve Mock, Reg Bacon ("Mr. Slim"), Tim Graham and Ron Meyers may be showing one another new ways to defy gravity with three or four boxes.

The manipulation of cigar boxes is a specialty developed comparatively recently. One expert practitioner, Kris Kremo, learned from his father, Bella. Cigar-box manipulation was brought to the attention of American audiences by the tramp juggler, Harrigan, from about 1895 to the early 1900s. He inspired W. C. Fields, who immortalized that particular art on film in his classic movie, The Old-Fashioned Way. However, the manipulation of wooden blocks and boxes was first performed in Europe by Japanese artists who, in turn, had learned it from the Chinese.

Traditional apparatus from China has always fascinated Western jugglers. The howl of a diabolo is heard above the general hubbub of the room, as it climbs a string to the ceiling. At the bottom, Larry Kluger can be found revving up a second diabolo. This whistling top, now made of plastic but formerly fashioned of bamboo, first came to France from China in the seventeenth century and became a sport rivaling tennis in popularity. The several European troupes of renown who currently play with diabolos all owe allegiance to the German artist McSovereign. From 1907 to 1947 he wore the crown as King of the Diabolo players and even obtained patents for three diabolo-related inventions.

The tap-tap-tap of a devil stick shared by Todd Strong and Andrew Allen draws one's attention. Devotees of this implement can trace its path from China to Europe and America. The original Chinese implement had pom-poms that looked like flowers affixed to both ends of the central stick. The name was changed from "flower stick," or *hua kun* in Chinese, to diabolo, meaning "to toss across'" in Greek. "Diabolo" was originally used for both the diabolo and the devil stick, but in the English language the two implements were separated. When we return to the source of this piece of apparatus, we find that the acrobats of Shenyang have paid the most attention to its development and specialize in combining folk music, dance and acrobatics with skillful manipulation.

Circus jugglers often appear at the IJA convention to participate in workshops or competitions. The juggler has always been part of the circus in both Europe and North America. When skill and showmanship permit, the juggling act can even play solo in the center ring of a three-ring circus. Francis and Lottie Brunn are examples of jugglers who could hold the attention of the most distant spectator. When John Ringling North first saw them in Madrid in 1947, he immediately offered them a contract. Francis, assisted by Lottie, was a featured solo center-ring performer with Ringling Brothers' Barnum and Bailey Circus from 1948 through 1950. Lottie, however, was too great a juggler herself to remain in her brother's shadow and has from 1951 performed alone as the "fastest female juggler in the world."

Many other activities at the IJA convention have deep historical roots in medieval Europe. These include the annual parade through the center of our host town or city, the gala costume ball, a picnic on the green and our annual banquet. The IJA itself could be likened to the European artists' guilds which flourished during the Renaissance.

ACHIEVEMENT
AWARDS
Endorsed by the International Jugglers' Association

The International Jugglers' Association or IJA was formed in 1947 to further the art of juggling. An IJA convention is held each year somewhere in North America, and local affiliates hold regional meets and festivals throughout the year. At these gatherings jugglers compete as individuals and as teams, winning trophies, cash prizes and recognition. Workshops are held to help you progress and to share skills; and there is always a public show.

Now you need not compete at an official event to be a winner, but can advance as a juggler in your own home town. To help you measure your progress, we have developed the certification program presented in this book. The first pin can be yours as soon as you learn to juggle. Simply demonstrate the cascade to two people and send in the form at the back of the book (or a copy) with $2.

After that first pin the requirements are tougher. You must demonstrate the required skill to one of the following:

- A panel of IJA members established by an IJA affiliate; or if that is not available

- A certified Juggling Institute instructor; or if that is not available

- A certified teacher, a camp director or a recreation director; or if that is not available

- A panel of 12 people (your audience), two of whom must sign your application.

For these higher level pins, send in $3 for each one along with a completed form from this book (or a copy).

A separate, but complementary, achievement system may be helpful to those who want to measure their growth as "numbers" jugglers. Simply add up the number of balls, rings and clubs which you can effectively handle. For instance, if you can juggle 4 balls, 4 rings and 3 clubs, your level is 11. When you can juggle 7 balls, 7 rings and 5 clubs, your level is 19. You have control over a specific number of objects when you can demonstrate two rounds of throws and finish with a clean catch. Thus with five balls you need 10 throws and 10 catches.

Not every juggler will use the achievement awards system. For some, juggling is its own reward. The feeling of competence and self-esteem which you achieve when you conquer gravity, or the applause of family, friends or strangers may be reward enough. For others of us a system of recognition and certification is helpful. It gives us a set of standards against which to measure our own progress, and challenges us to keep improving.

Whether you set out to earn pins or not, we recommend that you join the IJA. When you join you will be informed of your nearest affiliate, and will learn about juggling activities and events close to home and around the world. The IJA address is included in Appendix 1: Useful Resources and Addresses.

APPLICATION FOR
BEGINNER PIN

This pin is yours for learning the cascade. You pay only $2 to cover handling and shipping charges. Send the following signed statement with payment to:

JUGGLEBUG
7506 J Olympic View Drive
Edmonds, WA 98020

Please allow 2-3 weeks for delivery. Use separate application form and enclose $2 for each pin ordered. Washington residents add 16 cents state sales tax.

I ___print your name_____ certify that I have learned to juggle and can do 20 or more throws without dropping.

_____
Witness
Signature

_____
Witness
Signature

_____
Sign your name

_____
Address (please print)

_____
City   State   Zip

_____
Your age (optional)

APPLICATION FOR ACHIEVEMENT PIN

The undersigned certifies that _____

_____

has performed for an audience of 12 or more on _____

at _____

_____

I/we the undersigned have read and understand the requirements

for earning the _____

achievement pin. The juggler named above has fulfilled those

requirements.

(One signature required if witness is IJA Affiliate Coordinator, Juggling Institute Instructor, certified teacher, Camp director or recreation specialist. Otherwise, 2 witnesses are required.)

Witness Name	Signature
Address	
City	State Zip
Witness Name	Signature
Address	
City	State Zip

Applicant Name	
Address	
City	State Zip

Note: Use separate application form and enclose $3 for each pin ordered. Washington residents add 25 cents sales tax. Payment by cash, check or money order to:

JUGGLEBUG
7506 J Olympic View Drive
Edmonds, WA 98020

JUGGLING PROGRESS CARD

NAME _____

DATE									
NAME OF TRICK	DURATION OR # OF SUCCESSFUL THROWS AND CATCHES								

How to use this card:

1. Put dates across the top.
2. List tricks down the side.
3. Every day fill in one column with the duration in seconds or the number of successful throws and catches.

APPENDIX I:
USEFUL
RESOURCES AND
ADDRESSES

To buy juggling equipment, check your local Yellow Pages under "Magicians' Supplies" or "Juggling Equipment." Call sporting good and toy stores in your area and ask if they carry juggling supplies.

To order juggling equipment by mail, write and ask for a juggling equipment catalog from:

Andy's Odd Sports
358 Trevor Lane
Bala Cynwyd, PA 19004

California Juggling Institute
15651 Eden
Westminster, CA 92683

The Bezdekian Collection
P.O. Box 2712
Columbia, MD 21045

Klutz Products
P.O. Box 2992
Stanford, CA 94305

Hank Lee's Magic Factory
24 Lincoln Street
Boston, MA 02111

Louis Tannen, Inc.
6 West 32nd Street
New York, NY 10001

Illinois Juggling Institute
143 N. Pershing
Bensenville, IL 60106

U.S. Toy Company
2008 West 103rd Terrace
Leawood, KS 66206

If you want to order juggling equipment in quantity for physical education or recreation programs, contact:

Flaghouse, Inc.
18 West 18th Street
New York, NY 10011

School Tech, Inc.
P.O. Box 1941
Ann Arbor, MI 48106

Gopher Athletics
P.O. Box 0
220 24th Avenue NW
Owatonna, MN 55060

Snitz Manufacturing Co.
2096 S. Church St.
East Troy, WI 53120

Graves-Humphries
P.O. Box 13407
Roanoke, VA 24033

Sportime
Select Service and Supply
2905 E. Amwiler Road
Atlanta, GA 30360

Mosier Materials
61328 Yakwahtin Court
Bend, OR 97702

Things from Bell
P.O. Box 706
4 Lincoln Avenue
Cortland, NY 13045

Passon's Sports
1017 Arch Street
Philadelphia, PA 19107

Taffy's
701 Beta Drive
Cleveland, OH 44143

If you own a store and want to carry juggling equipment, contact:

Jugglebug
7506 J Olympic View Drive, Dept. JB
Edmonds, WA 98020
(206) 774-2127

In addition to the juggling equipment sold by Jugglebug, a two-hour instructional video series, "Juggling Step by Step," is also available. The video follows the same general plan as the instructional portion of this book.

If you want to stay in touch with jugglers and juggling, join the International Jugglers' Association (IJA). Membership brings you four issues of *Jugglers' World* magazine and a roster of members each year. Your IJA membership keeps you up to date on local juggling events and the annual IJA regional and national conventions. When you join the IJA, you will get a current list of prop makers who manufacture juggling equipment for professional performers and recreational jugglers. To inquire about current cost or to join, write IJA, P.O. Box 29JB, Kenmore, NY 14217, USA.

To network with jugglers and juggling in Europe, and to find out about the annual European Jugglers' Convention, subscribe to *Kaskade*. For subscription information, write to *Kaskade*, Annastrasse 7, D-6200, Wiesbaden, West Germany.

The best lists of festivals and fairs around the country are:

- *Chase's Annual Events*, a calendar of activities published annually by Contemporary Books, Chicago

- *Directory of North American Fairs and Expositions*, an exhaustive list published annually by Amusement Business, Box 24970, Nashville, TN 37202

- The Chamber of Commerce of each state or Canadian province, which usually publishes a list of festivals, fairs and street or neighborhood events

To get in touch with the street scene and to stay up on the legal issues involved, write to Steven Baird, *The Street Performers' Newsletter*, P.O. Box 570, Cambridge, MA 02238-0570.

To learn about the history of juggling and the life stories of the great jugglers of the past, the author recommends *Juggling—Its*

History and Greatest Performers, by Francisco Alvarez, which presents a readable narrative and line drawings of some of the greats of the past. It is available from Francisco Alvarez, P.O. Box 8795, Albuquerque, NM 87108. Far more elaborate and more expensive is *Juggling, The Art and Its Artists,* by Karl-Heinz Ziethen and Andrew Allen. This coffee-table book includes 290 black-and-white photographs, eight color plates and 93 drawings. The text is sparse and humorous. This book is published by RLV—Rausch and Luft, Hasenheide 54, D-1000, Berlin 61, West Germany.

To explore the world of club passing in depth, the 450-page book *Patterns* can be ordered from Richard Dingman, 64 Wendell, Cambridge, MA 02138.

If you would like to arrange for a speaker for corporations, associations or professional groups, using juggling as the medium for presenting a variety of messages, the following individuals may be available:

Steve Allen, Jr., M.D.
735 Watkins Road
Horseheads, NY 14845
(607) 739-8778

Dr. Allen (son of entertainer Steve Allen) teaches juggling to help patients reduce stress. His entertaining programs are in demand by corporations and health professionals.

Dave Finnigan (AKA Professor Confidence)
7506 J Olympic View Drive, Dept. PC
Edmonds, WA 98020
(206) 774-2127

Having taught over 350,000 people how to juggle, Professor Confidence is not going to fail with you or your group. His program includes full participation by everyone in a joyous learning experience.

To arrange for a juggling team to come to your school or recreation center, present an assembly and teach juggling, or if you would like to undertake training for such a program, contact the Juggling Institute, 7506 J Olympic View Drive, Dept. JI, Edmonds, WA 98020; Tel.: (206) 774-2127.

To audition for the college circuit and to find out about regional and national showcases, contact the National Association of Campus Activities, P.O. Box 6828, Columbia, SC 29260; Tel.: (803) 782-7121.

APPENDIX 2:
GLOSSARY OF
JUGGLING
TERMS AND
INDEX OF NAMES

This glossary is intended to define juggling terms and to help jugglers develop a common language. It is also designed as an index. Page numbers, where pertinent, are given after the entry. When an example has been given in the text (as opposed to a demonstration of a certain technique or point), that has been indicated. An index of people well known in the juggling world follows the glossary.

Albert throws A club-juggling pattern in which the clubs are thrown between the legs from front to back without lifting the feet off of the floor. Throws made from back to front are reverse Albert throws, or "treblas." Named for Albert Lucas, who has popularized this pattern. (Example on p. 195)

American club A juggling club which has a wide bulb.

Anchored stick A stick, held firmly at the base, on which plates are spun. (p. 382)

Applause point A moment in the routine when the audience can see that it is appropriate to applaud. Often marked by a pause or body catch. (pp. 54–59)

Back to back A passing pattern where the jugglers stand back to back and pass to one another. (pp. 129, 228, 315, 344)

Back to front A passing pattern in which one juggler stands behind the other, facing his back. (p. 128)

Back crosses The props are carried behind the back and thrown across the back and over the opposite shoulder, first on one side, then on the other. The right hand throws over the left shoulder, and the left hand over the right shoulder. (pp. 69, 196)

Back roll To roll a ball from one hand down the arm and across the back to the other hand. (p. 401)

Balance To bring an object to a state of equilibrium while it is resting on a part of your body or on another object. (pp. 165, 182, 311–12, 367, 380–81, 407–15)

Ball on a ball A double balance in which one ball spins on top of another, which is balanced and spinning. (p. 396)

Beanbag A sphere, cube or other shape with a covering of cloth or leather, filled with grain, plastic pellets or other stuffing.

Behind the back The prop is carried behind the back and thrown across the back and over the opposite shoulder on one side. This move is one half of a back cross. (pp. 66–69, 182, 305, 399)

Blind trick (or blind move) A move in which the juggler cannot see the prop or the place to which it is being thrown. Example: catching a ball behind the back. (Example on p. 69)

Body bounces Objects are not grasped but are hit to be kept in motion. Most common bounces are off the head, knee, foot, arm and hand. (pp. 79–80)

Body catches Objects are caught without the use of the hands. Common body catches include back of the neck, foot, forehead or crook of the elbow. (pp. 54–59)

Body rolls A ball is caught on a part of the body and rolled to another part. Example: a ball is caught on the top of one foot. The juggler raises his leg and bends at the waist, and the ball rolls up the leg, across the back and shoulder, and out the arm to rest on the extended fingers of the back of the hand. (pp. 400–402)

Body shots Throwing under, around or behind some part of the body while juggling or while passing with a partner. (p. 65)

Box formation A passing pattern in which four jugglers form a square, facing the center. Each juggler throws to the person directly across from him. Partners stagger the timing of their throws in order to avoid collisions. (p. 249)

Bulb (or belly)   The widest part of a juggling club. (p. 170)

Butt   The base of a juggling club. (p. 170)

Carousel   A feed with three people and six clubs in which the jugglers change positions while passing. (pp. 246–47)

Carry   To move a prop from one position to another in a juggling pattern without throwing. (pp. 48–49)

Cascade   The basic juggling move, in which objects are thrown from the inside to the outside with a scooping underhand motion, ascending up and across the midline of the juggler's body. The most common juggling pattern for odd numbers of objects. A rest position to which the juggler can return easily. (pp. 8–12, 26–32, 87)

Chest roll   To roll a ball from hand to hand across the chest. (p. 400)

Chop pass   A passing move in which the club is thrown overhand from an upraised hand held at about shoulder height. (p. 216)

Chops   While in the Cascade, the prop is carried down and across the juggling pattern with a rapid motion which looks like a karate chop. (pp. 50–51, 192–93)

Cigar box   A prop that originated in China, was developed in Japan, and popularized in the West by W. C. Fields. These are strong, lightweight boxes that are manipulated and/or balanced. (pp. 259–77)

Clawing (or the tax collector)   Balls are caught with palms facing down and thrown with palms facing out. (pp. 36–37)

Club   A lightweight prop designed to be thrown. Juggling clubs evolved from Indian clubs, which were heavy and made of wood and were swung by the knob. (p. 168)

Color change   A ring move in which the props are turned over while juggling, to present the opposite side to the audience. (pp. 160, 165)

Columns   A move in which the prop is thrown straight up and comes down in the same pathway. (pp. 15, 44–45, 186–87)

Combined moves   Changing from one juggling pattern to another in a routine. (pp. 16–18, 198, 398)

Combination trick   A number of different tricks are performed at one time. Example: juggling with one hand, balancing an object with the other hand and spinning a ring around one ankle. (p. 398)

Configuration   How jugglers are physically arranged relative to one another while passing.

Count   The beat or rhythm of a juggling pattern or of a passing pattern (p. 126)

Curl   While an object is spinning on the finger, bring the hand down, raise the elbow, and bring the spinning object under the elbow and up the back of the arm, returning to the original position. (pp. 377, 391–95)

Crossed arms   Juggling with one arm over the other. (pp. 52–53)

Dead ball   A ball that does not bounce.

Devil stick (or flower stick)   A prop of Chinese origin. A central stick is tapped back and forth by two hand sticks, and appears to be suspended in mid air. (pp. 279–316, 547)

Diabolo   From the Greek, *Dia* = across, *bolo* = to throw. A prop of Chinese origin. A spool made of wood, plastic or rubber which is spun, thrown and caught with the aid of a string tied to two hand sticks. (pp. 317–51, 546–47)

Diagonal passing   While standing face to face with your passing partner, throw across from your right to his right, or from your left to his left. (p. 127)

Double balance   To balance a prop on another prop which is being balanced. (pp. 396, 406, 414)

Double feed   In passing, when two feeders pass with three or more feedees simultaneously. (pp. 255–57)

Double sticking   A method for keeping a devil stick moving by hitting the central stick with both hand sticks at the same time—one on top, and one below. (pp. 287–91)

Doubles   A move whereby a linear prop such as a club or torch turns twice. (p. 230)

Drop   A prop that falls out of a pattern to the floor. (p. 248)

Drop back   A passing pattern in which a prop is thrown over the juggler's head or shoulder to another juggler standing to the rear. (p. 315)

English   A spin put on a ball when it is bounced so that the direction or angle of rebound differs from the expectation of an observer. (pp. 77–78)

European club   A juggling club with a slim bulb developed by European performers.

Fake   When the arm goes through the motion of throwing a prop, but the prop is not released at the end of the move.

Feed   A passing pattern where one juggler, the post or feeder, passes to two or more jugglers in turn. (pp. 238, 248)

Feedee   A juggler who receives passes from a feeder or post. (p. 238)

Feeder (post)   The juggler in a feed who passes to the feedees. (p. 238)

Fingerplex   Catching and throwing with the backs of the fingers. (Example on p. 56)

Flash   To throw any number of props rapidly in succession so that there is a moment when all of the objects juggled are in the air. (p. 188)

Flash pass   To pass rapidly to your partner so that all of the objects are in the air at the same time. (p. 117–18)

Flats (or floaters)   To throw a club or other linear object in such a manner that it does not turn end over end. (p. 180)

Flat throws   When rings, plates, or similar props are thrown so that, with the juggler facing forward, the audience sees the flat side of the object, rather than the edge. (p. 365)

Flip (or turn or spin)   Each end-over-end rotation that a club or other linear object makes in the air. (Example: A triple flip) (pp. 290–93, 301–2)

Floor rolls   Balls or other props manipulated on the floor.

Forced bounce   In a bouncing pattern throw the balls down with palms down so that they rebound higher than if merely dropped. (p. 77)

Fountain   A pattern for juggling an even number of props in which the props in each hand are thrown from inside to outside and do not cross. A reverse fountain is from outside to inside. (Example on p. 92)

Half-shower   Objects from one hand follow a cascade pattern, and from the other hand a reverse Cascade. (p. 102)

Handle (or neck)   The long, narrow part of a club, by which it is caught and thrown. (p. 170)

Hands reversed   A tricky method of throwing and catching where the elbow, forearm and wrist turn inward so that the fingers are pointed outward and to the back. (pp. 63–64)

Heading   Bouncing one or more balls repeatedly with the forehead. (p. 403)

Head piece (or head pedestal)   An object which is set or balanced on the head or forehead to hold props. (Illustration on p. 412)

Head roll   A ball caught on the head or neck and rolled around the head by bending the neck. For instance, the ball can be rolled from ear to ear, over the nape of the neck, across the forehead or to the back of the neck. (p. 402)

Head spin   A club or other linear object makes a horizontal spin on the top of the juggler's head. (pp. 194–95)

Helicopter spin (or horizontal spin or flat spin) When a club or other linear object turns in a horizontal plane. (pp. 217, 298)

Hoop A prop shaped like a bicycle-tire rim that can be juggled, rolled on the floor or rolled over the body. (p. 426)

Indian clubs Wooden pins, shaped like modern juggling clubs, used for swinging and acrobatics, especially in the nineteenth century. (p. 539)

International Jugglers' Association Membership organization for jugglers worldwide. (pp. 437, 454, 545, 548)

Juggle An act of dexterity; an act of manipulation; to toss, hold, balance, handle or manipulate objects in a skillful manner; a show of manual dexterity.

Juggling Institute A network of instructors who teach juggling professionally. (pp. 433, 507, 542)

Kickback A method for retrieving a dropped ball by stepping down and back on it while it is at the top of its rebound, imparting spin to the ball and causing it to bounce up into the pattern. (p. 83)

Kickups Using one foot or both feet to toss a prop into a juggling pattern. (pp. 60–61, 184, 296–97)

Kissing When two props hit in midair. (p. 45)

Knob Part of a juggling club. Refer to diagram. (p. 170)

Lacrosse balls Balls used in the game of lacrosse from which the modern juggling ball was developed.

Line passing A formation in which three or more jugglers stand in a line. (pp. 241, 243, 250–51, 256)

Live start (or quick start) In passing, your first throw is from the passing hand and goes across to your partner. (p. 131)

Mills' mess A complex pattern credited to Steve Mills, where the hands are crossed and uncrossed as the balls are caught, thrown, and carried through the pattern.

Mouth stick A stick held in the mouth to support a prop. (p. 404)

Move (or trick) An action, feat or series of repetitive motions learned as a result of practice. In juggling, a move or trick generally involves the manipulation of objects in a manner intended to amuse or amaze an onlooker.

Multiplex When more than one prop is thrown at the same time with each throw. (pp. 88, 140–53)

Neck catch A ball is caught and balanced on the back of the neck by bending at the waist. (p. 57)

Nested cups (or shakers)   A prop developed from cocktail shakers. Several cups are placed one inside another. The outer cup is held and the inner cups are thrown and caught again.

Over the shoulder   A move in solo juggling where the prop comes over the shoulder of the hand that threw it and lands in that same hand again. In passing, the object comes over the shoulder and goes straight across to your partner. (p. 70)

Pancakes (or butterflies)   A move in which rings are flipped like pancakes. (p. 162)

Pass through (or cuts)   While two objects are juggled in one hand, the other hand carries a third object through the pattern.

Passing   Exchanging props between two or more jugglers. (pp. 117, 121–39, 238–57)

Pattern   The path props follow in the juggle.

Pause   A planned temporary halt to the juggling routine by catching or balancing an object in a skillful or startling manner. Often used as an applause point. (pp. 54–59)

Pick-up   A method for putting a dropped object back into a passing pattern without stopping. (pp. 136, 295)

Pirouette   A 360-degree turn executed by the juggler. (p. 188)

Pistons   Four or more objects, thrown in separate columns in a staggered rhythm.

Pivot   A passing configuration wherein the jugglers change partners while passing by turning to face another person on a specific count. (p. 252)

Plates   Dinner-type plates that are juggled in a manner similar to rings. (pp. 370–83)

Post   *See feeder.*

Propeller spin   When a linear prop is turned like an airplane propeller (pp. 300, 310)

Recovery   To pick up a dropped prop in a skillful manner and continue juggling. (pp. 60–61)

Reverse Cascade   A basic juggling move where objects are thrown from the outside to the inside in an overhand arc, descending down and across the midline of the juggler's body (pp. 13–14, 35, 103)

Reverse curl   While spinning an object on the finger, bring the hand down behind the back and raise the elbow, bringing the spinning object under the arm and back up the front.

Reverse spin   A club-juggling move in which the knob goes up and toward the juggler. (pp. 181, 217)

Ring   A circular prop used by jugglers. (pp. 155–66)

Rola bola (or Bongo Board)   A cylinder placed horizontally on the floor with a board balanced on it. The performer stands on the board with one foot on each side of the cylinder.

Rolling globe   A large ball that is moved around by a person balancing on top of it.

Routine   Moves that are put together in a set order. (pp. 416–18)

Running three   Passing three clubs between two people. (pp. 119–20, 212–15)

Run-around   A move involving two or more jugglers sharing one set of props and continuously circling one another to take over the props in turn. (pp. 113–15, 223–24)

Scoop   The underhand motion which your hand makes in throwing self-throws across the chest in a cascade pattern. (p. 171)

See-saw   A three-ball move where each hand throws one ball up and down in a column while the third ball goes back and forth from hand to hand. (pp. 46–47)

Self-throw   The throw in passing that crosses your chest, usually from the left to the right hand.

Sharing   Juggling three or more props between two people where each person uses one hand. (Example on p. 222)

Shoulder throw   The prop is thrown over the shoulder from back to front and is either caught by the same hand that threw it, or is passed to a partner. (p. 217)

Shower   Juggling in a roughly circular pattern with one hand doing all of the throwing and the other hand doing all of the catching and passing the props across to the throwing hand. (pp. 19, 39, 86, 105)

Shower passing (or every right hand or two count)   A rhythm for continuous passing where every throw from a designated hand (generally the right) goes across to your partner, and every throw from your other hand goes across your chest to your own passing hand. (pp. 126, 225)

Side by side   Juggling three or more props between two people who are standing next to each other. Each juggler may use one or both hands. (pp. 23, 116, 130, 222, 343)

Simultaneous   A rhythm with four objects where both hands throw at the same time. (p. 91)

Single, double, triple   A club-passing move where one juggler passes three clubs in succession to his partner, the first with a single flip, the second with a double flip, and the third with a triple flip. (p. 231)

Single sticking A method for manipulating the devil stick by tapping once on each side in an upward direction. (pp. 284, 301–2)

Slap up Striking the prop with the sole of the foot, causing it to jump up toward the juggler.

Slow start (or lead start) In passing, the first two right-hand throws are self-throws and the third right-hand throw goes across to your partner. (p. 131)

Solids A passing rhythm in which both hands throw every throw in the same pattern. (pp. 132–33)

Spinning ball A ball that rotates on a finger, a stick, another ball or any other object. (pp. 384–405)

Spinning plate A plate with a rim around the bottom that rotates on a finger or stick. (pp. 370–83)

Split (or spread) Objects are juggled in columns with a wide distance between the columns. Usually seen as a four-object split with the two right columns being thrown at the same time, alternating with two left columns being thrown at the same time. (pp. 20–21, 203)

Stack Cigar boxes that are balanced one on top of another in different patterns. Usually done with eight or more boxes. (pp. 276–77)

Stage balls Large juggling balls, around 4 inches in diameter, that are very visible to the audience.

Staggered A rhythm with four objects where each hand throws and catches in an alternating count. (p. 92)

Star pattern A passing formation where five jugglers stand in a circle equidistant from each other. Can be extended to seven or nine jugglers. (p. 253)

Starts Moves for beginning a juggling routine or reinitiating a juggling routine after a pause. (pp. 29, 81–82, 131, 190)

Statue of Liberty (or Waterfall) Balls are showered with the catching hand held straight up in the air. Balls are thrown up to the catching hand, caught and then dropped down to the throwing hand. (p. 49)

Sticks (or batons) Wooden rods or dowels which were traditionally used by jugglers in place of clubs before the development of modern juggling equipment. The juggler can catch either end.

Stuck behind the back (or under the arm) A move where the jugglers arm goes behind the back and the hand comes out under the opposite arm.

Synchronized juggling When two or more jugglers execute the same move at the same time. (Example on p. 91)

Take away (or stealing) Two or more jugglers share a set of props without interrupting the pattern. (pp. 110–12, 316)

Tennis While juggling in a cascade pattern, the juggler throws one ball back and forth over the top of the pattern, creating the illusion of a tennis ball going back and forth over a net. (p. 40)

Three-three-ten A common passing rhythm where the jugglers pass every third right-hand throw three times, every second right-hand throw three times, and every right-hand throw after that ten times. (pp. 122–25)

Three and two A five-object pattern in which one hand juggles three objects while the other hand juggles two.

Three with four A pattern in which four props are juggled, one is thrown high and the remaining three are juggled in a Cascade until the fourth prop falls back down far enough for the juggler to resume the four-object pattern. Also a pattern in which four balls are juggled and one ball is thrown to the side, where it bounces once and reenters the pattern. In each case the juggler must shift from a four-object Fountain to a three-object Cascade and back to the Fountain.

Thunder shower Passing every throw to a partner with both hands and no self throws. (p. 229)

Transition A change from one move to another in a juggling routine.

Triangle A passing configuration with three jugglers. (p. 240)

Trick *See* move.

Two-high One person stands on the shoulders of another while one or both juggle. (pp. 244–45)

Under the leg A self-throw or pass to a partner in which the juggler lifts his leg and throws under it. (pp. 65, 179, 226, 304, 399)

Vamp To gain a beat in a passing pattern by throwing across the chest.

Weave A passing configuration in which three or more feedees walk around one another in a figure-eight pattern while passing to a feeder. (p. 248)

Y A passing configuration in which the jugglers form the letter "Y". (p. 252)

Yo-Yo Two balls are juggled in one hand and a third ball is moved up and down in the other hand, just above one of the balls being juggled. The upside-down Yo-Yo with the held ball under the juggled ball is often called the "Oy-Oy." (pp. 42–43)

INDEX
OF NAMES

NOTES

NOTES

NOTES

NOTES

NOTES

About the Author

Dave Finnigan (aka Professor Confidence) has a B.A. in sociology and anthropology from Cornell and an M.A. in public health education from the University of California at Berkeley. From 1966 to 1975 he worked in population- and family-planning programs in Korea, Taiwan, the Philippines, Indonesia, Thailand, Nepal, and Turkey. He has worked for the Ford and Rockefeller foundations, the Population Council, various U.N. agencies, the World Bank, and the U.S. Agency for International Development. In 1976, while a Ph.D. candidate at the University of Washington, he learned to juggle. Since then he has taught over 350,000 people to juggle, performed and taught at over 300 schools, presented workshops for physical educators in 12 states and 3 provinces, produced a video teaching series, and served as education director of the International Jugglers' Association. He lives in Edmonds, Washington.